Other Works
by Bill Campbell

Sunshine Patriots
My Booty Novel
Koontown Killing Kaper

Pop Culture

Politics, Puns, and "Poohbutt" from a Liberal Stay-at-Home Dad

Bill Campbell

Rosarium Publishing
Greenbelt, MD

Published by Rosarium Publishing
P.O. Box 544, Greenbelt, MD 20741 U.S.A.
www.rosariumpublishing.com

Covert Art and Design by Gerald Mohamed

What the Bloggers Are Saying about *Pop Culture*

"If Bill Cosby was hipper and less cranky, he'd be Bill Campbell. Equal parts historian, cultural critic, and comedian, Campbell takes on a host of topics including "paper patriots," hip-hop cold cases, Catholicism, "lefty films," economics, and fatherhood. Whether riffing on the race card, waxing nostalgic about the summer of '88, or reviewing Philip Roth, this "liberal stay-at-home dad" delivers. *Pop Culture* is a delightful fix for the pop culture junkie!"

Deesha Philyaw, co-founder, *CoParenting101.org*

"Bill Campbell tackles race and religion, culture and class, politics and parenthood in this whip-smart collection of articles, essays, and rants. Both urban and urbane, his writing is sharp and modern, adorned with moments of great humor, insight, and tenderness (and not only where his little daughter is concerned)."

Shani Ferguson, *Ratphooey*

"The smart woman's daddy-blogger! When I want to get the pulse of the current political scene, I turn to Bill Campbell. I don't watch any of the plethora of 3-lettered news programs, I read Bill. And when I want to giggle and smile at the not-your-average Daddy stories, Bill does not disappoint! His witty diatribes surprise and titillate. The range of history that he knows and draws from is impressive and I come away from reading Bill feeling informed and inspired. If you like politics, history, and satire with an added dose of parent humor, you've got the right book."

– Andi Fisher, *Misadventures with Andi*

"Bill's essays are by turns funny, serious, angry, insightful, and always compelling. He made me rethink much of what I thought I knew. I loved seeing politics and pop culture through his eyes."

– Steve Denton, *Monkey Muck*

"Hip-hop, Obama and Poohbutt, what more do you want? Wistful and open, this book is a Gen-X look at hope through politics and family. It says all those things you were thinking, only funnier."

– Iasa Duffy, *Blissfully Unaware Lounge Singer*

"Campbell gives us interesting mini history lessons as they relate to current events. And makes us LIKE them. Dude cracks me up."

– *politickybitch*

"One well-deserved criticism of the blogosphere is, it's too white. Bill Campbell's book amplifies a very smart, happily irreverent, and beholden to no one African-American blog voice above the progressive blog cacophony. It's very welcome."

Frances Langum, *Blue Gal and Crooks and Liars*

"I first got turned on to Bill's blog because of the name. It just fascinated me. Then I actually started reading and...well, he had me at hello. Bloggers, for the most part, aren't really writers. That's why it's always refreshing to find someone who can actually do both. Bill has put together some of his most insightful and refreshing posts and observations about the current American cultural and racial scene, and it's a must-read for anyone who is interested in where this country has been, and, ultimately, where it's going. Pick up Bill's book, and, like me, promise you won't put it down."

Wayne M. Bennett, Esq., *The Field Negro*

"If ever there was a time when we needed a blogger like Bill Campbell (or a reasonable facsimile) to weigh in on a world that's so screwed up it denounces gay marriage but accepts torture, it was at the tail end of the 'W' era, 2008-09. This almost 40-year-old, half-Jamaican, half-African-American's almost-daily rant covered those years like nothing else. Acerbic, outrageous but always imaginative, Campbell lent historical perspective to every outrage."

Paula Behnken, *Birds on a Wire*

Contents

Poohbutt

Foreword

The undisputed Sage of the Seventies and the man who briefly brought the funk to the Beatles, Billy Preston, once asked the timeless question that has plagued humanity for time immemorial: "Will It Go Round in Circles?" Well, I gotta tell ya, when it comes to my life and blogging, the answer is most definitely, "Yes."

Some time in the early 2Gs, I kept hearing about these curious little "weblogs," where people wrote daily about their own lives for the whole internet to read. While my ego is rather sizeable (and what artist's isn't—after all, we believe you should actually *buy* any old fancy that springs from our minds—that your life would be incredibly *enriched* by doing so—and that, one day, you'll be eternally *grateful* for the *privilege* of having done so), I simply thought that my life was too boring to be able to sustain a weblog.

However, I soon became intrigued by the idea of having a fake blog, of sorts, about a fictional character, where I'd chronicle the daily events of some poor schlep on the make. By 2004, I'd been with my wife for over nine years, so it would've been a real challenge to remember what it was like being single and I would've had to invent all these different scenarios pretty much from whole cloth. So, realizing I just didn't have that kind of fortitude to maintain that kind of project, I abandoned that blog idea.

But, out of that idea, came *My Booty Novel*. For those of you who haven't read *MBN*, it's the story of 32-year-old writer, Damian Cross, who, fresh off his first book tour, finds himself single for the first time in seven years. So, he has to write a second novel and find love. Since reading Junichiro Tanizaki's *The Key*, I'd been fascinated by the idea of writing an epistolary novel (a novel written in letter form). So, I figured, why not update the notion? So yes, *My Booty Novel* is written as a blog.

The challenge of writing a book as a blog is that the blog cannot appear to be a book. The book has to be plotted (it is a book, after all), but it can't appear to have been too heavily-plotted. After all, aside from "you're born, you age (if lucky), then you die," no one can really say, with any degree of certainty, what the plot, what the overriding arc of our lives really is. So, I had to write *MBN*, always keeping the randomness of real life in mind—to provide it with a kind of "controlled randomness," if you will.

There are digressions and rants—as any blog would have—a lot of fits and starts that would happen in anyone's daily life. There was a bit of cheating, of course. As one reader (a blogger herself) pointed out, there sure was a lot of dialogue in that book for a blog. Knowing that no one can actually remember exactly what someone says at any given time, I made the dialogue in *MBN* hyper-exact, full of the "Um"s and "Ah"s common in everyday speech. But the overriding challenge was to make sure that the author of the *blog* wasn't *too* aware that he was merely fulfilling the machinations of the author of the *book*.

It was a challenge well-worth taking up. Writing *My Booty Novel* was a lot of fun. I think it's a fun book. But the whole experience left me with one nagging question, a question many readers kept nagging me with after reading the book: "Why not start your own blog?" And they would always add, "It could help sell your book."

Fast-forward to January 2008. My wife and I had just had our first child, a daughter (herein referred to as "Poohbutt"). Mrs. Unknown (her *nom de Tome*, if you will) was just about to go back to work. We'd always wanted one of us to stay with the kid for her first year on this planet. Since I'm a bum writer—sorry, "Unknown Writer"—we'd decided that she'd go back to work and that I'd take care of Poohbutt during the day and work at night. I figured it would be a great opportunity to watch the li'l un grow and bang out a third novel. Of course, it didn't work out that way. We parents know … it never does.

Now, Oprah says that motherhood is the toughest job anyone can ever have. I'm sure Mr. Obama would disagree with that. He seems to be having a pretty tough time at his job right now. And I don't know where that sentiment leaves us dads—especially us stay-at-home-ish dads who work nights. I didn't necessarily find watching the infant the "toughest." In fact, I kind of considered my time with Poohbutt to be a blessing. The greatest gift a man who's never won the lottery can ever receive.

But, I won't lie, it *was* labor-intensive. And there were times when I couldn't tell who was crying louder—Pooh or me. But it was also a blast. As you'll be able to tell when reading, I had a lot of fun with it—as incompetent as I was. You'll also be able to surmise that I didn't write that third novel, yet. It was simply amazing how much *work* it took tending a kid who, at the time, couldn't even crawl. And, once she did start crawling, it was all over.

However, I am a writer. I had to write something.

At the time, the Presidential election was in full-swing. I'm a bit of a political junkie, and I spent most of my days chasing my daughter around, changing diapers, and being addicted to *NPR*. As the primaries heated up and ended and the general campaign started, I was growing more and more anxious (as we all were). I just felt like I needed to do *something*.

Finally, my anxiety reached a boiling point when John McCain's camp accused Obama of using the "race card" after the latter mentioned the fact that he didn't look like all those dead white guys on our money. The very idea of the "race card" has always infuriated me. The absurdity of the notion that we African-Americans can somehow "play" our blackness as some sort of *carte blanche* (hmmm …) to gain privilege over white folks is only trumped by the absurd fact that some people actually *believe* this phenomenon actually exists.

So, I wrote "Play That Funky Race Card, White Boy" (the first essay in this collection) as a response, opened a Blogger.com account, and posted it for folks to read. *Tome of the Unknown Writer* was born.

It's been going strong ever since (having today celebrated my 500th post on the site). I don't know how it ranks up there with other blogs, quality-wise (Technocrati and Google Analytics tell me the other stuff), but I'm rather proud of what I've accomplished so far on *Tome*. It's full of politics, history, my own twisted sense of humor, and, most importantly, Poohbutt. It has allowed me to connect with readers in a way that my two novels haven't. I've met lots of cool and interesting "cyberfriends." And I'm proud to be a small part in the Vast Left-Wing Conspiracy that is the liberal/progressive blogosphere.

And back to the Preston Circle I was talking about: the idea of blogging led to a book, *My Booty Novel*, written in blog-form, which led to my actually writing my own blog, *Tome of the Unknown Writer*, which led to this collection of my favorite blog posts, *Pop Culture*.

I don't know the future of *Tome* nor blogs, in general. But I hope and pray that both can keep going strong. I think blogs are a hard thing to maintain (especially for little or no money) and could see how they may ultimately wither away. Sometimes, I feel quite "daunted" with the task of coming up with something humorous, entertaining, and/or pertinent on a not-quite-daily basis. But I feel that blogs contribute a very valuable voice in the Cacophony of Ideas that is modern-day American politics. They are voices that have seldom been heard in the past, but voices that indeed need to be heard. They are *ours*, after all. I only hope that you find *mine* worth listening to, as well. Or at least that you have a good chuckle (even at my own expense) while you do.

Bill Campbell
Washington, DC
March 15, 2010

Politics

**(with a little Culture thrown in for good measure—
we've gotta respect the book's title)**

Play That Funky Race Card, White Boy

Friday, August 8, 2008

"So nobody really thinks that Bush or McCain have a real answer for the challenges we face, so what they're going to try to do is make you scared of me. You know, he's not patriotic enough. He's got a funny name. You know, he doesn't look like all those other presidents on those dollar bills, you know. He's risky. That's essentially the argument they're making."
-- Barack Obama

"Barack Obama has played the race card, and he played it from the bottom of the deck. It's divisive, negative, shameful and wrong."
-- Rick Davis, John McCain campaign manager

Ah, that all-powerful Race Card. I don't know about you, but I knew it was coming. It was bound to. Barack Obama's being the Democratic presidential nominee flies in the face of 400 years of this continent's history, 90% of which was dominated by slavery and Jim Crow. His very presence brings that history to the fore, which is very uncomfortable for many. Most prefer not to think about it. Many point to the past 40 years and think that equality has been achieved. But, despite the great gains made by black people in this country, there's still a lot of work to be done.

Instead of acknowledging this, many like to paper over this ugly sore with laudatory proclamations of what a great, multicultural society we have today. Yet, despite these claims, Obama has been suffering a whispering campaign about how he's a closet Muslim terrorist, his wife a black radical, etc. But it is not the whisperers who are accused of using race as a weapon, but Barack Obama. And all because of that pesky, little Race Card, which, apparently, we blacks have constantly used to get where we are. While I'm still waiting for my Card and still can't quite figure out what one looks like or how to best use it, the latest claims by the McCain campaign have made me wonder where the Race Card came from. This is what I found:

According to the UK's *Guardian*, the term "race card" originated in

Bill Campbell

Britain in 1964. After waves of colored immigrants, race had become such a hot-button issue that politicians on both sides had a gentlemen's agreement not to exploit it. That was until Tory Peter Griffiths rode the slogan, "Want a nigger neighbor, vote Labour" all the way to victory. Instead of giving the man credit for a catchy slogan, they accused Griffiths of using race like a trump card in whist. Thus, "race card" was born.

Slower than the *Mayflower*, it took some 30 years before the term became popularized here in the US. I wonder what event in the '90s could have coined a new racial term. Why, the most racialized event in the past 15 years: the OJ Simpson trial!

After the trial was over, Simpson defense attorney Robert Shapiro evidently decided that his client wasn't innocent after all, and started hitting the talk show circuit to spread his newfound belief. There, Shapiro claimed that Johnny Cochran, Simpson's black defense attorney, had "played the race card, and dealt it from the bottom of the deck."

Bringing us to the present, I find it interesting that the McCain camp would hearken back to the OJ trial to find techniques to criticize Obama. But what is more interesting is how the Race Card got flipped. While the idea of using racial division to one's own political advantage hasn't changed, it has gone from a term of white, racial bigotry to white, racial *victimization*.

Of course, this was the '90s, which saw the rise of Rush Limbaugh and the Angry, Oppressed White Male. With all the civil rights legislation, prejudice was over for women and minorities, and now the pendulum had swung the other way with affirmative action, racial quotas, and reverse discrimination. Everything was backwards (is *that* what *reverse* discrimination means?).

This Race Card had become so powerful that the racial tables had turned. Good, God-fearing, hardworking white Americans had become so paralyzed with guilt that minorities and liberal Feminazis had taken over the world. A good, white man couldn't find a job. The 1990 Jesse Helms "white hands" ad during a Congressional campaign against black challenger Harvey Gantt sums up the sentiment perfectly: "You needed that job, and you were the best qualified. But they had to give it to a minority because of a racial quota. Is that really fair?"

I gotta tell ya, as a black man, I feel utterly cheated by this whole Race Card phenomenon. While I don't feel particularly oppressed at the moment, I haven't received my Race Card in the mail yet, so I'm not reaping the privileges either. I guess being a minority helped me get into college – though I fit well within my alma mater's academic parameters. But I definitely know it didn't help me get that dream job at Goldman Sachs: "Well, Mr. Campbell, you have absolutely no qualifications to be a financial analyst. *However*, we *have* to hire one more minority today. So, I guess you're it!"

But I'm not alone in this. So are most African-Americans. There seems to be an entire socio-scientific industry built on chronicling the disparities between blacks and whites. (So much so that when *Freakanomics* reported that test score differences are more class-based than race-based—in other words, middle- and upper-class blacks score the same as their white counterparts and poor whites score just as badly as blacks—it was wholeheartedly ignored.) Blacks come out on the short end when it comes to infant mortality, life expectancy, HIV infection rates, diabetes, and a whole slew of physical ailments. While black and white drug use is the same, the chances for first-time black offenders of being incarcerated are 48 times greater than whites.

Folks with "white-sounding" names are 50% more likely to be called back for job interviews than those with "black-sounding" ones. (William Robert Campbell at your service!) And, my favorite, in 2003 the *American Journal of Sociology* found that white men with criminal records are slightly more likely to get a call back for an interview than are black men with a totally clean record.

Where are these people's Race Cards? As I said, I'm still waiting for mine. I got big plans. As soon as I get it, I'm going to go buy that $1.4 million house in my old Cleveland Park neighborhood with no money down and 2% interest (I'm willing to work for what's mine). Then, I'm going to Georgetown University Hospital and become a well-paid neurosurgeon. Sure, I have neither credentials nor training, but I'm black, right? White folks will feel sooooo guilty that they'll let me crack open their skulls. And then I'm going to flash my Race Card and make my books, *My Booty Novel* and *Sunshine Patriots*, international best sellers. See, I can't wait to get minez. I just wish Jesse Jackson and Al Sharpton would stop bogarting them all!

I'm guessing that's not how the Race Card works. I couldn't tell you. Nobody I know has ever gotten one, either. It's a mystery to us all. We're starting to think it doesn't exist—almost as though it's a … a myth.

If the Race Card is indeed a myth (and I have my doubts), it would just be one in a long line of racial myths that have graced our shores since the Middle Passages. There was the "happy darky" who absolutely *loved* being a slave—just a-pickin' and a-grinnin' in the cotton field. The negro didn't want freedom and, yet, was too child-like and feeble-minded to endure the rigors of slavery. Phrenology scientifically proved that the negro skull was too small to contain real intellect. The Bible definitively stated that black enslavement was the result of the curse on the sons of Ham. White people were just following the Word.

What these and so many other myths did was help excuse, defend, and justify white privilege. It had been proven unequivocally that blacks were inherently inferior. Whites were not *oppressing* them. They were doing blacks a favor. After all, it was the "White Man's Burden" to colonize the world, subjugate its darker peoples, and extract its natural resources because, without them, the colored masses would be living in a world of darkness absent God's Light.

In a way, the white man was the victim in all this. Sure, he was getting rich off the whole venture, but these people didn't understand the stress and strain of this civilizing enterprise. In fact, those coolies and niggers were downright ungrateful. Slave revolts, malingering, colonial uprisings, independence movements ... when would it all cease? And even when Europe gave in and *gave* those countries their independence, when America *gave* blacks the right to vote and all that civil rights legislation, they still kept coming at them, charging white people with "racism" all the time. They just kept playing the Race Card!

Look, I understand, nobody wants to admit that they somehow live a privileged existence. I, as an American, don't like to think that the cheap shirt I just bought cost so little because some kid in Asia was locked up in a sweatshop being forced to make it for next to no wages. I work hard and try to do right by people. And so do most white people. Neither of us wants to hear that our little world might be built on the backs of others' suffering. Besides, this is America, the Land of Opportunity, where, if you work hard, you can make it, because in America everybody gets a fair shake.

The abovementioned statistics, and so many more, fly in the face of that belief. And it's hard to reconcile the two. Most refuse to even acknowledge them. And, inevitably, some become hostile to those stats and start getting angry at the people who produce them. They're struggling, paying bills, and people are out there complaining about "white privilege" and "racism". Are those people accusing *me* of being racist?

Well, I'm not racist! They're racist! They're the ones playing the Race Card. Not me. Hence, the effectiveness of the Race Card. It charges that those complainers are not just grandstanding whiners, but it also claims that they are using race as a weapon to further their own ends. They want more money for welfare (mistakenly believed to be mostly for African-Americans), they want more affirmative action, more racial quotas, they want to take away more jobs and more college slots from hard-working, deserving white people. It preys on white insecurity and blames the victims for their own victimization as well as conveniently turning whites into victims themselves (look at the White Hands ad—the white worker *and* employer were powerless in the face of racial quotas).

By charging the racial disparity commentator of racism, Race Card victims are attempting to silence her/him. It denies white privilege and seeks to shore up its defenses with that silence. We can easily dismiss those stats as racist as well and never be forced to address the inequalities in this supposed Land of Equality.

That's why I find it curious that John McCain has taken this tack the past week. When he accuses Obama of using the Race Card "from the bottom of the deck," what is he really up to?

Race is not exactly new to American politics. The idea of white victimization ain't all that novel, either. In more recent times, we've had Nixon's "Southern strategy," Bush, Sr.'s Willie Horton, Reagan's Welfare Queen. McCain himself has fallen victim when W. surrogates claimed that his adopted Bangladeshi daughter was actually his black love child back in 2000. Some claim it lost him South Carolina.

So, no, race and American politics have often been bedfellows. And, with Barack Obama's historical candidacy, it can't be avoided— no matter how hard we try. After all, nobody's looking at him, saying, "Hey, who's that half-white guy?" Because of that, there are going to be people who vote for Obama because he's black, and there'll be folks who will vote against him for the same reason. People are inspired by racial pride, and operatives are out there preying on racial and religious fear.

And the latter are definitely out there. There's Fox News, which constantly refers to the Dem as "Barack *Hussein* Obama." There's Sean Hannity suggesting that electing Obama "would mean a racist and an anti-Semite would be President of the United States." Rush Limbaugh claims that Obama has "disowned his white half" and that he's the "Affirmative Action" candidate since he "probably didn't get out of Harvard without affirmative action." Ann Coulter has called him a racist and advises people to read Hitler's *Mein Kampf* in order to better understand Obama. There are also bloggers and emails circulating that accuse Obama of being a Muslim, black radical, closet al Qaeda, etc., fanning the flames of fear and racism.

McCain knows this stuff is going on. He can probably guess that these attacks are not just coming from whack jobs and Fox News (redundant?)—that some of these people are probably attached to, associated with, maybe even funded by Republican sympathizers or backers. McCain himself has denounced some of these attacks.

Before you get all pissed, I am not accusing McCain of being a racist himself. Hell, I don't know the man. I can't look into his heart. Joe Lieberman claims that McCain "doesn't have a racist bone in his body." While I refuse to call him a racist, his record doesn't exactly jibe with Joe.

McCain has come clean about originally voting against the MLK holiday. What he forgets to mention is that he supported Arizona governor Evan Mecham's decision in 1987 to rescind an executive order creating a state holiday for King. Nor has he said anything about siding with our man Jesse Helms in voting to prohibit federal financing for the Martin Luther King Jr. Federal Holiday Commission. Oh, and has anybody heard about why he reportedly voted against the Civil Rights Act of 1990 four times?

And can we forget: "I hated the gooks. I will hate them as long as I live." But hey, he was a prisoner of war, captured and tortured by the people he made a living *bombing*. He later reversed his support of Mecham's decision. He's apologized for the MLK vote, protested the South Carolina Confederate flag, called the Religious Right "agents of intolerance," and he's got that black love child. So, no, I wouldn't accuse McCain of being racist. I think his record, like most of ours, is just a bit ambivalent when it comes to race.

What I will accuse McCain of is what he's saying about Obama, and that is that Obama is using the Race Card. By employing the Race Card accusation against Obama, he hopes to silence the man's complaints or, if Obama does actually complain about the whispering campaign against him, to paint those grievances with a "racist" brush. "Oh, there you go again, injecting race into the campaign." But race has been a part of this campaign since Clinton campaign staffers sent an e-mail that Obama attended a madrassa, and it hasn't stopped. If McCain's ploy is successful, it will silence Obama on said racial attacks and allow those racial attacks to continue unabated.

Meanwhile, McCain himself hopes to look as though he's above the Race Issue (though his statements and voting record could suggest otherwise). *And* he can look like the victim in all this, suffering the slings and arrows of Obama's racist attacks. In fact, this past weekend pundits reported that the McCain camp fears that anything they say will be misconstrued as racist by Obama supporters.

Pretty clever.

And downright disingenuous. When you claim that Obama's inexperienced or is an empty suit, when you claim that his policies won't work, nobody finds you to be racist at all. When you say he'd rather lose a war in order to win an election or that he wouldn't visit wounded troops in Germany because there'd have been no cameras there (even though he'd visited wounded troops in Iraq and Afghanistan that same week), we don't find those at all racist—distasteful, but not racist.

But, in all honesty, what people find offensive or not isn't really the point, is it? The McCain campaign is attempting to put out that they are the victims of racism and will continue to be as long as this campaign continues (meanwhile, providing cover fire for the Fox News pundits, Rush Limbaugh, and random bloggers—nothing they say will be accused of being racist now either). And, if Obama was being taken to task for the comments of Jeremiah Wright, why isn't McCain suffering the same fate for all these comments being said about his opponent? I'm assuming that that will never happen. McCain is never going to have to give a contrite speech about race before the nation. No, in the race debate, McCain is going to be seen as the victim of racialized tactics. See, that's the beauty of the Race Card—it turns victimizer into victim and vice versa. And it has been a very effective tool in getting people elected. Just ask Jesse Helms, who was behind in the polls until the White Hands ad. Or Bush, Sr. The Willie Horton ad did wonders for his campaign. Ask McCain himself. His "black love child" cost him South Carolina. Better yet, just ask Peter Griffiths. "Want a nigger neighbor, vote Labour."

Gotta love it.

Popular Politics

Tuesday, August 26, 2008

Why do we have to like our public figures? Why do we have to know so much about them? Do we really need to relate to these people? Why does it matter in the least? Why aren't even the dead exempt?

Why do I have to hear speculation about whether Abraham Lincoln were gay or not? He fought that Civil War. That's all I care about. Hemingway may have been a cross-dresser? Oh, really? That still doesn't tell me why I had to read *A Farewell to Arms* in high school. And if you told me Thomas Hardy was actually a black nationalist transsexual Satanist, I'd still be pissed about having to have read *The Mayor of Casterbridge*.

But still, we have to know. And we have to approve. Of people's past and present behavior. LeBron James curses out his mama. Christian Bale pimp-slaps his. Paris shaves, Lindsay shaves more, and Britney cuts it *all* off.

The paparazzi colonoscopy is constantly searching. Even politicians get the anal probe. Mark Foley wanted to give one to many of his young pages, Larry Craig was looking for one—or just his shoe laces—in an airport bathroom. John Edwards had to confess to probing a former employee. John McCain got in trouble for just *looking* like he wanted to probe a lobbyist.

All because we need to like not only our celebrities but our politicians as well? Not their policies, but their personae? "Sure, he started a pre-emptive war and lied about it, but he seems like a good guy." Really? Is that why my brother pulled a tour in Iraq? Because you felt that you, working-class commoner, you could have a beer with W., whose family has been rich for a century and a half? Was he inviting you to the Skull and Bones Country Club or was he meeting you at the Bumblefuck Bar and Grille? Or was it that you looked into your TV screen, looked into his eyes, and just knew that he was pretty cool? Now, I realize that that's a sound way to run foreign policy—and it's working wonders for us in Russia and Pakistan—but it seems like a completely ridiculous way to vote for a politician.

And what's even more ridiculous is that now we have to like a candidate's spouse as well. I mean, why are Cindy McCain and Michelle Obama in the news at all? Cindy has a half-sister she won't claim; Michelle's an "angry black woman"; Cindy broke up John's first marriage; Michelle had some shady dealings with a hospital board; they both love their "black" daughters.

Enough already. It's petty and annoying. And I'm pissed that I fell for it last night at the Democratic National Convention. I mean, Michelle Obama's a pretty impressive woman. She struck me as a strong, intelligent, talented, and incredibly dynamic woman in her own right. Her speech—her story—was utterly compelling. She seems to me to be a woman who can definitely hold her own and would definitely do us proud as the First Lady.

Michelle Obama is most definitely a strong woman, and weak men generally don't fall for strong women. Russian mail order brides, trophy wives—or in Donald Trump's case—both—but hardly ever a multiply Ivy League-trained attorney. It made me a bit more impressed with Barack himself.

But, in all honesty, Michelle Obama's speech, no matter how eloquent, is not going to have me voting for her husband. I already have my reasons to do that. She's had no effect on that whatsoever. And if he keeps up with that FISA crap, he could still lose my vote. And if Cindy McCain ends up being Mother Teresa, the Virgin Mary, Lucille Ball, Marilyn Monroe, and Vanessa del Rio combined, I still won't be voting for McCain. Even if the three of us got drunk at a Redskins game and pissed on Daniel Snyder, I couldn't do it. No matter how much I loved those two fools, no matter how many candlelit evenings we spent together, gazing lovingly into each other's eyes, how could that determine my vote? There are wars to be ended, jobs to be found, bridges to fix, healths to be cared for. What does a winning smile and dewy eyes have to do with anything? I can get those and much better music with Prince … but that doesn't mean I want him in the Oval Office.

Though it would be cool to paint the White House purple.

Summer of '88 – Bring That Beat Back!

Thursday, August 28, 2008

A few years back, I was itching to write a book about the summer of '88. It was supposed to be about four high school friends who had formed a rap group but were about to graduate and go their separate ways—that pivotal moment when the future lies so breathlessly ahead, filled with excitement and trepidation, and the dread of leaving the familiar behind. But mostly, *Summer of '88* was supposed to be about the music—hip-hop. I mean, damn, look what came out between May and September that year:

Public Enemy—*It Takes a Nation of Millions…*
Eric B & Rakim—*Follow the Leader*
Boogie Down Productions—*By All Means Necessary*
EPMD—*Strictly Business*
Big Daddy Kane—*Long Live the Kane*
Schoolly D—*Smoke Some Kill*
Jungle Brothers—*Straight out the Jungle*
Marley Marl—*In Control*
Biz Markie—*Goin' Off*
Run-DMC—*Tougher Than Leather*
De La Soul "Potholes in My Lawn"
Rob Base & DJ E-Z Rock "It Takes Two"
MC Lyte—*Lyte as a Rock*
Salt N Pepa—*A Salt with a Deadly Pepa*
Doug E. Fresh—*The World's Greatest Entertainer*
Stetsasonic—*In Full Gear*
Kid N Play—*2 Hype*
Audio Two—*What More Can I Say?*
Eazy-E "Eazy-Duz-It" *EP*

My original thinking was that, while there have been great moments in music (1968-72 in all genres; the birth of jazz, be-bop, punk, etc.), but rarely—if ever—have so many important records in any given genre been released in such a short time.

But ultimately, nobody seemed terribly interested. I started to think that I was deluding myself. I mean, I know music is associative—that we often imbue songs with meanings they don't necessarily have— we often associate what's going on in our lives with the music we love. I heard Sting once marvel that couples considered his stalker ode, "Every Breath You Take," *their* song. Reactionary patriots' heads explode singing the protest song, "Born in the USA" on the Fourth. Booker T & the MGs' "Green Onions" was a Civil Rights anthem, and that's an instrumental.

So, maybe the summer of '88 wasn't all that. After all, that was the year I was graduated from high school. I was on top of the world, full of optimism, going off to the college of my dreams. It was a great time in my life. The soundtrack had to be great, too.

Or maybe I was just being nostalgic, pulling that annoying, "You kids don't know music. Now, back in my day, *that* was music!" Hopefully not. I'm hoping that summer's music was really as great as I remember it.

I feel that nostalgia is a trap. It looks at the past through a distorted lens, harkening back to an idyll that never really existed. We forget the bad and mediocre and treat the extraordinary as the norm. The '80s Reaganites always heralded a queer, *Leave It to Beaver* 1950s— conveniently forgetting the segregation, sexism, homophobia, and HUAC of the era. Baby Boomers still drone on and on about how they "changed the world" like they were all on that bus, got shot at Kent State, and high at Woodstock. They never seem to mention that the rates of crime, divorce, and pretension were never higher than in their heyday (they also forget that W. is a Boomer—well, he definitely did change the world).

Doom and gloom are telltale signs of middle age. No longer optimistic about their own futures, folks start condemning the present and lionize their own past. Reality, statistics don't matter. You can't tell a WWII vet that it was his generation that started the divorce boom because "you kids just don't respect the institution of marriage." You can't tell a Boomer that these American streets haven't been this safe since 1910 because "you kids just don't respect the rule of law."

And now we Gen X hip-hop heads are starting to do the same with our own experience. We are walking three miles uphill to school *each way*, calling ourselves the "Hip-Hop Generation" and the music we listened to "the Golden Age of Hip-Hop." Now we decry the detritus on the radio. Yeah, I think it sucks, too. But that's because I'm 38 and their target audience is 12-25, not because it necessarily does. I just don't get most of it. Neither do my compatriots, but they won't admit it. Instead, we talk about how degrading the music is to black people, black women, and how it glamorizes gangs and drugs.

As though all the music before 1995 was one, big P.E. concert. Well, it wasn't. If you care to remember, Eazy E's "Boyz N The Hood" came out in '87. Before that, Ice T, Schoolly D, and ultra-conscious KRS-One were celebrating the "gangster" lifestyle ("Listen to my 9mm go bang!"). The Geto Boys were around. Eric B & Rakim's "Follow the Leader" video was an ode to Capone.

For misogyny, what about LL's "Dear Yvette" or the entire Just-Ice catalogue? How about a little Slick Rick? The Beasties said foul shit about women and boasted of shooting folks—just like EPMD. All the things that the "Hip-Hop Generation" lambastes in today's music, we ourselves consumed. How many of us danced to "Girls L.G.B.N.A.F. (Let's Get Butt Naked and Fuck)" or "Bitchez Ain't Shit"? And we all loved Digital Underground, didn't we?

Sure, we had more "happy rap," like Kid 'N' Play and Kwame, and we had sisters spit instead of swallow Sprite cans; but this is of our own making. Yeah, we liked our Digables, but we went ape-shit over *The Chronic*. Common Sense was cool, but he was no "thug" like Tupac. Those afrohippy Roots were nice—but damn! Did you see the ice on Biggie and Puffy?

Corporations heeded our call and modeled their future acts on the stuff we bought the most of. That's what corporations do. Kids went crazy over the Beatles; we got the British Invasion. People loved disco so much the Fatback Band was replaced by Abba, and even Queen and the Stones came out with disco tracks. The early success of Van Halen and Motley Crue gave us the hair band. So, our love of Dre, Snoop, Tupac, and Biggie has given us the blinged-out thug in all his regional variations. We middle-aging heads have no one to blame but ourselves.

But wait! This is *not* how nostalgia works. Rewind, Selector! The music today is just total bullshit! All that bitchez and hoz nonsense! We used to respect our women. We called them "skeezers" and "strawberries". Not that foul shit these fools are saying! We treated them like *prostitutes* not tricks! Where is the respect? Where is the love? Where are all the positive messages we *always* used to listen to back in the day?!

Hm … all this sex talk … Jane! Yvette! Roxanne! Latoya! Let's go! Me so horny, me love you long time!

Palin Comparison

Wednesday, September 3, 2008

I spent much of last Friday in confusion. That *maverick* John McCain really threw us for a *maverick* loop with his *maverick* choice (did I mention John McCain is a *maverick*?) for VP. Like the rest of you, I had no clue who the hell Sarah Palin was, and, before I could even start to wrap my head around her bio, my boy, Nameless (a staunch Republican), sent me a triumphal email over the pick. We traded our usual, faux-combative emails where I warned him, though not knowing why, that the GOP was going to live to regret this one.

At the time I couldn't figure out McCain's logic. I'm thinking that most Hillary Clinton supporters are middle-aged, pro-choice feminists. Especially with *Roe v. Wade* in the 5-4 balance and Ruth Bader Ginsburg stunt-doubling for the Crypt Keeper, how would they find the NRA, pro-life governor at all appealing?

Just because she's a woman?

And why would McCain negate his most effective argument against Obama—his lack of experience—by nominating someone with arguably less experience to be a "heartbeat away" from the Presidency? Sure, I'll admit that she has roughly two years of executive experience. But it's Alaska, for godsakes—one of the smallest, most homogenous states of the Union that gets the most federal funds of any other and every citizen gets an annual welfare check from the oil companies just for living there. How hard could it be to govern that place? Even W. couldn't mess that one up!

And now, with every day revealing a new surprise about the woman, I'm even more baffled. The abstinence-only advocate has a pregnant teenage daughter (note: many conservatives are claiming this reportage unfair, that family should be off-limits, but Palin's been the one touting her own "hockey mom" credentials, her military-bound son, and her Down's syndrome baby as reasons to vote for her; if it was fair to scrutinize Kerry's military record since he brought it up, why isn't Palin's motherhood fair game—after all, only 2.2% of teens get pregnant in this country, which makes her situation *extremely* rare and Palin advocates abstinence-only, which clearly isn't working in her own family). The *maverick* Palin hired a Washington lobbyist to get $27 million in earmarks for her town of 9,000 when she was mayor—the same amount Boise, ID, population 100,000, got—wrote a letter to Ted Stevens requesting $200 million in earmarks for the state while governor, and was for the Bridge to Nowhere before she was against it. She's also apparently a supporter and/or member of an Alaskan secessionist party. The Pentacostal governor, like our President, also believes she's doing God's work—even when trying to get a $30 billion natural gas pipeline built through Alaska. "I think God's will has to be done in unifying people and companies to get that gas line built, so pray for that."

While I definitely don't understand McCain's logic in choosing *her*, I see why he would choose a woman. The Republican brand is rusted, and demographic studies show that it will continue to erode. In less than 40 years, there will be no majority race in the United States. Any party that wants to survive has to reach out to women and minorities. The GOP, however, has a lot of recent history to overcome. They were the "party of Lincoln," as they often claim, but those Radical Republican days are long gone. Black folks stayed Republican until 1960 when JFK made that famous phone call to Coretta Scott King while MLK was in jail. After his loss to Kennedy, the card-carrying NAACP member Richard Milhouse Nixon devised his Southern Strategy, exploiting whites' anxieties and racism to electoral victory. Those anti-segregation former Dixiecrats also jumped to the GOP ship, and ever since we have had "Welfare Queens," "reverse racism," and Willie Horton ads. Blacks now feel quite alienated by the GOP and feel that that party exploits prejudice to blacks' detriment and their gain. Most black folks can't help but feel suspect to any overtures made by Republicans, still smarting over past slights.

I don't think Latinos feel much better about the party. After all, it's the GOP that drives 187-like, heavily-racialized anti-immigration crusades, often claiming that "those people" can never truly become American, how they ruin American culture, you know the drill.

Much to their defense, it was also the Republicans who first advocated for the Equal Rights Amendment. It was an official part of their platform from WWII until the 1970s—when Phyllis Schlafly had it expunged. Ever since, they have been notorious in excoriating "Feminazis," being anti-choice, and generally deriding most feminist causes.

This is the legacy current Republicans have to overcome if they truly want to reach out to women and minorities. And they will have to run female and minority candidates. But running those candidates isn't the point. It is not simply a matter of throwing up a black, Latino, Asian, or woman. A black candidate can be just as racist as any Klansman, and many of the (to quote a friend) "self-loathing Negroes" the GOP throws up makes you wonder. And Phyllis Schlafly has proven that a woman can be just as sexist as any male chauvinist pig.

I don't know if Sarah Palin's a sexist, or not. I'll give her the benefit of the doubt. I see that she has definitely energized the conservative base. But I don't see how her views and her record will appeal to liberal or moderate women—self-described feminists or not. I also don't see why, if McCain were compelled to choose a female running mate, he wouldn't pick someone with more of a proven track record, a Christine Todd Whitman, Kay Bailey Hutchison, or Condoleeza Rice, a woman who one might not agree with but one who has earned her place at the table. When you compare Palin to these women or Hillary Clinton, she is most definitely lacking.

In fact, the Palin pick smells a bit like the choice of Clarence Thomas. The only thing that qualified that man for the Supreme Court was that he was black and conservative. It was the condescending tokenism of his choice that outraged blacks. So far, it seems the same, tragic logic was used for Sarah Palin. With her spotty, short record, it is hard to fathom what qualifies her to be veep except that she's young, conservative, and, to quote a leering Orrin Hatch on *Charlie Rose* last night, "quite feminine."

I don't know if feminists will ultimately end up as resentful over her choice as blacks are over Thomas. I do have a feeling, though, that they aren't going to fall for the okey-doke nor vote for McCain just because he's picking a woman to be second-in-command. The Republicans do need to reach out, but nobody's looking for that type of tokenism. The next time they decide to pick a female for a prominent position, they need to make sure that that candidate truly and sincerely addresses female issues—such as equal pay for equal work, health care, education, maternity *and* paternity leave. The same holds true for minority issues. Until they do that, no amount of tokenism will erase their legacy, and they will forever be the party of Phyllis Schlafly and the Southern Strategy—and will probably be relegated to the dust bin of history.

Six Degrees of 9/11

Wednesday, September 10, 2008

No one under the age of 15 can forget where they were when they heard the news of September 11, 2001 (like our politicians will ever let us forget). I'd just moved to DC and was about to drive down to Atlanta to move some stuff that day. My wife had taken the car to run some errands first and was running late. I had a 10-hour drive ahead of me and was getting irritated.

She came home, harried. "Bill, I think you're going to have to cancel your trip."

"What?"

"Terrorists have flown a plane into the Pentagon. The Twin Towers, too."

"Well, it was bound to happen sooner or later," I said, dismissively, ready to go. And then ... "Wait! What?!"

You know the rest—the shock, confusion, the dismay. Even though we lived in DC and the anthrax letters soon followed, I wasn't one for the fear—or the duct tape—the event caused in a lot of people. I mean, this wasn't Tel Aviv or Kashmir or Sri Lanka where you can walk into a café and get blown to bits. I figured al Qaeda had tapped themselves out on that one, and we weren't going to get attacked again any time soon. How could I live in fear of something that most likely wasn't going to happen?

But that view was easy for me. I didn't live in New York, barely lived in DC at the time. I didn't have any friends or family who died or were injured. For me, 9/11's like any other tragedy—Darfur, Afghanistan, Georgia—I've seen on TV—sad, but hardly affected me personally. I am so far removed from the tragedy, I can only feel sympathy for the victims but hardly feel any loss myself. It remained an abstraction.

That changed a bit for me in the spring of 2004. I was about to go on tour for the first book and was trawling the internet for old acquaintances—college, high school, work, whatever—just to say, "Hey, I'm coming to your town." As anyone on Facebook or Myspace knows, once you start thinking up old names, others can't stop popping into your head. Soon, you're looking up your cousin's third-grade teacher's baby-sitting niece.

That's when I typed in Melissa Doi. She and I had work-studied together at the student union building my freshman year in college. We weren't great friends or anything, just co-workers—bantered during work hours, stopped and chatted for a minute if we bumped into each other outside of work. Nothing special. Her name just popped into my head for the first time in ages. So I Googled her. That was how I discovered that she had died in the Twin Towers.

As I said, we weren't friends. I couldn't even tell you the last time I'd thought of her before that moment. The most I can say is I always thought she was cool. So, it wasn't like I grieved or felt particularly sad. I just felt … weird. Like 9/11 wasn't anything I was personally connected to, but then suddenly, that tragic day had a face. Melissa's. It soon had a voice, too. During the Zacharias Moussaoui (the original "20th hijacker") trial, the prosecutors played the 911 tapes of Melissa's calling in. The media picked it up, and for two days straight, I heard her croaking, "I'm about to die, aren't I?"

The media always play that stuff to shock and horrify. I usually ignore it, but when you knew the person on the tape, it just kind of freaks you out. And it made me feel … I don't know. I mean, what can be more private than your last moments on this Earth? And she was terrified—and who wouldn't be, going to work on the 83rd floor on a perfectly ordinary day to realize that you're trapped in a fiery tomb about to be murdered – and you could hear it in her voice. I just didn't feel that I had the right to hear it at all. Something like that, something so raw and fragile and heart-rending, should be heard—if it must be heard at all—by close family and friends only. Not some guy who barely knew her decades ago and definitely not by complete strangers. And it shouldn't be played for shock in the courtroom or ratings on TV. By the end of the Moussaoui trial, I was outraged for ever having heard Melissa Doi's last words.

I think what upset me most was that none of the September 11 victims' deaths were their own. It was, indeed, a public tragedy. But it was also 3,000 private ones. And the victims have no say in how the public uses them. Pundits, politicians, chicken hawks, and doves all invoke the name of the 9/11 victims to push their agendas, viewpoints, laws, and wars. But it's not as though we can ask the victims themselves. They've been being used for seven years now, and we'll never know if any of them are cool with that. How many of them were actually pacifists? How many would never have wanted the wars we're fighting or the freedoms we're eroding? How many would've been cool with all of it?

It doesn't matter. Because the victims of 9/11 are simply abstractions for our public figures to use however they please. Their deaths are to justify whatever agenda strikes politicians' fancy. After seven years, their power has definitely waned. September 11 no longer engenders the passion and terror it once had. But some still fear, and politicians continue to run on it. But death, no matter how public, is still a private affair. One's death should not be used to further another's ends. I don't know. Personally, I still don't feel all that connected to what happened seven years ago. In many ways, I refuse to. However, for me, whenever politicians do utter those words (which is why I try never to listen to Giuliani), "September 11" now has a face.

Sambo-Bitchgate

Friday, September 12, 2008

I first came across this Sarah Palin accusation while reading the *Field Negro* blog last week. Yesterday, my boy Dabalu sent me an email about it. Curious, I Googled it and realized that this rumor's gone viral. Even Michelle Malkin has blogged about it. If you haven't heard, Sarah Palin's being accused of once calling Obama "Sambo" and Hillary Clinton a "bitch."

Here's the email:

Alaskans Speak (In A Frightened Whisper): Palin Is "Racist, Sexist, Vindictive, And Mean"

September 5, 2008
by Charley James —

"So Sambo beat the bitch!"

This is how Republican Vice Presidential nominee Sarah Palin described Barack Obama's win over Hillary Clinton to political colleagues in a restaurant a few days after Obama locked up the Democratic Party presidential nomination.

According to Lucille, the waitress serving her table at the time and who asked that her last name not be used, Gov. Palin was eating lunch with five or six people when the subject of the Democrat's primary battle came up. The governor, seemingly not caring that people at nearby tables would likely hear her, uttered the slur and then laughed loudly as her meal mates joined in appreciatively.

"It was kind of disgusting," Lucille, who is part Aboriginal, said in a phone interview after admitting that she is frightened of being discovered telling folks in the "lower 48" about life near the North Pole.

Then, almost with a sigh, she added, "But that's just Alaska."

Racial and ethnic slurs may be "just Alaska" and, clearly, they are common, everyday chatter for Palin.

Besides insulting Obama with a Step-N'-Fetch-It, "darkie musical" swipe, *people who know her say she refers regularly to Alaska's Aboriginal people as "Arctic Arabs" — how efficient, lumping two apparently undesirable groups into one ugly description — as well as the more colourful "mukluks" along with the totally unimaginative "f**king Eskimo's," according to a number of Alaskans and Wasillians interviewed for this article.*

But being openly racist is only the tip of the Palin iceberg. According to Alaskans interviewed for this article, she is also vindictive and mean. We're talking Rove mean and Nixon vindictive.

No wonder the vast sea of white, cheering faces at the Republican Convention went wild for Sarah: They adore the type, it's in their genetic code. So much for McCain's pledge of a "high road" campaign; Palin is incapable of being part of one.

Now, Field (whose blog I *seriously* love and read every day) decided to treat this internet rumor as true. I have to respectfully disagree. Not because I'm a Palin supporter (quite the opposite) but mainly because it's way too convenient to be true—like all urban myths.

All too many of us are willing to believe that a Republican can be racist (warranted or not—I mean, "genetic code" was a bit much, don't you think?). So, of course, the Republican governor would be spitting "Sambo" on the diner floor. It just reinforces what we already think. But for those supposed Hillary voters who are about to jump the fence, look, Palin called your girl a "bitch." How can you vote for her?

Despite the image the GOP's trying to mold around the woman, I don't think Palin's a saint. I don't think she's all that qualified to be VP, but I also find it hard to believe that she's a complete moron. And it would've been completely moronic for a trained politician to say something like that in public. It wouldn't be the first time—but it's still unlikely—especially since it dovetails so nicely against her.

Unlike those right-wing bloggers out there, I'm sure this rumor didn't come from the Obama camp (they aren't morons either). Just like I'm sure that McCain's not responsible for the Obama-Anti-Christ-abortionist-jihadi rumors. I'm just tired of all the bullshit.

Look, I'm not some kind of political naïf, singing "Kumbaya," wondering why we all can't just get along. Bitter partisan rancor, vicious rumors, baseless accusations have been an intrinsic part of American politics since Washington hung up his spurs. Claims of bastard children, questionable parentage (did you know Warren G. Harding was our first black president?), alcoholism, debauchery. Our politicians have been some of the most evil sons- and daughters-ofbitches on the planet—or so their opponents would have you believe. It's just that this campaign has been going on for way too long. People are anxious. *I'm* anxious. This election is a watershed moment in our nation's history. Not just race and gender will be affected. Currently, our country's problems are so vast and numerous, and Obama and McCain see governance fundamentally differently. We have two seriously divergent paths to choose from for our future. And because these paths are so disparate, because so much is at stake, I just wish … just wish … just …

Ah, screw it.

Sarah Palin is a racist, neo-Nazi lesbian dominatrix who killed and ate Cambodian children when she led Khmer Rouge troops back in '75! That's right, when she was *nine-years-old*! All the while selling state secrets to al Qaeda! And John McCain is her love child!!!

Yeah. That's right. You heard it here first!

Bill Campbell

Black Muggers for Obama™

Friday, October 24, 2008

Yeah, nigga! We *big, we black, and we* deep, *nigga!" boasts Nucka D., president and founder of Black Muggers for Obama™. "We was pissed, yo, pissed wif all dese racist, cracker muthafuckas poppin' they shit, votin' fo' Palin 'n' shit. So, we got our asses ohga—ohgan—we got our shit togever, nigga! An' we goin' to* all *them swing states,* swingin'! *We on the attack! So, to all yall racists votin' fo' McCain, if you see a gang a niggas bumpin' to 'Ride of the Valkyrie'—"*

"Wagner's one deep nigga," interjects T. Coon Pickens, the group's treasurer.

"Yall better change yo' votes to Obama. Or else, you gonna git got!"

"Yeah, and make sho' you carryin' at least *a 20," advises Pickens. "Or it ain't just gonna be a 'B' in yo' cheek, but the whole, damned name. Barack Hussein* Obama. *And we gonna misspell it, too—to make yo' ass look stupid."*

This nightmare vision of racial, political violence is the latest boogeyman terrorizing the blogosphere Right after reports of such violence came out of my hometown, Pittsburgh, yesterday. For those who haven't heard, a 20-year-old McCain volunteer, Ashley Todd, was robbed at knife-point at an ATM Wednesday night. The mugger (reportedly a 6'4", 200-pound black man), after getting the cash, suddenly noticed the McCain bumper sticker on her car, became enraged, socked her in the eye, and, in order to "teach her a lesson," carved a backwards "B" on her cheek.

The story went nationwide. The Obama/Biden campaign released a statement: "Our thoughts and prayers are with the young woman for her to make a speedy recovery, and we hope that the person who perpetrated this crime is swiftly apprehended and brought to justice." The McCain/Palin campaign released a statement, and both candidates have talked to the woman. Almost immediately, folks smelled a rat. And not just the liberal blogosphere and their vast, liberal, MSM conspiracy. No, even the rabid Michelle Malkin has gained a little sanity on this point, comparing Todd to Sarah Marshak, the George

Washington University student who caused a national furor when she drew swastikas on her own door to call attention to anti-Semitism on campus.

Now, I don't really want to get into a "blame the victim" post here. But one does have to question the veracity of Todd's tale. Many question the superficiality of the cut and why the B is backwards. Todd, herself, now seems to be changing her story, now claiming she was also sexually assaulted.

Personally, I can't help but think this is a hoax. I'm not saying my brothers and sisters in Pittsburgh aren't above mugging someone. But, come on, this story is just too weird. A **big, black** mugger suddenly becomes enraged because this young, white woman isn't backing **the black candidate** and wants to ... teach her a lesson? And then he also wants to sexually assault her? In this racially-charged election season, what better story to drum up even more porch-monkey paranoia than an Obama racist raping white McCain women? Clutch your children, and vote for the GOP!

No, I am not, not, not, not, NOT putting this one on the McCain/ Palin campaign. There is no way in hell they're responsible for this nonsense. What enrages me is that I'm sick of the attacker *always* being black. Almost 19 years to the day (October 23, 1989), Charles Stuart shot and killed his pregnant wife in Boston and shot himself in the abdomen and then went on to claim that a black guy "with a raspy voice" shot them both. According to the Boston Globe, "Police swarmed the area and a black man, Willie Bennett, was arrested on unrelated charges and became a prime suspect in the case."

Almost 14 years to the day, Susan Smith rolled her car into a South Carolina lake, killing her three-year-old and 14-month-old sons. She immediately told the authorities that she had been carjacked by a, yes, black man. For nine days, the entire world was looking for a black man, two white boys, and a Mazda Protégé before the woman confessed to the crime.

And it's not just these whack jobs who blame black folks for all their ills. Black folks have damned near always been the *bete noir* of American politics. We were blamed for our own slavery, being too stupid, child-like, and cursed by God. Despite the evidence, blacks were considered too cowardly to fight and weren't integrated into the armed services for centuries. Crack cocaine, welfare abuse, all of it has been placed at our feet. It's hard to believe that Jerry Falwell didn't blame us (along with the feminists and gays) for 9/11.

Currently, the GOP is blaming the housing crisis on Fanny and

Freddie lending to too many "high-risk" blacks and Latino, and the McCain camp are claiming that ACORN is trying to steal the upcoming election, illegally registering all these black and poor to vote. It feels that they are reaching into the white, reactionary past and stealing signs from the Hoke Smith playbook.

For those who don't know, Hoke was an Atlanta politician and publisher of *The Atlanta Journal* during the turn of the century. While running for the governership in 1906, Smith realized that the black vote might ruin his chances. Needing to suppress the black vote so that blacks would "know their place," Hoke started running stories of black men attacking whites and sexually assaulting white women. The other Atlanta dailies got into the act, ultimately inflaming a race riot, leaving dozens of blacks and two whites dead.

Maybe I'm being too sensitive here, but that is why I find the Todd story so disturbing. While I think she's just a kook and a flake (like the equally egregious Tawanna Brawley and Duke rape cases), it seems that there are dangerous strains running through this campaign that some people are all too willing to believe. "Real American," "America First," "patriotic America," "Joe Six-Pack," "hockey mom," blaming brown folks for the financial crisis, the "ACORN swindle," it feels as though the GOP is mustering up animosity and rabid hatred among their constituents. Though they have toned down a little after the "kill him" controversy, the McCain/Palin campaign is edging perilously close to an American past most of us truly want to leave behind.

Todd will, I feel, be soon revealed as a hoax, but it won't matter. Twenty years later, people still believe that Tawanna told the truth. No amount of evidence will convince them that the girl smeared herself with dog feces and etched "KKK" into her own skin. People who want to believe will not believe that Todd carved that B into her own cheek. They are going to believe that racist blacks committed voter fraud to get their boy elected. As I said, I don't blame the GOP nor the McCain campaign for this woman's story. But I do blame them for fostering a climate that makes this tale seem the least bit credible. The Republicans seem to be more than willing to throw more wood under the racial cauldron this election season. I just hope it doesn't boil over—like it did in 1906.

The Plot Against America

Friday, October 31, 2008

This past Wednesday, the *Diane Rehm Show* featured Philip Roth's *The Plot Against America* for its October's Readers' Review. Since the Rehm Team sees fit to ignore each and every of my *constant* emails and I'm afraid of restraining orders, I've decided to relegate my complaints about the book to *Tome*.

For those of you who aren't familiar with *Plot*, it's Roth's attempt at alternative history. Charles Lindbergh, famous aviator, national hero, and reputed anti-Semite, beats FDR in his re-election bid of 1940. So, instead of the US entering the war with Hitler, Lindbergh (a fan of the Fuhrer) signs a peace treaty. As a result, we never enter the war and anti-Semitism crashes upon our shores. Roth fictionalizes his family and talks about what it would've been like being a Jew in this harrowing time for the Jews.

My problems with *Plot* were twofold. While I'll admit that anti-Semitism *has* been a problem in America, it has paled in comparison to the racial strife that America has suffered throughout its history. The war years were indeed turbulent on the home front, but it wasn't anti-Semitism that rocked the country to its foundations. It was racial strife.

In 1943, Los Angeles erupted in bloodshed with the Zoot Suit Riots, where thousands of sailors and Marines targeted Latinos (but also blacks and Filipinos). The police escorted the servicemen during the melee and arrested over 500 Latinos for "rioting." Some 500 people were injured during the riots, and the local press heralded our boys in uniform for the riot's "cleansing effect." They even went so far as accusing Eleanor Roosevelt of stirring racial discord when she spoke out against the riots and claiming she had Communist leanings.

There, of course, was the internment of mainland Japanese-Americans during the war. There was the Jim Crow South, and race riots in Mobile when the wartime industries were desegregated, as well as other race riots in Chicago, Harlem, and Detroit (so much for Americans banding together to beat the bad guy).

My point being, if one were to write an alternative history about prosecuted minorities during the war, it seems that race was the overarching conflict—not religion. Even as allegory, I thought that *Plot* dodged the real story to make it more Eurocentric than it really was. Hollywood does much the same thing with Civil Rights movies like *Mississippi Burning* or *Long Walk Home* and this latest batch of Civil Rights/Sports films (*Hurricane, The Express*), conflating the roles of white mentors to diminish black heroics.

My other problem with *Plot* was simply the cartoonish ending. Charles Lindbergh is defeated in his own re-election bid, everybody sees the light, and America instantly goes back to becoming the great nation it was destined to be. The gripe I have with this ending is the same I have, as a science-fiction writer and fan, with dystopian Hollywood SF films.

Dystopias don't happen overnight. The Holocaust didn't either. It's not as though the Germans just woke up one day and decided to kill all the Jews. The Holocaust was the culmination of centuries of anti-Semitism, Jewish persecution, and pogroms. The Nazis built upon a framework that existed way before they mass-produced murder.

Hollywood routinely ignores this—all in an attempt to blame dystopias on one, reeeeaaallly evil bastard. As I said, these things don't happen overnight. Philosophies are developed, attitudes are changed and cemented, institutions are built. Dystopias are *systems*. One person's never responsible for this. They may capitalize on these existing strains, but they don't create them out of the ether. Therefore, getting rid of the person does not get rid of the system. *Strange Days, Minority Report*, and a slew of other films always rely on the trope of the Bad Guy (actually, *Strange Days* blamed an entire police state apparatus on two "rogue" cops).

T   he *Plot Against America* does the same thing. It's an understandable trope for movies. If one concedes that dystopias are systems, we can't really have a happy ending. You can't just kill one person and have an entire society wipe away its entire history (ya hear that, W.?) and become paradise on Earth. That's far too unwieldy for a movie to tackle.

However, I would expect that type of scrutiny from a novel— especially from a novel by Philip Roth. If America had gotten to the point of flirting with its own holocaust of the Jews, simply defeating Charles Lindbergh at the polls would not have stopped it. America would've been a fundamentally different place. Would Jews really have been granted full citizenship afterwards? And what about the blacks, Latinos, and Asians who were roundly ignored in the book?

These are exactly the questions alternative histories are written to address or at least ruminate over. Roth completely ignored his responsibilities in writing such a speculative work. And since he did ignore them, I ultimately couldn't figure out his point in writing the book and found it all too wanting.

The Definitions of a Terrorist

Saturday, November 22, 2008

You heard the words so much they penetrated your dreams, turning them to nightmares, jarring you awake, screaming, trembling, praying that it would all soon be over. "Palling around with terrorists … palling around with terrorists … palling around with terrorists…" Of course, Gov. Sarah "John McCain's Biggest Mistake" Palin was referring to Barack Obama's supposedly intimate relationship with former student radical, SDS member, and founder of the Weather Underground, William Ayers.

Though countless news outlets repeatedly reported that there was just no there there, Palin and McCain continued the Ayers attacks, which started (along with most of the GOP's attacks this fall) with the Clinton campaign. And throughout it all, Bill Ayers remained disquietingly silent. But now, with the campaign over and the re-publication of his memoir, *Fugitive Days*, the former radical has finally found his tongue and is wagging it over the airwaves.

I'm sure for Ayers (like so many during that vicious campaign) it was more than a bit disconcerting to be thrown into the middle of Presidential politics. And no one else had to deal with people chanting "Kill him!" when their names were uttered. Aside from wanting to continue their tried, tired, and true culture war against the '60s, the GOP just loved linking Obama (who many believe is a closet Muslim and, therefore, a jihadi) with terrorism. Ayers was just a convenient vehicle (as was Rashid Khalidi in the campaign's final weeks); after all, Bill was a member of a group that had bombed the Pentagon. Though the Weathermen never killed anyone but themselves, the Republicans knew the very word "terrorist" would link them in folks' minds with al Qaeda—another "Obama bin Laden" marketing coup.

This attempted conflation of the Weathermen with al Qaeda was totally disingenuous, but Bush started it when he declared war on terror seven years ago. Suddenly, any group that had ever used terror was supposed to be on the same footing with al Qaeda. Therefore, at least rhetorically, the US would consider the IRA, ETA, the PLO, etc., as though they'd blown up the World Trade Center. Of course, it didn't work out that way. Ultimately, that tactic just seemed to ring a false note (everybody knew they weren't bombing Belfast any time soon). But what also sounds a bit off is Ayers's response to the attacks on him.

To his credit, he refuses to join what he calls "the Culture of Apology" by saying "I apologize if I offended anyone" or "Mistakes were made," but at the same time, he refuses to label himself a terrorist and instead says he carried out "acts of extreme vandalism."

I can understand why Ayers refuses to be painted with the same brush as bin Laden; but terrorism has had many faces, and his is one. The French Revolution kicked it off with Robespierre's Terror, killing every "enemy of the Revolution" in sight. There have been countless incidents of state terror ever since—including too many of our Latin American allies during the Cold War. On the other end, we have religious terrorists like Timothy McVeigh, Hamas's suicide bombers, and al Qaeda, where it's all about the body count—guilt or innocence mattering for nothing. The Weather Underground along with the early PLO, Jewish Defense League, Baader-Meinhof, etc., lie in different places in the middle. These groups used bombings, kidnappings, vandalism, and killings to *terrify* the general populace and further their political goals.

The Weather Underground itself was formed as a rebuke against non-violent protest, calling for "militancy" and a "white fighting force" to achieve "the destruction of US imperialism and achieve a classless world: world communism." They were perfectly willing to embrace violent means. It wasn't until three of their own died while making a bomb in Greenwich Village in 1970 that they decided that human casualties were no longer acceptable. The fact that they didn't kill anybody beforehand was a happy accident. Afterwards, they took measures—bombing only after-hours and calling ahead of time—to avoid death, but the fact that they continued bombing shows that they were still willing to accept them.

Despite the lengths they went to to avoid death, their aims still stayed the same, "the destruction of US imperialism." Now, I know they were idealistic flower children, but even they knew this could only be achieved through violent means. They accepted this. And they accepted the use of violence to achieve their political ends. In other words, they were perfectly willing to use terrorism. The Weathermen were definitely no sansculottes, Ton Ton Macoute, "freedom-fighting" Contras who attacked hospitals and schools, and definitely no al

Qaeda, but they were definitely terrorists and not extreme vandals.

So, while Ayers says he refuses to apologize, in a strange way he has by trying to cloud what he truly was. Being seven years into the "War on Terror," it is probably too late for us to have an honest dialogue on terrorism: its different forms and tactics; whether it's an effective tactic or simply "cowardly" and "evil"; how we can effectively combat it. If we can't expect such honesty from our political leaders, I definitely shouldn't have expected it from "an old washed-up terrorist." It's just a shame that Ayers himself is more than willing to continue muddying the waters. After all, bombing a hopefully empty Pentagon (whether one agrees with it or not) is still terrorism; "bombing" an empty subway train with spray paint like early graffiti artists TAKI 183, Lady Pink, and Fab 5 Freddy is "extreme vandalism."

Mugabe Will Continue to Plague Zimbabwe

Friday, December 12, 2008

It was lifetimes ago, way back in 1980, when Robert Mugabe was hailed as a revolutionary Moses delivering his people from the racist chains of Rhodesia's white government. In April of that year, the country was "given" its independence by the British. It was renamed "Zimbabwe." Blacks finally ruled. Mugabe was made Prime Minister. Bob Marley wrote and performed a (great) song.

Though Mugabe's had blood on his hands pretty much from the git, he'd been treated fairly well by the West's media (even with his Communist-trained troops). By letting the colonials keep their land, money, and privilege, Mugabe and Zimbabwe were held up as a possible model of future governance for apartheid-era South Africa. Zimbabwe was a place where everybody supposedly got along.

This "rainbow coalition" facade was blown out of the water in 2002, when our press reported that Mugabe was expelling white farmers from their lands and giving the estates to former soldiers. Only then did we start hearing what a political mess Zimbabwe had actually been for decades.

Ever since, MugabeLand has treated us to one shit-storm after another: hyper-inflation (I actually have a Zimbabwean $50 billion note worth about 10 cents US); rampant violence; mass evictions; an election so fixed it took them a month to fix it; Zimbabweans fleeing to South Africa only to be violently repulsed; mass starvation; and now cholera.

It now seems that the former Moses has turned into a modern-day Pharaoh, visiting plague upon plague upon his land in a stubborn refusal to abdicate power. The world wrings its hands, hopeless, every effort rebuffed, wondering why the man just doesn't leave Zimbabwe and give his people a chance to recover, to survive.

It seems like a reasonable enough question. The man's almost 85. He and his peeps have had damn near 30 years to rape and murder and steal all they can from their citizens. They've probably pilfered billions of dollars on which to retire. Why can't Mugabe just do like so many of his despotic predecessors—buy his black ass a Swiss chalet in the Alps and just chill, worry-free? That's what I'd do. Who knows? Maybe that's what Mugabe himself would do—if it weren't for Augusto José Ramón Pinochet Ugarte and what happened to him on October 17, 1998.

That day the former Chilean dictator was arrested while receiving medical treatment in London on a Spanish provisional arrest warrant for murdering Spanish citizens in Chile during his reign. He was slapped with another arrest warrant from Spain five days later for forced disappearances, illegal detentions, and systematic torture and murder. Pinochet's own country signed an amnesty law, freeing Augusto and his cronies from prosecution. However, the Spanish judge in this case cited the principle of "universal jurisdiction"—the idea "that certain crimes are so egregious that they constitute crimes against humanity and can therefore be prosecuted in any court in the world."

Though Pinochet died before the issue of the legality of universal jurisdiction could be resolved, both the British and Spanish courts later ruled that it was indeed legit. The principle has not been utilized too often, but it has been utilized. And it did get Chad's former president, Hissene Habre, thrown in a Senegalese clink back in 2005. As Secretary General of Amnesty International, Irene Khan, has said, "The detention of Augusto Pinochet heralded a turning point in the practice of universal jurisdiction by recognizing that heads of state are not above the law and could be arrested and tried internationally for crimes committed in their own country."

For Mugabe and his people, that means any judge in any court in the world can issue an arrest warrant, any cop on any corner can slap on the cuffs. They could possibly be hunted down no matter where they tried to hide.

Personally, I think all dictators, no matter who their allies are, should face judgment, and, if they got the Nuremberg treatment, so be it. However, people don't become ruthless, bloody dictators because their instinct for self-preservation is weak. They fight. *Hard.* Knowing that they will face judgment only means that today's dictators aren't going to quietly slip away like a Marcos or the Shah of Iran. They're not going to simply flee like an Amin or a Somoza. And, knowing that The Hague is in their future, they're damned sure not going to let themselves be voted out of office.

So, we can have "The Elders" try to fly into Zimbabwe and cajole Mugabe, et al., to leave the country. We can try to shame Sudan's regime with accusations of genocide. We can pound our breasts to a pulp over Burma and North Korea, condemn every two-bit dictator around the globe until we're blue in the face. Shame will not get these bastards to leave power. They have too much to lose and a nice, little jail cell waiting for them if they do.

The concept of universal jurisdiction was indeed a victory for the international human rights movement, but, for the people suffering under today's dictatorships, it's a Pyrrhic one at best. They can die reassured that one day their tormentor will go to court?! Maybe. But today, thousands of people are dying each week in Zimbabwe from starvation and cholera because Mugabe and his crew don't want to die in jail. If we want more to die, we only have to keep dangling universal jurisdiction before the octogenarian's eyes. However, if we want to save the lives of those innocent people, we will probably have to let Mugabe's people walk away with all their spoils without fear of prosecution. Until we make that painful decision, the man dies, or he is ousted, Mugabe's pestilence will most likely continue.

To Hell with "Condi"

Sunday, December 21, 2008

This morning, watching Condoleezza Rice's *Meet the Press* swan song with the Muppet (sorry, David Gregory), I realized what a relief it'll be to finally let go of my eight-year disdain for that woman. For the longest time, I simply hated the sister, thought she was a self-loathing true believer like an Uncle Clarence or Ward Connerly. Then, there was her head cheerleader role in the run-up to the Iraq war, which simply infuriated me: "Smoking Gun! Mushroom Cloud! Siss-boom-bahh!!!" Though mediocre at best, Antonia Felix's biography, *Condi*, made me somewhat modify my opinion of Rice. I no longer thought her unqualified to be National Security Advisor, and, learning she was a student of Josef Korbel (Madeleine Albright's father) and a disciple of Brent Scrowcroft, I realized she wasn't a neo-con harpy but a conservative "realist." Not a true believer—but a sell-out.

I've even had to give her *some* begrudging respect with her stint as Secretary of State. Finally, someone has corralled those wannabe cowboy, neo-con draft dodgers, and Bush's foreign policy has made a little bit of sense lately—ignoring the lunatic rantings of Dick Cheney and John Bolton and using diplomacy (what a quaint notion) with the likes of Iran and North Korea.

Don't get me wrong. I still loathe Madame Secretary. I can't think of a time I've actually admired her nor a time that Bush and the Gang have filled me with anything other than contempt. But the other thing I've found utterly contemptuous is the press's treatment of Rice.

There's been speculation about her sex life and the endless scrutiny of her wardrobe. Unfortunately, those are things that all women in public life have to deal with. What has really pissed me off all these years is how the media have somehow deemed it appropriate to constantly call Dr. Condoleezza Rice, former provost of Stanford University, former National Security Advisor, and current Secretary of State, "Condi."

Now, I realize that Rice—like so many of our oppressed black brothers and sisters—is shackled to a messed-up, made-up name. I know that "Condoleezza" is a mouthful (I'm getting carpal tunnel syndrome typing it out so damned much). However, she *is* the Secretary of State, fourth in line for the Presidency, and the third most powerful woman in the world (behind Oprah and Nancy Pelosi).

"Condi" is reportedly a nickname used by friends and intimates. I have never seen the woman smile coyly before the cameras, and vamp, "Call me 'Condi.'" Yet, in newspaper after newspaper, countless telecasts, books, etc., journalists have taken this liberty.

It's one thing when politicians like Clinton or Richardson go by "Bill" or those old Republican Revolutionaries are "Dicks" (Sweat and Armey). They choose to call themselves those names. Elizabeth Dole, in 1996, decided to disingenuously position herself against the "Feminazi" Hillary Clinton by calling herself "Liddy" during Bob's Presidential run. But, as I said, Rice has never done any such thing, yet she continues to be disrespected.

Some would claim your run-of-the-mill sexism. A cutesy way to somehow belittle such a powerful woman (like the fashion critiques and sex speculation). But Madeleine Albright was never called "Maddie"; you'll hear "Bill and Hill," but Senator Clinton's generally referred to by her given name (there's even a book titled *Condi vs. Hillary*); Sen. Feinstein isn't called "Di"; and Sen. Boxer ain't "Babs."

Secretary Rice's *white* female counterparts have been given the dignity of being addressed and referred to properly. Yet, this black woman's constantly infantilized by a nickname she doesn't use in public. I don't know if it's been subconscious on the media's and politicians' part. That they couldn't quite grasp or come to terms with the fact that an African-American woman had reached such heights and felt some need—no matter how juvenile—to knock her down a peg. I don't know if it was just journalistic laziness, and folks just wanted to knock a couple of syllables off her name (didn't they call Boutros Boutros-Ghali "Secretary-General Booty," after all?). Personally, I've always suspected it to be the former. And it pissed me off. And it pissed me off that it pissed me off. Because I just don't like the woman nor her policies. It's just the principle of the matter. Black women deserve respect—especially one who got to where she's gotten. They should've referred to her by her given name or title. "Condi" should've never crossed their lips.

Redemptive Blackness

Saturday, January 3, 2009

"Sneer not at the nigger, for today it is in him we must find our Lord, and in serving him that we are to serve the church of God."

--Orestes Brownson, 1863, after the New York draft riots

Every millennium or so, Western civilization becomes so lost, so desperate, they look to the black man to save them. First, there was Jesus, of course. Then there was Prester John, the mythological Indian or Ethiopian or Malian Christian king who was supposed to save Europe from Mohammedan rage during the second Crusades. And, this past November, we Americans, knowing we needed a radical break from the past, radically broke with almost 400 years of history and voted a black man, Barack Hussein Obama, our Savior-in-Chief.

Despite these examples, whites have historically perceived *themselves*, despite overwhelming historical evidence to the contrary, as the messiahs of their darker brethren across the globe. This perception started in the very beginning of the colonial era over 500 years ago and still persists in our own present-day. Even when coming face-to-face with their own New World barbarity, many Europeans believed they were the only ones who could possibly save the natives from barbarism. As Father Bartolome de las Casas (who himself saw Spanish atrocities against the Arawaks on Espanola) stated in the 1500s, "there are no races in the world, however rude, uncultivated, barbarous, gross, or almost brutal they may be, who cannot be persuaded and brought to a good order and way of life, and made domestic, mild, and tractable." As las Casas's own words intimate ("made domestic," "tractable"), accepting this form of white salvation only opened oneself up to exploitation. Las Casas himself, seeing the Arawak dying under the oppressive Spanish yoke, strongly advocated the abolition of Indian slavery and replacing it with its African cousin. This legendary humanitarian's advocacy (today las Casas is hailed as Spain's first anti-colonialist and anti-racist) did absolutely nothing to stop the extermination of the Arawaks and brought countless African tribes across the Atlantic to populate the New World.

Ironic, ain't it?

Not really. This European notion of "The White Man's Burden" has always cloaked exploitation with notions of beneficence (no matter how sincere or disingenuous) from las Casas to Kipling to Sir Henry Stanley's ("Dr. Livingstone, I presume") trumpeting the abolition of slavery in Africa to the public while begging the European powers to open up Africa to colonization and the exploitation of African markets (after all, he ended up working for the most brutal colonial regime of all, King Leopold's "Free Congo State").

In the United States, we can find the same sort of duplicity. After all, Andrew Jackson considered himself the Indians' "Great White Father." Yet he was the one who initiated the Trail of Tears. The very notion of the reservation was thought to be a way of saving Native Americans from the brutality of western expansion. And Liberia and the repatriation of American blacks to Africa was thought to be another way to "save" former slaves.

However, here in America, the queer idea arose that bringing salvation to the downtrodden Negro would, in some way, redeem whites from the very inception of our nation. And, like all things American, the notion was imbued with religious zeal. Benjamin Franklin, in an appeal to abolish slavery, wrote to the first Congress in 1790:

"A just & accurate Conception of the true Principles of liberty, as it spread through the land, produced accessions to their numbers, many friends to their Cause, & a legislative Co-operation with their views, which, by the blessing of Divine Providence, have been successfully directed to the relieving from bondage a large number of their fellow Creatures of the African Race."

As we all know, Congress ignored Franklin and retained slavery. Though there were minor abolitionist victories (by 1804 slavery was "abolished" everywhere north of the Mason-Dixon line though there were still some "permanent apprentices" in the North by 1860), America was too busy fearing invasion by the European powers to give much of a hoot about enslaved Africans. It wasn't until the 1830s with such radicals as William Lloyd Garrison, Theodore Weld, and, later, Frederick Douglass did the abolitionist movement and this notion of racial redemption really start taking hold.

Bill Campbell

Born within the millenarian fire-and-brimstone of the Second Great Awakening, this generation of zealots believed that America as a nation could only be redeemed by expunging from its soul America's Original Sin, slavery. America was God's chosen land and all of its troubles (there was a depression from 1837 to 1843 and another in 1857) were God's punishment for the abomination of slavery. It was a divine mission from the Lord Himself. As John Brown said, "I am as content to die for God's eternal truth on the scaffold as in any other way."

The abolitionists believed that freeing the slaves would not only rescue blacks from their physical chains but would also loosen whites' spiritual ones. "... [N]o one who has not been an integral part of a slaveholding community, can have any idea of its abominations.... even were slavery no curse to its victims, the exercise of arbitrary power works such fearful ruin upon the hearts of slaveholders, that I should feel impelled to labor and pray for its overthrow with my last energies and latest breath," stated Angelina Grimke.

It was a belief and a fervor that brought us the Civil War (despite what many revisionists like to state, the Civil War *was* fought strictly over slavery), Reconstruction, the demise of Andrew Johnson, and women's suffrage.

Though this fervor eventually died out with the rise of Jim Crow and America's own colonial aspirations, it did reappear in the 1960s Civil Rights movement, with whites volunteering in the South to combat desegregation (some, like Viola Liuzzo, Andrew Goodman, and Michael Schwerner, actually sacrificed their lives for the cause). That, too, eventually petered out, but the notion of black salvation/white redemption still holds today in, what I like to call, the "White Messiah" film.

You know the plot: well-meaning white person finds some oppressed, dark masses, and, through their own self-actualization, delivers the darkies from their own oppression, ignorance, etc., to the promised land, thereby, you guessed it, finding their own redemption.

This deliverer can be a teacher (like Jon Voigt in *Conrack* or the Dylan-spewing Michelle Pfeiffer in *Dangerous Minds*). S/he can go native like in *Dances with Wolves* or *The Last Samurai*. Or the savior can simply feel guilty and temporarily "risk everything" like in *The Long Walk Home*. The White Messiah rarely dies, but when he does, he gives reaalllly long soliloquies like Leonardo DiCaprio in *Blood Diamonds*. He can actually be two people simultaneously—as the ahistorical mindfuck *Mississippi Burning* (the FBI as the hero of the Civil Rights movement?!) proved with Willem Dafoe and Gene Hackman. And

Bruce Willis has proven that the White Messiah can, time and time again, resurrect a career (*Pulp Fiction, Die Hard 3,* and *Tears of the Sun*). Now, all things being ... whatever they are in our "post-racial" world, the black man has emerged to save the white man's day in the form of the "magical Negro." You may have heard of him or at least have seen him. Hell, you may have one of your own (Will Smith played one in *The Legend of Bagger Vance,* but I hear he can be a bit pricey). This supernatural African generally "appears out of nowhere" and, with his "Oh, Lawdy" folksy wisdom and his undying, self-sacrificing love of all things Caucazoid, will often sacrifice himself to rescue the white man from imminent disaster like our good friend, Gunga Din.

This past year many have speculated in the press and blogosphere whether Barack Obama could indeed be said Negro. I'd have to say no. It's mostly a class thing. The magical Negro is most definitely a social inferior. His help is seldom wanted, and he is mostly condescended to throughout his existence. It is only out of his love and sacrifice for the white man that he gains begrudging respect. He is never (even in death) looked upon as an equal and most definitely not a superior. At best, he's a curious oddity and will never be looked upon as more than the belittled exception to the rule. Even if the magical Negro saves the day, he will never be invited to sit at the big table, won't be dating your daughter, and most definitely would *never* be elected to the White House.

Obama's not viewed as Gunga, Will Smith, or Morgan Freeman. He is more in line with Prester John—the African Christian king who was supposed to save all of Christendom. This bi-racial brother is neither a "magical Negro" nor a "White Messiah." He is more, to borrow from the late, great Isaac Hayes, a "Black Moses." He is not supposed to rescue our asses. He is supposed to deliver America and the world from the hell we have wrought these past eight years. He is supposed to *redeem* us.

You could see this hope all throughout the 2008 campaign (in the talk surrounding his candidacy and even Will.I.Am and YouTube videos). Obama became an empty vessel of hope into which we poured all our despair, all our dreams. A lot of these expectations were definitely because of Obama's apparent talents. But his race was also a major factor. We wanted a major break from the past, and electing a black man president would definitely be that.

Blacks and whites alike found hope in his black flesh. Muslims found hope in his very name. Some Asian-Americans speculated on whether or not he could be America's first Asian president. Some pro-life, fundamentalist Christians supported him. Even white supremacists celebrated his possible presidency.

If elected, Obama would get us out of both wars, fix the economy and the environment and our disastrous medical industry; he would grant gay rights, provide government transparency, erase 400 years of racial oppression, restore America's primacy in the world, bring peace to the Middle East, fix our nation's school system, end the partisan bickering in Washington, end political corruption. I could go on for days. Basically, as Monica Crowley put it, Obama was going to be "Abraham Lincoln, FDR, and Jesus combined." As the abolitionists believed that ending slavery would redeem our country, so today many believe that electing Barack Obama would ultimately do the same.

Oddly enough, in some ways, it already has. With his election, nobody will look at America quite the same again. After all, while India has a Sikh prime minister, what other country would elect a minority as despised as we African-Americans have been to its prime leadership position? Ayman Zawahiri *tried* to castigate Obama as an Uncle Tom, Limbaugh and Hannity and the like try to paint him as the anti-Christ commissar who'll install Communism across the land, Fred Armisen *tries* to spoof him, Don Rickles bombed trying to lampoon him; but all these things fall on deaf ears. There is so much hope wrapped up in Obama's epidermis that we've become humorless and way too protective of the man. Who has the right to criticize or even poke fun at our last, greatest hope?

That hope was expressed on election night in Chicago's Grant Park, with people dancing in the streets of DC, Baltimore, all across America's cities, in Kenyan villages, all across the globe. Allies who've been icy during the Bush years have suddenly warmed up to us. Even belligerents like Russia and Iran have congratulated Obama on his victory. It's as though the entire world is once again viewing America with hope.

Ultimately, though, Barack Obama is not a magical, messianic Moses. He's simply a human being—and a Democrat to boot. He cannot possibly do *all* the things we want him to accomplish. That would require a revolution—not an election. He is going to disappoint. You can see some of that disappointment already in some of the criticism. So many can't stand all the Clintonians he's selected to join his Administration (though they were the last Dems to run anything and are, unfortunately, logical choices). There was the hubbub over Rick Warren (though, what did people think "reach across the aisle" actually meant?). However, W. has not simply lowered the bar. He's utterly obliterated it. *Any* sign of progress will be greeted with cheering and flowers in the street (you know, like the Iraqis greeted us when we invaded). It seems that, no matter what Obama does, he will ultimately be seen as a deliverer. Let's hope that his presidency is so spectacular that we rid ourselves of the White Messiah *and* the magical Negro and become the post-racial world all these liberals, with not just a little self-congratulation, say we're already in. Perhaps, we can finally say goodbye to at least *those* racial stereotypes and create a whole new one.

W Made Me Vote—RNC Made Me a Democrat

Tuesday, January 20, 2009

According to family lore, I was practically *born* political. Little William, all of four years of age, as my father likes to brag, stood up before his dad's business school students and proudly proclaimed, "They're gonna *'peach* Nixon away!"

For the next 18 years, I was a staunch Democrat. I vaguely remember loving the election results in 1976. I wanted Kennedy to beat Carter and then wanted him to step down because he was making it too easy for Reagan. I was disgusted all throughout the Reagan/Bush years. I was even depressed that the 1988 Pennsylvania primary happened five days before I reached my majority, and I would never be able to vote for Jesse.

As a lifelong Dem, I should've been ecstatic over Clinton, but I wasn't. I was disgusted. Just the year before I was canvassing for the party, going door-to-door, to drum up support for what ultimately became the Family Medical Leave Bill. I'd gone out of my way to make sure Harris Wofford beat Dick Thornburg for the Pennsylvania Senate seat. But by '92, Rodney King and the riots had happened. I just couldn't believe in the American Experiment any longer, and nothing Clinton could say would make me think differently. I did vote for Carol Moseley Braun for Senate, though, and Lenora Fulani for Prez. that year. But that was it. I didn't want to vote again.

I'd become a Leftist, an anarchist to be more exact (don't laugh). I didn't want to vote anymore. I didn't want to give my stamp of approval to a system I no longer believed in. And, while I believed there were some philosophical differences between Democrats and Republicans, I didn't think those differences were fundamental. They still believed in the System. It was chicken or beef with them—no vegetarian option in sight. And I had a big beef with a country that allowed Rodney Kings, Desert Storms, death penalties, etc., to exist. Things had to change, and our system was not built for the fundamental changes I wanted. In fact, I *thought* the system was built so that one, elected official couldn't make that much of a difference in how this country was run.

W. changed all that. Leftist Bill, of course, greeted his "election" with self-satisfied smugness. While the true believers screeched that the election "proved" that "every vote counts," 2000 actually proved quite the opposite. When all was said and done, Justices Scalia, Thomas, Rehnquist, O'Connor, and Kennedy had the only votes that truly mattered in a country of over 250 million people. Quite the opposite of the Democracy we've been taught to value.

2000 seems like a lifetime ago. I was smug in my own ignorance, I soon came to realize. I thought Bush was just a harmless, little savant who'd be gone in four years. Then 9/11 happened, and everything changed. I knee-jerked and was against the invasion of Afghanistan until I came to realize that every elected official in the history of the world would've invaded. It was the PATRIOT Act, the mass deportations, GITMO, FISA, all of it, that made me realize how dangerous the Bush Babee truly was.

The Iraq invasion put me over the top. Not only did I not believe the spiel about Saddam's being connected to al Qaeda, I actually got off my lazy duff and protested the invasion. The thing that got me, though, was that this was one place where I could point to where it actually *did* matter who we had elected to the Presidency. Al Gore never would've ousted Saddam. No other elected official would've dared to get us into this elective war. None of them would've casually thrown out 30 years of military policy and committed our armed forces to a long, drawn-out war of occupation. No, this was *personal* for Bush, and if he'd have lost the Supreme Court vote, we never would've been bogged down in Mesopotamia.

The man had to be stopped. W. had to go. So, I registered to vote and, for the first time in 12 years, I did vote. For Kerry. And nothing depressed me more than W.'s re-election.

When 2008 rolled around, I figured I'd vote for the Dem who eventually won the nomination. I just knew that I didn't want the GOP in the White House again. When the primaries started, I only cared as a political junkie. I'm into the race horse, too, but I didn't feel personally invested.

I figured, despite common wisdom, Hillary would not win because of her baggage and lack of a (scrotal) sack. I thought Richardson was the most qualified, but America wasn't ready for a Latino POTUS. I liked Obama enough, but I thought he was a flash in the pan, someone white folks liked because he made them feel better about themselves ("See, I'm not racist—I like Barack Obama"). I just couldn't take the brother seriously. I figured, when the rubber hit the road and all those white people had to pull the lever, they'd ultimately go with the white guy, and the cutest white guy around was John Edwards.

But then Iowa happened, and I had to change my thinking. I mean, if all those lillies of the cornfields voted for the black man, I had to take Obama seriously.

Unfortunately, the Clintons came to the same conclusion. The attack was on, and it was dirty. There was Hillary belittling MLK and lauding LBJ for the Civil Rights movement (while I always marvel at LBJ's courage in pushing the legislation through, knowing his party would forever lose the "Solid South," let's be honest: LBJ died of old age; MLK from a bullet), and then Bill totally discounted the black vote (after we vigorously supported him through thick and thin), saying "of course" we'd vote for Obama because he was black—never caring to admit that we black automatons didn't vote for Al Sharpton nor Carol Moseley Braun during their Presidential runs nor that we'd *never* support Alan Keyes. Our former Civil Rights heroes exposed themselves for chitlin'-eatin' table-scrappers perfectly willing to attack one of their own for the good of the almighty white folk. Andrew Young came out saying that Obama wasn't black, that Bill Clinton was blacker than him, and, in fact, Bill has "slept with more black women than Barack" (yeah, so did Strom Thurmond and Thomas Jefferson, what exactly *was* your point, Andy?). Then John Lewis was on *The News Hour* claiming that Obama was actually running a racist campaign. And I don't even want to talk about all the anti-Muslim shit the Clinton campaign pulled.

I watched and listened to all this in horror with my 16-month-old daughter, RNC (henceforth, "Poohbutt") in my arms. I can't speak for every black parent, but I was raised to believe that you fight the good fight, the right fight, in the hopes that those who come after you won't have to fight it. That you cannot end racism, maybe racism will never end, but you've got to do what you can to chip away at its armor. That's what the generations before you—through the Middle Passages, through slavery and Jim Crow, through all of it—have done for you, and that's what you must do for your own children. I don't know how much I've actually done, but I had a child now. And there I was—with her and bottle in hand—watching Obama going through some of the same things I went through growing up writ large: attacks from blacks and whites for being too black, not black enough, a black radical, a sell-out, being all about race, not enough about race, of constantly using the Race Card. And I kept thinking, "This shit has got to stop."

So, for RNC and her future, I did what I thought I'd never do: I registered to vote as a Democrat (Maryland has closed primaries), and, because of my baby girl, I voted for Barack Obama. For her, I voted, I blogged, and while we were out campaigning for her grandfather (who was running for local office in the neighboring state), I (foolishly?) hoped that those white Virginian voters would look down at my little brown girl, while talking politics, and perhaps think that Obama might not be so bad, after all. Of course, none of this was enough nor decisive nor influential, but I did what I could.

And now, here we are, Inauguration Day. Barack Obama is now the 44th President of the United States (five minutes late--in true, *black* fashion). I don't know what all that means. None of us will for years to come. Perhaps we'll never know. I do know that a lot of my views of my country have definitely been changed forever. I know watching all the pomp and circumstance on the television while Poohbutt plays innocently with her blocks, I keep finding myself choking up. I know for the first time watching one of these things, I really and truly feel proud to be an American.

Having seen Lester Holt and Michael Eric Dyson choke up after speaking on NBC, I know I am not alone in this. I keep smiling, I keep choking up, I keep crying and holding my daughter and kissing the hell out of her chubby, little cheeks. I can't help thinking that this is the greatest event I've ever witnessed, and I feel blessed to be sharing it with her. I'm so glad my parents are around to see this. I wish my grandparents were, my great-grandparents. I wish that every African who survived *and* died during the Middle Passages could see this, every black person who suffered and died these past 400 years of oppression and humiliation could sit down and take this all in.

If somehow they can, I wonder what they're thinking. I wonder if they feel the pride I do at this very moment. I wonder if their eyes are also filled with tears of joy and honor.

Poohbutt has no clue why I'm crying right now. And nothing makes me happier than knowing that she will *never* exactly understand why her father was crying on Tuesday, January 20, 2009. She'll never know why I'll so fervently keep preaching to her, "You can be *whatever* you want to be in this world." She'll never understand that, on this beautiful day, I could say those words and actually *believe* them—unlike all the black parents before me. And she'll never, ever, ever quite get her old man and his hearty laugh when she screws up her face and rolls her eyes, and huffs, "Yeah, yeah, Dad. First black President. Whatever."

God, how I love this day!

Bill Campbell

The Arts Tsar

Monday, January 26, 2009

One can only imagine the first week of any President's administration as the opening scene of *The Godfather*. Last week, I could see President Obama sitting in the Oval Office with cotton stuffed in his cheeks with *consigliere* Rahm Emmanuel off in the corner giving his creepily silent "Yea" or "Nay" as supplicants approach asking for everything from the legalization of marijuana to boosting the Department of Defense's budget.

Of course, Don Corleone, being a fictional Mafia boss, did not have to deal with the court of public opinion nor his interlocutors courting said court. Last week, with Obama barely able to warm his new seat, Quincy Jones became head jester for what I consider one of the most ridiculous causes I've heard so far (after all, don't we have two wars and an economy in the shitter?): that of Secretary of the Arts.

Apparently, Sir Quincy has been outraged over our present-day teenagers' inability to tell him who Duke Ellington and John Coltrane were. His ruffles ruffled, Jones started an on-line campaign for a federal Department of the Arts. He then took himself and his collected 150,000 electronic signatures and came to Washington buzzing his new brainchild into the ears of any who would listen.

As a novelist, I wholeheartedly support the encouraging of American arts. Hell, I'd even take a Republican-led tax-cut initiative to help us artists. (Seriously, do the Republicans think tax cuts are the remedy for everything? Like would they treat a gunshot wound with a 30 percent reduction in capital gains taxes?) I feel this corporatized drive to maximize profits within the arts has left our country's culture somewhat lacking. In popular music, we haven't had a scene-shifting new genre since grunge almost 20 years ago; house is about 25 years old; and hip-hop is looking at 35. Hollywood, in a constant search for bankable hits, will remake *anything*—old TV shows, comic books, old Hollywood hits *and* flops, amusement park rides, you name it. Broadway has turned so many movies into musicals I'm waiting for them to stage *Dude, Where's My Car?* We black authors have been ghettoized into producing "ghetto lit" almost exclusively. And I'm still waiting for us Gen X'ers to produce our own Morrison or Hemingway or Scorsese, for that matter.

But I don't see how a Secretary of the Arts would remedy any of that. What exactly would SoA, if created, actually accomplish? Would her/his weekly briefings to the President ignite an international crisis within the University of Iowa's MFA program? Would it lead to the strategic bombing of the Indian subcontinent and its diaspora so they stop producing Booker Prize winners? Would federal agents flood the Mississippi delta and the Appalachian Mountains with guitars and banjos to ensure that the blues and old-timey live on? Would there be molding clay in every pot? A piano in every parlor? Would Serrano (creator of the "Piss Christ") agents give each child coffee, a jar, and a crucifix to enliven the controversial artist's legacy?

I think Jones tipped his hand with his intentions for the Cabinet position with his invoking the names of the Duke and Trane. What he and the Ken Burnses and Wynton Marsalises of the world wish to do is elevate jazz as "America's Classical music." It's an annoying trend—if well-intentioned. Just because these men know that "serious," white cultural connoisseurs with their serious, white money laud Classical music, they chase after that moniker for the music they love best. But jazz—and all its subgenres—is jazz. Classical—and all its subgenres—is Classical. Jazz is great in its own right. Why try to mix the two? They have very little in common, and I feel this shotgun, dialectical "Me, too" marriage only *diminishes* jazz's greatness.

My diatribe aside, it shows that Jones doesn't really want to promote American art to this country or the world. He really wants to promote *his* art. After all, why isn't it equally disheartening that these kids don't know who Bill Monroe and Kool Herc are? If Jones were to get his Cabinet Secretary position or even a lesser "Arts Tsar," he would more than likely give state sanction to the art he loves. Jazz would definitely be elevated to what he feels is its rightful place, "America's Classical music." Perhaps he would branch out and give blessings and federal funds to the Harlem Renaissance's elevation. His replacement may be a modern art lover, and we would have nationwide celebrations of Jackson Pollock and Robert Motherwell. Maybe the next one will celebrate the life and art of Sam Bush. Either way you slice it, the SoA or Arts Tsar would sooner or later codify an official "American Art" to be celebrated and imitated nationwide in order to gain legitimacy and/or federal financing. The end result could be just as suffocating as the corporate-controlled media we have today (television being the sole bright light where corporate competition is actually improving the art). Either remedy turns into a malady in the eyes of truly innovative artists—no matter the genre.

Instead, if Jones, who has more money than God, really wants to promote American arts and culture, why doesn't he take some of that moolah and create private/public ventures in our nation's schools to do just that? If he's really worried about the state of American music, why doesn't he fund primary- and secondary-school music programs? After all, if it hadn't been for such programs in the past, with those poor children learning the art of the European marching band, would we have ever had jazz or funk? Not only would his maligned teenagers learn of the genius of Duke and Trane, but think of the new music they will ultimately create.

Jones and his Hollywood horde could fund extracurricular drama programs. They could hire local, starving actors to come in and train aspiring or simply curious students in week-long, quarterly drama workshops. They could do the same for the visual and material arts. Local writers could also chip in to promote their craft. Other philanthropic media moguls could open up middle-school "news stations" to teach kids what that takes to produce.

Writers could also lobby to come up with better literature syllabi for high school readers. I've wanted to be a writer since I was nine-years-old, and yet, even I found high school literature classes a bore at best and mostly torture. High schoolers become totally divorced from literature as entertainment or self-edification while being tortured with works from Hardy and the like—which are completely irrelevant to their own situation. Of coure, finding more relevant reading for teens is fraught with disaster in a land where parents want to burn *Harry Potter* for teaching witchcraft. I would love to give every teenager Sapphire's *Push*, but I'm sure the story of a pregnant, molested, AIDS-infected teenager would instigate a putsch in any local high school. However, I feel the effort to find such material would be worth it and pay dividends well into the future.

While I am generally not a fan of such "private-public" ventures, it seems to me that Jones and his ilk could better serve our arts and culture by doing something like this (since our own schools seem to have mostly given up) as opposed to erecting a federally-sanctioned "American Art." Not only would it promote a more proper respect for our culture's past, but it would also bolster a future, more vibrant art than we find ourselves with today.

The Arts Tsar—much as her/his corporate cousin does currently—

would only create an American, Stalinized, "Capitalist-Realist" art that would codify conformity and thwart innovation. We need a more "bottom-up" approach to revitalize the culture. Jazz was born in brothels; hip-hop in Bronx projects; country in the Scots-Irish hills of Appalachia. That is American art. That is our culture. Not some government official telling us what is "Art" from on-high.

Ridin' Dirty

Friday, February 6, 2009

We Americans are not as naive nor as stupid as many politicians may think. We know that campaign promises are more like *suggestions* and that Washington really isn't built for rapid change. Yes, Obama did really get us with his "Change" message, but we knew that it wasn't going to be overnight, if it happened at all. I think that's where all that "Hope" came in.

One of the things that we did hope for is that he really could change how Washington works. Every politician runs on "Washington is broken," but, with the disaster of the Bush Babee administration, those words seemed truer than they have since 1980. With all the scandals, all the sniping and back-biting, and the disastrous economy, we all know things have to change in DC.

We're still hoping that Obama can be that instrument for change, but it's looking to be a lot harder than we could've ever imagined.

The "revolving door" between pols and lobbyists and special interests have even hit Obama's own nominations. Just weeks after The Big Brother had been lauded for his prudent, damn-near sagacious choices for his cabinet, he's being hit left-and-right with exactly how insidious these relationships are. These latest controversies are starting to make me wonder what exactly is going on with our politicians, how dirty are these fools, and can Obama "clean up Washington," as he's promised or at least manage to acquire a dust-free cabinet.

Just look at what's been going on.

In a slap-to-the-face to his own "no lobbyists" decree, Secretary of Defense Robert Gates got a waiver for his Raytheon lobbyist bud, William Lynn, so he can serve as his deputy. Tom Daschle had to withdraw because of tax evasion and questions in how the hell he's made so much money as an "unofficial" lobbyist over these past few years since he was ousted from the Senate. Timothy Geithner had tax evasion issues. His nominee for White House Chief Performance Officer, Nancy Killefer, had to bow out over similar, though much less dramatic tax concerns. His nominee for Labor Secretary, Hilda

Solis, is having her Senate confirmations held up over her husband's tax problems. And now retired Gen. Anthony Zinni had the offer of his being US Ambassador to Iraq rescinded in part due to his being an executive vice-president for DynCorp, a huge military contractor who's all over Afghanistan and Iraq.

Of course, the nascent Obama administration will ride over these bumps in the road. All administrations stumble out of the gate. It's just his turn. But there are larger questions to ask here: If Obama, who's trying to run a squeaky-clean operation, can't find nominees who clear the bar, is it because of his people's lack of vetting skills or is it that everybody gets a little dirty once they enter Washington politics? Just look at some of the scandals our nation's Capitol has been dealing with these past few years:

Charlie Rangel (D-NY)

I love my Bronx Jew/Black Harlemite, I love his voice, I loved his autobiography, I hate his hair, but I love his candor. Now, he's been held under suspicion for his cozy ties with corporate honchos, a relationship way too cozy for the Chairman of the House Ways and Means Committee. But now he's dodging tax evasion charges. Makes you wonder, don't it?

Randy "Duke" Cunningham (R-CA)

What this guy did was more than felonious. It was *treasonous*. Taking $2 million in bribes from defense contractors, especially while our nation's at war, makes you really wonder how many men, women, and children died in Afghanistan and Iraq because of this bastard's greed.

William Jefferson (D-LA)

Now, all you middle-class black folks know that feeling of dread that turns your stomach when a spectacular crime's teased on the news. You sit up there praying, "Oh, please, don't let him be black." Jefferson definitely piqued my middle-class black sensibilities with his brazen crimes. Not only was he bilking our African brothers, but he didn't even have the decency to hide his graft in an off-shore account. I mean, damn, $900,000 in your gotdamned *freezer*?! What kind of ghetto bullshit was that?!

Bill Campbell

Mary Landrieu (D-LA)

One of the only politicians who came out clean over the Katrina mess has since been muddied up over having received over $2 million of earmarks for $30,000 in campaign contributions from a *reading program*. Shaking down illiterate children. Now that takes ovaries.

As we all know, every day was Christmas for Ted Stevens.

People are *still* being convicted over the Jack Abramoff (who was convicted back in '06) scandal.

And the Biggest Scandal That Wasn't

How Republican Congressman Billy Tauzin didn't end up in jail after he fanagled that horrible Medicaid bill, which was nothing but a huge payday for the pharmaceutical industry, and then got the cushy, $2 million-a-year gig of president and CEO of that industry's largest lobbying group, PHRMA, is beyond me.

What that list and the latest flap over the Obama picks prove to me is that Washington does indeed need a big broom but it also needs to scrub the baseboards, lighting fixtures, and a severe douching of its septic tank. With the mind-boggling amounts of cash that flow in and out of Washington, we have hordes of lobbyists rushing the Capitol Steps every day. No matter how much Congress tries to disingenuously purge themselves of their influence, lobbyists still have a way-too-cozy relationship with our politicians and government officials. And we Americans pay the price. The Madoff scheme was probably not investigated for years because the Madoff family was literally in bed with the SEC. And what about last year's Sex-for-Oil scandal over at the Interior Department?

Our politicians always have been and always will be a privileged caste. However, it seems that they have let this privilege blind them to their primary responsibility: to represent the *citizens* of the United States of America. Instead, they have become way too identified with whom the lobbyists represent. They have decided that they too are immune from paying their taxes. They've decided that it's only "busines as usual" to trade campaign contributions for earmarks. In exchange for these political favors, many politicians like Tauzin and Daschle feel that it's only to be expected that they're rewarded with lucrative jobs from the industries they'd formerly regulated.

Washington is drowning in a miasma of corruption and "improprieties." We need to make it impossible for the Daschles and Tauzins to do what they did. We need to seriously audit these pols' tax returns during and *after* they leave office (hear that, Mr. Clinton?). We need to make sure that there is no ultimate pay-off for any person who serves this nation's government.

Unfortunately, the only people who can legislate such reform are the very ones who grow fat on the life rafts of cronyism while the rest of the nation sinks to the bottom.

We can clown Obama for his nomination missteps all we like. It is the easier news story. But what we really need to do is find out exactly how dirty Washington actually is and how the hell we can clean it all up.

15 **Albums That Changed My Life**

Sunday, February 15, 2009

All right, I got this from Gail at the blog *The Worley Gig*, who got it from one of those lists floating around on Facebook. I was unaware of that one, but blogger *Skunk Gal* has a hysterical response to the *25 Things You Don't Know About Me*, which is so popular it was even featured on *The Today Show* this morning.

I've yet felt compelled to fill that one out, but the *15 Albums* seemed like fun. Gail contends that her list doesn't contain anything from beyond 1987 because of a dearth of kick-ass music. I'd argue that it's not the music's fault. We just generally feel things more strongly in our youth. For example, close your eyes, think back to that crush you had back in eighth grade, how you would just *die!* if you weren't together *forever*. Now, open your eyes, turn around ... Where are they?

So, I won't claim that my *15 Albums* are the greatest of all-time, or even the ones I think are the greatest. However, these albums all represent something important to me—even if I don't listen to them now. I hope you enjoy.

1. **Prince** *–1999*

My Uncle Rodney got me hooked on Prince at a very early age. My Uncle Rodney surprised me with a ticket to my first concert, *1999*, and I got to go with him, my cousin, and my cousin's best friend, who I had a huge crush on. A few years ago, when my uncle lay dying in a drug-induced semi-coma in the ICU, I put one bud in my ear and another in his ear and played *1999* for him. That was the last time I saw my Uncle Rodney alive.

2. **Prince** *—Purple Rain*

While Prince is my favorite artist and "When Doves Cry" is my favorite Prince song, *Purple Rain* isn't even my second favorite Prince album. Despite that, at one time, I took the success of this album so personally, you'd have thought I was getting royalties.

3. X-Clan—*To the East Blackwards*

Yes, I, too, loved Brother J Funkin' Lesson and Professor X, The Overseer, sisssssyyyyyyy!!! While I don't think X-Clan was the most innovative group of the period (though the one with the best mythology), I credit them for getting my young, angry ass to look into vodou, santeria, obeah, and other Africanist religions, which really influenced my first novel, *Sunshine Patriots*. I gotta give credit where credit's due.

4. Various Artists (but mostly the Bee Gees)—*Saturday Night Fever* [OST]

Steve Miller's "The Joker," "The Theme from S.W.A.T." and "Welcome Back" (from *Welcome Back, Kotter*) were my first 45s, and this soundtrack, bought when I was a mere 7-years-old, started my music addiction that has not been slaked to this day.

5. LL Cool—*Radio*

Most people forget the early days of hip-hop when even black radio wouldn't play rap music. In a lot of cities at the time, they were violently opposed to the music. And I, being young and bourgie, fell into their classtrap. LL brought me out of my delusion. I've been a hip-hop head ever since. I still blame him for the horrendous concept of the "rap ballad" (after all, who remembers MC Shan's "Left Me Lonely"?), but LL was the man.

6. John Coltrane—*Giant Steps*

Back in high school when I wanted to hear more jazz, I bought this album, *My Favorite Things*, and Thelonious Monk's *Brilliant Corners*. But this is the album I kept coming back to. This is the one that gave me my life-long love of jazz.

7. Public Enemy—*It Takes a Nation of Millions to Hold Us Back*

I think before this album came out, I was just a *peeved*, young black man.

8. Fela—*Original Sufferhead*

It's hard to believe with all my pro-black, pan-Africanist militancy back in the day, it took me until I was 25 before I discovered Fela Anikulapo (Ransome) Kuti. Of course, it's totally believable that it was an older white guy from Alabama who made the introduction. Supremely funky, militantly outspoken, Wole Soyinka's cousin, Fela's everything I love in an artist—no matter the medium.

9. Ice Cube—*Death Certificate*

Face it, nothing beats Cube's children's movies, but, not only was O'Shea at the top of his game and on top of the world, *Death Certificate* perfectly encapsulated the rage we were feeling after the Rodney King beating.

10. R.E.M. —*Document*

All right, this is a weird one because *Document* marks more of a negation than any of my other picks. Because of MTV's racial policies of the time, I was more into rock than I'd ever been before or since. So, in the mid-80s, I was really into R.E.M., U2, The Police, Talking Heads, Kate Bush, Tears for Fear. But in '87 I got BET, and it was pretty much over for rock. *Document*'s the last rock album I'd buy for almost 20 years.

11. Billy Eckstine—*Everything I Have Is Yours: The Best of the M-G-M Years*

Being from Pittsburgh, I'd heard homeboy Eckstine's name all the time. So, in college while I was a jazz DJ for the radio station, I dubbed this album and became addicted to him and "corny" jazz vocals. So, by day, I'd pump Digital Underground, but at night, I'd while away the time with Billy and Sarah.

12. Wu-Tang Clan—*Enter the Wu-Tang (36 Chambers)*

After spending almost a year in the Czech Republic, I was pretty much out of sorts. I'd missed African-Americans, our culture, our music, everything, and I missed all the food options America can offer. Of course, with all that stuff now available, I was suffering culture shock like you wouldn't believe and didn't know exactly where I belonged in this world. Then I heard one little word spelled out, and I knew I was, indeed, where I belonged. "M-E-T-H-O-D."

13. D'Angelo—*Voodoo*

This album made it OK to love (R&B) again. I thought D'Angelo had firmly established himself as the ruler of R&B and that he'd ushered in a new day for the stale genre. Boy, I was wrong on both counts. But that's all right, this was a great album.

14. Jazzanova—*The Remixes 1997-2000*

I hadn't really been into electronic music since I'd left Chicago's House-plagued land after college. Then I got a hold of this two-disc set, and I really went ape-shit. I ended up being an electronica critic for *BPM* and ink19.com for years and did something I was always loathe to do: go to clubs (generally to review and/or interview DJs—but still).

15. The Slits—*Cut*

A few years back, I was contemplating writing a coming-of-age book set in the '80s. It was to concentrate mostly on hip-hop, but, for background, I picked up the great *Rip It Up and Start Again: Postpunk 1978-1984* by Simon Reynolds. Because I liked their names, I first checked out The Slits. God, I love these women. I totally got into Post-Punk (Devo, Gang of Four, ESG, A Certain Ratio, Pere Ubu, James Chance, Young Marble Giants, the list goes on and on). Soon thereafter, I got into the White Stripes, Coheed and Cambria, and a whole bunch of other rock. After some 20 years, I like rock, and it all starts with the Slits.

Bill Campbell

For the Love of Jesus

Wednesday, February 18, 2009

To say I'm a lapsed Catholic would be a gross understatement. I went to Catholic elementary school, and, because of motherly pressure, I became a *converso* at 14. However, since confirmation, I haven't really been to mass and don't miss it much. *Forgive me, Father, for I have sinned. It has been 25 years since my last confession.* In fact, the last time I went, a wedding a few years back, I drank so much communal wine (I know, I shouldn't have been up there in the first place) the deacon thanked me for bogarting the blood of Christ.

But, no matter how hard you try, you can never quite deny what you grew up being. I'll always be a Catholic. And, as such, I can't stop being pissed over my church and the man they'd chosen to lead it, that RatZinger, Benedict XVI.

I confess. I wasn't a big fan of John Paul II. I'll always feel his open hostility toward liberation theology got a lot of priests, nuns, and lay people killed in Latin America, which is probably why evangelicals are taking over there today.

Of course, Latin America's not alone in shedding its Catholic identity. Africa and Asia see its paltry numbers growing, but in North America and Europe, folks have fled the Church like it's a rampaging Cossack. When JPII died in April 2005, Rome found itself at a crossroads.

They could have addressed the problem of their fleeing flock, opened up, liberalized, become more inclusive like they had with Vatican II. Instead, the beleaguered Cardinal College circled their wagons and retrenched, electing someone so reactionary, so venomous, I wouldn't be surprised if he jumped up, screamed, "No one expects the Spanish Inquisition!" and started burning witches in St. Peter's Square.

In 2004, under the ancient regime, American cardinals threatened to deny John Kerry communion for his pro-choice stance. In 2007, RatZinger upped the ante by threatening pro-choice candidates with excommunication. No doubt he emboldened the American clergy to bully from their pulpits last year and exhort/-tort parishioners that they "risked their immortal soul" by voting pro-choice. South Carolinian

Reverend Jay Scott Norman even told his flock they shouldn't take the Host if they voted for Barack "the most radical pro-abortion politician ever" Obama.

BREAK FOR RANT-WITHIN-RANT

While I definitely don't agree, I can respect the Church's *official* pro-life position. *Every* life is sacred and should not be destroyed. Therefore, they have always been against abortion *and* capital punishment. Officially.

They've been quite vocal, have campaigned vigorously against the former. No one doubts the Church's views on fetal life. But what about penal death? *Dead Man Walking* aside, where are they when a convict has her/his life flushed away by lethal injection? Why don't I see them protesting outside prisons?

More importantly, why don't I see them protesting Republican candidates or any and *all* candidates who advocate for the death penalty? Wouldn't that consistency be truer to Church doctrine? Since there are probably few if any politicians who espouses the Church's particular pro-life stance, shouldn't priests deny *every* American voter the Eucharist? Shouldn't RatZinger excommunicate *every* Catholic politician in these here United States?

So, either you excoriate all American Catholics for our political beliefs, or shut the hell up. You tell the liberation theologists to stop focusing so much on their politics and focus more on Jesus' being the Son of God. Hmmm, maybe *someone* should practice what they preach. And, if you're looking for a sermon, why not start with Isaiah? "My house shall be known as a house of prayer for *all* peoples."

END OF RANT-WITHIN-RANT

This November, 54 percent of American Catholics told their clergy they'd gladly risk their "immortal souls" to save their temporal asses and voted for Obama, anyway. But it's not as though this Pope will listen to those results or the pleas to expand women's role within the Church or end priestly celibacy or stop their homophobic blame game with the child molestation scandals. And they definitely won't stop hiding the crimes' main facilitator, Cardinal Law, in Vatican City and bring him to justice. Nope, they are obstinately deaf, dumb, and blind to our modern age. They are hightailin' it *outta* Damascus and breaking the sound barrier down the road to perdition.

And RatZinger is proudly leading the charge. The man isn't satisfied with just enraging Catholics. He is hellbent and determined to piss *everybody* off (remember how he attacked Harry Potter?). This Pope finds the ideas of Christian brotherhood, love, and charity anathema to his very being. He doesn't want to bring the world together in understanding and respect but would rather fling us all in a steel cage and have us fight it out in a no-holds-barred conflagration of religious fury. To make John's *Revelation* flesh.

Of course, RatZinger didn't get where he is by not being clever. He uses Bush Babee obfuscation to somehow cloud his true intentions.

He often praises women for their early roles in the Church; he thinks their contribution "always has been a determining factor without which the church could not live"; Catholic mothers have "given life" and introduce that life to a "friendship with Jesus"; he even calls Mary Magdalene "the apostle of the apostles." Should women become priests? Hell no! Didn't you see that? "The apostle *of* the apostles." And, if you don't get that, here: "Jesus chose 12 men as fathers of the new Israel, 'to be with Him and to be sent out to proclaim the message.'" Stick to birthing, ladies—or at least the rhythm method.

There was his 2006 speech where he took on Islam: "The emperor comes to speak about the issue of jihad, holy war. He said, I quote, 'Show me just what Mohammed brought that was new, and there you will find things only evil and inhuman...'"

When furor naturally erupted, he did his best Lucille Ball mischievous blush to the world's outraged Ricky Ricardo. "Who me?!" He tried to hide behind quotes, but only the mainstream media was fooled. After all, this is the same RatZinger who in 2000 claimed that Muslims and other religions are "gravely deficient" and "depend on superstitions or other errors ... [and] constitute an obstacle to salvation."

He hid behind this newfangled field of "gender theories" this past Christmas after he infuriated gays, transsexuals, feminists, and (who knows) orthodox environmentalists when he admonished us all to preserve God's "natural" order of man and woman, calling for an "ecology of man." "The tropical forests do deserve our protection; but man, as a creature, does not deserve any less."

Vatican spokesman Father Federico Lombardi hearkened to said gender theory and said that the Pope did not specifically attack homosexuality. But RatZinger has spent a lot of his time attacking gays. Within months of ascending to the papacy, he effectively banned gays from the priesthood. Before that he authored the Church's 2003 battle plan to oppose gay marriage and adoption and has also written that gay discrimination is "not unjust discrimination" and that homosexuality represents "an intrinsic moral evil."

The Vatican and MSM like to treat every new RatZinger controversy as a mere slip of the tongue, a clerical Spoonerism that the Pope (no matter how consistent these "slips" are with his past views) somehow didn't mean. But one does not become Pope without being a political being. As Prof. Chester Gillis, chair of the theology department at Georgetown University, has claimed, "He knows very well the kind of claims he makes have political implications. He wants to influence public policy in numerous places in the world and hopefully sway the powers that be to his side, especially on so-called social issues."

But it's RatZinger's *actions* last month that should've really told the world exactly where this Pope stands. As you've no doubt heard by now, the Pontiff rescinded the excommunication of four Society of St. Pius X bishops, a breakaway order started by Archbishop Marcel Lefebvre that basically wanted to repeal Vatican II. Among the group of four was Bishop Richard Williamson, a known Holocaust denier.

Outrage immediately ensued. Germany's Central Council of Jews, the Jewish Agency for Israel, Yad Vashem, and Elie Wiesel condemned the action. German Chancellor Angela Merkel called on RatZinger to issue a "very clear" rejection of Holocaust denial, and the Chief Rabbinate of Israel cut ties with the Vatican.

In response, Rome came out ringing a false note. Lombardi stated, "The condemnation of statements that deny the Holocaust could not have been clearer, and from the context it is apparent that it referred to the positions of Bishop Williamson and to all similar positions." They even told Williamson to "distance himself" from his Holocaust fantasies—though he's yet to do it. That doesn't really matter, though. As Monsignor Robert Wister pointed out, "To deny the Holocaust is not a heresy even though it is a lie. ... The excommunication can be lifted because he, Williamson, is not a heretic, but he remains a liar."

But Williamson *is* a heretic. He wasn't excommunicated for his anti-Semitism 20 years ago. He was booted because his unauthorized consecration was deemed "an unlawful and schismatic act" by JPII himself. RatZinger, who's always been sympathetic to the Society, reinstated the bishops as a thumb in the eye to his predecessor.

The fact that Williamson is a Holocaust denier is only an added plum (maybe his time as a Nazi Youth and German soldier affected him more deeply than the Pope claims?). It may even be more to the point.

The American press has been flummoxed by the move. They *claim* that Benedict has expended great effort in reaching out to Jews. Oh, he's made some cursory gestures, but he's exerted much more effort doing just the opposite. He's worked vigorously to accelerate the canonization of Pope Pius XII, who's believed to have turned a blind eye to the Holocaust. He's reinstated the Tridentine Mass, which includes a prayer for the conversion of Jews "from darkness to Catholicism." And now this.

I've heard a couple pundits claim that RatZinger's just attempting to "reach out" to unite the Church's disparate groups. I say he's reaching *back* to Catholicism's dark past. As Gillis noted, this man "knows very well" what he's doing, and what he's doing is courting reaction and disaster. All his little "malaprops" and "missteps" are designed to divide and drive the Church even further to the Right. He may occasionally pay lip service to this PC, multiculti modernity he finds himself in, and Lombardi will equivocate and parse and search for "context" when his Bossman makes a "boo boo"; but these mistakes are the point. He is hacking away at the modern age, attacking all he finds an affront to God, and his sexist, homophobic, anti-Semitic, anti-Potterite agenda is designed to destroy these "abominations" in order to restore the Church to its proper place—the primacy of Christendom.

Unfortunately for Catholicism, RatZinger's efforts will only fling the Church headlong into obscurity. His atavistic brand of hate has no place in our world (well, maybe YouTube). Benedict knows this, but he doesn't care. Like Bush Babee, this Pope is certain that history and God will bear him out. We Americans couldn't bring ourselves to impeach Bush, and we had to wait him out for eight, long years. Look where that's gotten us! RatZinger won't be excommunicated. He's Pope for life, baby. There's no telling how long his reign of horrors will continue. For the love of Jesus, I hope it's not much longer. However, until Benedict goes to that Great Auto da fé in the Sky, he will continue to outrage, he won't stop spewing his vitriol, he will continue to cover gays, women, Arabs, Jews, all he finds blasphemous with his vile. And, while he does it, more and more will join me in a decidedly un-Catholic flock.

Eat A Armey Award:
Sarah Palin and The Pips

Monday, March 23, 2009

(*In honor of* *everyone's favorite Dick, ormer Congressman from Texas, House Majority Leader, and "Republican Revolutionary," Dick Armey, I give you the second,* Eat A Armey Award, *handed out to the public luminary who's being an especial jackhole the previous week.)*

Singing the same old, tired doo wop of "the dangers of deficit spending," Sarah Palin and the Pips (Haley Barbour, Rick Perry, Mark Sanford, and castrato Bobby Jindal) are flooding the airwaves with their retread miss, "Fiscal Conservativism." The tune has changed and has been remixed several times over the past few years, but, no matter how hard they try, this song seems to be perpetually off-key and is currently falling on deaf ears.

For those of you who haven't heard, Palin and these other Republican governors have decided to reject *parts* of the federal stimulus package going to their states. A few were originally contemplating rejecting all their state's funds but realized that would be political suicide. And, since this is all really about positioning themselves for the GOP presidential nomination in '12, nobody's been willing to fall on their swords on "principle" just yet.

Even with this supposed compromise, Palin, Perry, Sanford, Jindal, and Barbour are going hoarse, screeching about their "conservative principles," "Trojan horses," and the Peloponessian War, for that matter. Barbour says he'll reject $56 million; Jindal, $98 million; Palin, $288 million; Perry, $566 million; and, after the White House rejected his ploy to use the money to pay off state debts, Mark Sanford claims he'll reject a whopping $700 million.

But what is the moral this GOP Greek chorus trying to sing? What exactly are these "principles" they're droning on and on about? Why are they only rejecting *part* of the stimulus package and not the whole thing? What part of it has their togas in a wad?

Bill Campbell

Why, unemployment benefits, of course.

Oompah!

They claim that the federal government's trying to stealthily change their states' unemployment compensation laws by extending the benefit to those seeking part-time as opposed to full-time employment. Their principles (I'm guessing those old shibboleths, "state's rights" and "welfare cheats") tell them that they don't want to reward people who are "unwilling" to seek full-time employment. Those same principles ignore the fact that most service employers refuse to *offer* full-time employment. But what does principle have to do with reality?

Of course, in the face of the economic crisis we're currently facing (much of it brought on by their principled Republican cohorts), this all begs the question: Who gives a fuck? Hundreds of thousands of people are being laid off monthly; Sanford's own South Carolina has the second highest unemployment rate in the country; and your "principles" are suddenly telling you to screw the ones who are most fucked by this economy. Yeah, I understand principles—not yours—but the principle of having principles. But principles are supposed to *guide* governance—not dictate it. As Pennsylvania governor, Ed Rendell, says:

"How do you sit across the table from a part-time worker working three part-time jobs, doing his best to keep his family afloat, didn't get health care, didn't get anything for it, all three of his jobs collapsing? What does that make you? Does that make you a good Christian?"

No, Ed, this whole song-and-dance doesn't make Palin and the Pips good *Christians*. It makes them good *Republicans*. Because none of these pols care about the suffering in 2009. They're looking at their prospects in 2012. And when that time comes, they won't point to the people they helped starve. They'll talk about how they stood up to "big, bad Washington"; how they wouldn't give in to "welfare cheats"; and that you'd have to pry "fiscal responsibility" from their cold, dead hands. But it's all a charade, a complex lip-synch routine replete with *Solid Gold* dancers, a "live studio" audience, canned applause, and a Top Ten chart that has nothing to do with reality ("Kill that metaphor, Bill! Kill it!"). Because while they rail against Washington and welfare, four of these governors are some of the biggest "welfare queens" this country's got.

Each one of their states (except for Rick Perry's Texas) receives more in federal money than they pay in federal taxes. South Carolina gets $1.35 for every dollar sent to Washington; Louisiana ranks fourth, receiving $1.78 for every dollar sent to Washington; Alaska's three

($1.84/$1); and Mississippi is number two, receiving a whopping $2.02 for every dollar sent in federal taxes.

So yes, my Four Tops, this is the same, old song. We've heard Republicans talk about fiscal responsibility, personal responsibility, we've heard them rail against deficit spending and pork and welfare for millennia now. But when the rubber hits the road, they are even *more* irresponsible than those dastardly "tax-and-spend" liberals. After all, Reagan, Bush, and Bush Babee are the ones who've given us record-breaking deficits. Even Deregulus Prime, Phil Gramm, that anti-whining "foot soldier of the Reagan Revolution" once confessed to being in Washington talking about slashing the pork while going home bragging about how he brought home the bacon.

And Palin and her Pips are some of the biggest swine swindlers there are out there. But reality and rhetoric never do have to meet in politics. They'll yodel all day long about their kosher politics while they gulp down their Lipitor with their Beltway bacon. They'll tell us how they stood up to Obama while they bent over backwards to get earmarks into his budgets. The one thing that will be consistent, though, is they'll continue to paint hard-working folks "welfare cheats" and deny them out of much-needed money.

So, while these people, who are "unwilling" to seek full-time employment while working two or three part-time jobs, become homeless, I hope Jindal will find it in his heart to open up the Super Dome to house them—if only temporarily. Then he and his fellow Pips could hold a benefit, hum a little phallic philharmonic, and asphyxiate on all the Armeys of the people they're screwing.

My Favorite Lefty Films

Sunday, March 29, 2009

Last night, I came across Distributorcap NY's *Must See Movies* list, which was inspired by Yahoo's *100 Movies to See Before You Die*. It all got me to thinking what were my favorite left-wing movies of all-time?

What do I mean by "left-wing" as opposed to, say, "liberal" movies? If you're liberal or leftist, you will naturally disagree with this (contention's in the DNA), but I look at it as sometimes simply being a matter of perspective: liberals believe in the system more than a leftist ever would. So (and I have to thank my friend Union Paul for this comparison), a liberal anti-corporation movie would be *Erin Brockovich*, where our heroine sees a wrong and through heroic, individual action she takes down the evil corporation because, in America, one *can* bring down the evil corporation and, in America, the justice system is *always* on the side of right. Oh yeah, and we can all get rich!!! in the process. A leftist, anti-corporation flick would be something like *Silkwood* where they kill the bitch off for startin' some shit.

The other way a film can be more liberal than leftist is when they get all Jack Nicholson "You can't handle the truth!" and tone down what needs to/actually was/should be said in order to (one assumes) better appeal to their audience. So, the teacher they based *Dangerous Minds* on used hip-hop to teach her inner-city students English while in the movie they used Bob Dylan, though it made absolutely no sense whatsoever.

The movie can also just make a bald-faced appeal to one's middle-class, bleeding-heart sensibilities, in order to gain your sympathies as opposed to just telling a story. *Boyz N The Hood* is a perfect example of a "liberal" ghetto tale. Ice Cube's no cold-blooded killer. He actually cries while blowing some dude's head off. Morris Chestnutt's character is murdered *just* before he scores high enough to get an athletic scholarship and escape the 'hood. And, if that ain't enough pathos fo' yo' ass, Ice Cube makes an open appeal with "Either they don't know, it don't show, or they don't care what's goin' on in the 'hood."

Menace II Society lies somewhere in between (if you excuse those horrible Charles Dutton speeches) because folks are just brutal. Our "hero" is no hero whatsoever. And, while he dies just before he gets out, you wonder if his moving to Atlanta would've really made him turn his life around. If he'd been moving to Des Moines, that would've been one thing. But the ATL's just as dirty as LA. Despite Jada's wishes, he still could've been pulling those "driiiiiiiiive-bys." She was just so ghetto in that movie. Ha!

However, I consider *The Wire* to be totally leftist. They never tried to appeal to your bleeding-heart sympathies. They'd have killed the puppy if it had made a better story. You're not tricked into feeling sympathy for their characters. It's the three-dimensional writing in the series that makes you connect with all the folks in it. And through that brilliant writing, they subvert your assumptions. There's something human in the drug dealers and dope fiends we've been trained to view as animal, as well as something animal in the police and politicians we're trained to view as our heroes. So, you're all pissed off that Bodie caps Wallace in Season One but somehow feel proud of Bodie for having gone out like a soldier in Season Four. It's that beautiful subversion that makes *The Wire* a leftist masterpiece.

I hope that long-winded, half-assed explanation helps you in reviewing my list. As with all lists, it's not as comprehensive as I'd wished and, of course, I would've liked to add more. But hell, coming up with and explaining 15 was hard enough.

1. Network (1976)

Much better and more eloquent people have waxed on about how brilliant this movie is. Paddy Chayefsky, Sidney Lumet, William Holden, (Oscar-winning) Peter Finch, Faye Dunaway (in her prime), Robert Duval (ditto), Ned Beatty. How couldn't it have been great? It's been inducted into the Producers Guild of America's Hall of Fame; the Writers Guild of America-East named the script one of the Top 10 of all-time; AFI named it the 64th greatest film of all-time (which is way too low in my opinion).

Frankly, *Network* is my favorite movie of all-time. As an aspiring satirist, this is the level of satire I aspire to. OK, that whole Holden speech to Dunaway about how she *is* TV is a bit lame, but the rest of it is absolutely perfect. The black revolutionaries ultimately arguing about market share. Ned Beatty delivering the word of God—money—to Finch. And the courage it took to have that ending!

Hollywood simply can't make a good satire these days *because* it doesn't have the courage to trust its audience and take the damned thing to its logical conclusion. *Bamboozled* came close, but then Spike felt the need to explain the entire movie at the end. *Thank You for Smoking* decided to bash us over the head with a "moral to this story is..." when the moral is the satire itself. And *A Day without a Mexican*, which had the potential to say so much, turned into some bullshit, liberal, PC claptrap about why can't we all just get along? I almost cried at the wasted opportunity.

But *Network* has balls coming out its ass (a serious medical condition where one should immediately consult a physician), and I love every minute of the movie for it.

2. Do the Right Thing (1989)

I think the thing that still amazes me about this movie is that the tension in the movie is still palpable. I don't think there's a better movie that captures anger and rage more than this movie. The one thing Spike's always been good at is casting, and this movie's just loaded: John Turturro, Samuel L. Jackson, Danny Aiello, Ossie Davis, Ruby Dee, Bill Nunn, Giancarlo Esposito, Robin Harris, Martin Lawrence, Rosie Perez's breastseses, the list goes on and on. The one thing Spike's always sucked at is just shutting the hell up every once in awhile, but the didacticism (is that a word?) in this movie doesn't seem so bad because everybody's all pissed off. The constant use of PE's "Fight the Power" was brilliant. Tuturro and Esposito are perfect racist counterweights to each other, and it's probably Lee's only "race" film where the white guy (Aiello) is multidimensional and the most sympathetic character. For the record, this is my second favorite film of all-time.

3. Matewan (1987)

Well, I was born a coal miner's grandson and another one's nephew. I'm heavily pro-union. Hell, my mom's from a small mining town outside of Pittsburgh that had no stop lights and one, huge slag heap. In other words, I was bred to love this pro-union, coal mining movie set in West Virginia. And this is one of many reasons why John Sayles is one of my favorite (if not my favorite) directors. I love Chris Cooper and James Earl Jones in this movie. And David Strathairn as the sheriff caught in between the striking miners and the Pinkerton boys is absolutely brilliant. I could watch this movie all day.

4. Conquest of the Planet of the Apes (1972)

OK, this is more of a childhood favorite than anything else. I mean, I used to *love The Planet of the Apes*. I watched all the movies, the TV series, the cartoon. I had the action figures. I still love the franchise as an adult (though that Mark Wahlberg movie sucked; and what was with that Charlton Heston ape being all anti-gun?). *Conquest* is my favorite movie of the bunch. I guess there was a fledgling black nationalist in my little boy frame. That's the only thing that could explain why I love this one best. After all, all the *Apes* movies are political. But this is the one where the ... uh ... apes take over.

5. The Battle of Algiers (1966)

I think (if I remember correctly) this movie's been praised throughout the ages for its gritty realism. It's definitely that. I think what struck me just now is just how relevant the damned thing still is. Minus today's Muslim fundamentalism (Algeria's was a post-colonial nationalist movement), the questions about a Western occupying power in a Muslim country and the uses of torture and terrorism are still plaguing our country today. Even without all that, *Battle* is still a brilliant movie.

6. The Conformist (1970)

This movie sparked my brief love affair with Bernardo Bertolucci, but it only lasted as long as this movie and *1900,* which is a long-ass movie in and of itself. The movie's set in Mussolini's Fascist Italy, where this spineless guy is sent to assassinate a former professor who's fled to France. You can watch it as a searing indictment of Fascism and its participants. Or you can choose to look upon it as some kind of highfalutin' existentialist tract. Either way, it's a great movie.

7. Putney Swope (1969)

Growing up, my Dad would always tell me how *Putney Swope* was the funniest movie he's ever seen. As a teenager, I didn't get it. But I don't think teens are physiologically able to understand satires. As an adult, *Putney* is definitely one of my favorite comedies ever. Like father, like son, eh? Much like *Conquest*, it's a speculative piece on what would happen if the ... uh ... apes took over. The CEO of a powerful

Madison Ave. ad agency dies, and everyone on the board votes for Swope to take over because they all assume nobody would vote for the token black guy. Of course, all hell breaks loose and hilarity ensues. I don't know what else Robert Downey, Sr., has ever done (aside from seriously screw up his kid), but this is a definite classic.

"The Boorman 6 Girl's *got* to have soul!"

8. Dr. Strangelove (1964)

Well, if you haven't figured it out, I love satire, and what better anti-nuke satire is there? This movie and Peter Sellers are hilarious through and through. 'Nuff said.

9. Burn (1969)

When people talk about great Brando performances, I don't think I've ever heard anyone mention this flick, but I think he's absolutely brilliant. *Burn* is about a British agent (Sir William Walker, not oddly enough) who tries to stir up a little slave rebellion on the Caribbean isle of "Queimada." Modeled very loosely on the Haitian revolution, I love how this movie has the rebellion and Walker's stooge turn the tables on the provocateur. It's as though Faustus finally got the upper hand on Mephistopholes. You can skip that *Emperor Jones* bullshit (though I love Paul Robeson) and just watch this bad boy.

10. City of God (2002)

I think I've admitted this before, but I was absolutely fanatical about this movie when it came out. It's one of the few movies I rushed back to the theater to see again right after I'd seen it the first time. I think what I loved so much about it was its utter brutality and seeming honesty. It was like, "Yeah, this is fucked up." But they didn't try to tug at your heartstrings or appeal to your empathy. They just showed it as close to how it T-I-is that a work of fiction can get.

(*PS. I'm so nutso about this movie, while in Mexico, I watched it in Portuguese with Spanish subtitles; yeah, you guessed it, I don't speak Spanish.*)

11. Paths of Glory (1957)

Yep, another Kubrick film, and probably my favorite anti-war film that I can think of. Based on a true story, Kirk Douglas plays a French commander who's forced to make an example out of some soldiers who refused to advance after the rest of their company was mowed down by the enemy. It's a brilliant study of the futility of war and the class politics that are played out in any conflict. Kirk Douglas is, well, Kirk Douglas, but Adolphe Menjou is perfect as the romantic, DeGaulle-esque, self-aggrandizing, blood-seeking general, Mireau.

General Mireau: I can't understand these armchair officers, fellas trying to fight a war from behind a desk, waving papers at the enemy, worrying about whether a mouse is gonna run up their pants leg.

Colonel Dax: I don't know, General. If I had the choice between mice and Mausers, I think I'd take the mice every time.

12. Salt of the Earth (1954)

This is one of those movies that you're pretty sure wouldn't be made today. *Salt of the Earth* is based on an actual strike against the Empire Zinc Mine in New Mexico, where Mexican-American miners hit the picket line for equal pay with their white counterparts. This movie deals with racism, union issues, discrimination, and is one of the strongest feminist treatments (the miners' wives are the bomb) you can see in American cinema

13. Serpico (1973)

All those great '70s actors (DeNiro, Nicholson, Pacino, Hackman) are now simply caricatures of their old selves and usually annoy the hell out of me whenever they're on the screen (except for Duval). But when I really want to remember how great Pacino was, I just throw in *Serpico*. Talk about your ultimate police corruption story. This movie also runs counter to most Hollywood stories. The hero generally sticks his neck out and saves the day. In *Serpico* (I guess because it's based on a true story), the hero sticks his neck out, gets shot in the face, and, while some things do change, he doesn't really do much good. Pretty much defeated and destroyed, he runs away to Europe probably wondering, "What the fuck was that all about?"

14. State of Siege (1972)

Bill Campbell

I think Costa-Gavras gets a lot more credit for making *Z.*, and he should really get slapped for having made that bullshit, *Betrayed*; but I really love this one. Yves Montand plays an American USAID official in Uruguay who gets kidnapped by the leftist Tupamaros. They use his interrogation as a backdrop to portray the conflict between the leftist guerrillas and Uruguay's military regime

Faux Netflix Feature: Those who liked *Four Days in September* also liked *State of Siege*.

15. Stalingrad (1993)

The Battle of Stalingrad is considered the bloodiest battle of modern history, with nearly 2 million casualties on both sides. What I love most about this movie is how they portray the romantic, youthful exuberance of going off to war that I think mostly every country enters a war feeling slowly and painfully turning into a mad, dog-eat-dog, desperate scramble for self-preservation. It's not a movie many politicians would take to heart (because none of them is immune to "war fever"), but it's one that more of us 'Mericans should.

Those 100 Movies You're Supposed to See Before You Die

Well, since I just did *My Favorite Lefty Films*, I figured I'd do the Yahoo *Movies to See Before You Die*, which inspired the former list. They claim that they selected these movies for their "historical importance" and "cultural impact" as well as picking "the most thrilling, most dramatic, scariest, and funniest movies of all time." So, please don't hate on me for their selections. I'm just telling you whether I saw the movie or not and what I thought. What a way to spend a hazy, lazy April Fool's Day, eh?

(*Author's Note: To get the full effect of my laziness, please listen to Xavier Cugat* while perusing this list. A good mambo never killed anyone—though a bad merengue can call for hip surgery.)

12 Angry Men (1957)

You know, when my wife and I first saw this, we said, "Oh, if only jury deliberations were actually like this." Funny thing was, when I was actually called on a jury (for a drug trial, no less), it *was* like *12 Angry Men*. There are several reasons I love director Sidney Lumet. This flick's one of them.

2001: A Space Odyssey (1968)

There are several reasons I love director Stanley Kubrick. I still can't figure out if this is one of them. I do like this film, but I don't know if it's because I'm supposed to like it or if I actually find it good. I'll always love the HAL part of the movie. The beginning with the monkeys still gives me flashbacks to when I was a bookkeeper at a collection agency.

Bill Campbell

The 400 Blows (1959)

I've always been meaning to see this Truffaut classic. But, since I saw Louis Malle's *Elevator to the Gallows* and loved it, I'll be one of those pretentious haters, and say, "Well, it's no *Elevator to the Gallows*."

8 ½ (1963)

After suffering through *La Dolce Vita*, I was so pissed off that Fellini's considered a "master," I have refused to see anything else of his. Yall can tell me what this one's like.

The African Queen (1952)

Who? Nefertiti? Ann Nzinga? Nope, sorry, missed this one. I like Hepburn and Bogart. I'm sure I'll actually see this one before I die. See, the list works.

Alien (1979)

I still find Sigourney Weaver in her underwear one of the most horrifying scenes in cinematic history. You may not remember, but her ass was so flat in this movie, she was actually showing plumber's crack. Other than that, I love *Alien*. Apparently so does Hollywood, since 90% of all SF movies since (no matter the topic) break down to become *Alien* in the end.

All About Eve (1950)

Growing up, I never did quite understand the whole Bette Davis thing. But watching this, you definitely get it. Damn, they could really be vicious back in the day. It still amazes me how clever so many of these old-timey movies were. We could use some of that today.

Annie Hall (1977)

No shame in my game (though a lot in his), I am an unabashed Woody Allen addict. This, of course, is my favorite Woody. I can watch *Annie Hall* all day long.

Apocalypse Now (1979)

When my mom was doing the whole single-parent-full-time-worker-night-school-student thing, she used to take me to some of her college courses at Pitt. Her Movie Appreciation course was my favorite. As a 10-year-old, I saw a whole bunch of movies I wouldn't have been allowed to see otherwise. This is one of them. As a genuine reflection of the war experience, *Apocalypse Now* strikes me as a pure piece of pretentious bullshit, but as a pure piece of pretentious bullshit, *Apocalypse Now* is a masterpiece.

The Battle of Algiers (1967)

See *My Favorite Lefty Films* above.

The Bicycle Thief (1948)

Yeah, this bad boy is a masterpiece. Yeah, it helped break the oppressive Hays Code. But, seriously, this movie still holds up. Especially in these trying economic times, one can relate to a father struggling to provide for his family.

Blade Runner (1982)

With this and *Alien* Ridley Scott was the man. I took my wife to see the director's cut at one of those movie theater/pub joints, and, at the last moment when you get that all-important clue that tells you for sure that Deckard's a Replicant, the waiter asked me a question about my bill, and I missed it. Bastard.

Blazing Saddles (1974)

I could go on and on about *Blazing Saddles*. Ask my wife, I can pretty much quote the entire movie verbatim. I might even be able to write the script for you and hardly miss a line. This is my favorite comedy of all time. I'm an absolute nut over this. White guys have *Caddy Shack*. I've got this. "They said you was hung." "And they was right."

Blow Up (1966)

I think I *tried* to watch this once in high school.

Blue Velvet (1986)

Bill Campbell

I think I actually *liked* this movie in high school. I pretty much hate David Lynch with every fiber of my being. So, I doubt if I'll ever revisit this one to see what I saw in it.

Bonnie and Clyde (1967)

I love the Serge Gainsbourg/Brigitte Bardo song. I love the Warren Beatty/Faye Dunaway movie. How could you hate on either one? And damn do they get lit up in the end. That is straight-up *gangsta*. Oh yeah, right. I guess that makes sense.

Breathless (1960)

Didn't Richard Gere try to rip this movie off in the '80s? I think I saw the rip-off.

The Bridge on the River Kwai (1957)

Since I can't whistle for shit, I've always been hostile to this movie. I've always been meaning to see it, but the closest I've ever gotten was *A Bridge Too Far*.

Bringing Up Baby (1938)

I fell madly in love with *The Philadelphia Story* (one of my favorite comedies) and immediately went out and rented *Bringing Up Baby*. I still like this one, but I was really disappointed. Just a case of bad timing, I guess.

Butch Cassidy and the Sundance Kid (1969)

OK, what the hell was up with "Raindrops Keep Falling on My Head"? I mean, I love B.J. Thomas as much as the next guy, but, damn, that song sticks out like a sore thumb. The shoot-out in *The Wild Bunch* is a hell of a lot better, but I still like this one. Redford's a stiff as always, but Paul Newman was the man.

Casablanca (1942)

I think it's actually illegal to say anything disparaging about this movie. So yeah, I *loved* it. I betcha Sam was still wondering what the hell he was doing in that part of Africa and was probably sweatin' his ass off wondering if the Nazis were going to off his black ass. If you ask me, he should've cold-cocked both Rick and Laszlo and gotten on that plane with Ilsa. Hmm ... I smell sequel!

Chinatown (1974)

Yeah, I like *Chinatown*—just not as much as I'm told I'm supposed to. If it had ended differently—like if that girl had ended up being Faye Dunaway's third cousin-twice removed—I bet folks would've remembered this one as the snooze fest it sometimes is.

Citizen Kane (1941)

What kind of asshole would I be if I didn't say this was THE GREATEST MOVIE OF ALL-TIME?!!! Well, it's no *Plan 9 from Outer Space*, but I guess Orson Welles deserves his props for this one. Though I think it would've been more believable if Rosebud would've turned out to have been a hooker who gave him the clap during the Spanish-American War than what it had actually turned out to have been.

Crouching Tiger, Hidden Dragon (2000)

I will always be indebted to this movie for introducing me to Ziyi Zhang. Our love *still* grows stronger by the day.

Die Hard (1988)

When thinking about this movie, I try to always block out the ridiculous sequels. I also try to block out the fact that people have been outrunning explosions ever since this movie was released. But yeah, this was fun. I'm sure Alan Rickman will probably go down as one of the best movie villains for this bad boy—oh yeah, and that *Robin Hood* joint he did with Kevin Costner. Ha!

Do the Right Thing (1989)

See **Lefty Films** again.

Double Indemnity (1944)

Bill Campbell

By their very nature, film noir flicks are misogynist. I'm not going to say that's what makes them entertaining, but you gotta wonder. Since Fred McMurray's the star of this one, you've got to constantly fight humming the theme to *My Three Sons*, but it's worth it. This is a gem.

Dr. Strangelove or: How I Learned to Stop Worrying and Love the Bomb (1964)

Lefty Films, y'all.

Duck Soup (1933)

I approach Groucho and his brothers like I do their distant cousin, Karl: I hope I'll understand them when I get older.

E.T. the Extra-Terrestrial (1982)

Even as a 12-year-old, there was something about *E.T.* that really pissed me off. I've refused to see it ever since, and I wouldn't be caught dead with some Reese's Pieces!

Enter the Dragon (1973)

Come on, people. Is there a black man alive raised on Saturday Afternoon Kung Fu Theater who does not love, adore, indeed, *worship* *Enter the Dragon*? I really and truly believe that Brutha Bruce is the reason Black Muslims started calling themselves "Asiatic".

The Exorcist (1973)

Aw, Linda Blair had me at "Your mother sucks cocks in Hell." What a darling.

Fast Times at Ridgemont High (1982)

Is there a Gen Xer alive who does not love this movie? Besides, everybody who was nobody in the '80s was in this one with Uncle Martin thrown in for good measure.

The French Connection (1971)

This movie's like those mix tapes we used to make: totally diminished by constant copying. This was the first movie that had the gritty city landscape, the cop of dubious morality, the hair-raising car chase. All of these things have been copied so often they're ingrained in our cultural cerebellum. When you finally see *The French Connection* you wonder what the big deal was. But it's still entertaining enough.

The Godfather (1972)

The Bomb!

The Godfather, Part II (1974)

The Bomb! Part II

Quick Question: Is there a single movie where John Cazale (Fredo) *doesn't* get punked?

Goldfinger (1964)

I don't care who you put in the role, I can't stand Bond. My Dad tried patriotism once: "But, son, James Bond was conceived in Jamaica." And I was like, "So was I. What's your point?" I give them props for getting *Octopussy* past the censors, but *Quantum of Solace* sounds like it was pulled straight out the thesaurus.

The Good, the Bad, and the Ugly (1968)

I've always wondered how Sergio Leone broke it to Eli Wallach that he was neither "The Good" nor "The Bad." I hope he didn't tell him he was born to play this role.

Goodfellas (1990)

I've never quite understood the big deal behind this one. And this movie paved the way for *Casino*, and I can never forgive it for that.

The Graduate (1967)

Hey, weren't Ann Bancroft and Dustin Hoffman the same age in this movie? Wasn't Ann Bancroft hot as hell? And isn't "Plastics" still

Bill Campbell

funny as all get-out?

Grand Illusion (1938)

I know I'm gonna get my Movie Pass revoked, but I haven't seen *Grand Illusion*, yet. Sorry.

Groundhog Day (1993)

I know you're not going to believe this, but I've never actually seen *Groundhog Day* all the way through. Unfortunately (and this isn't meant to be a joke), when I do catch it, I always catch the same scenes over and over again.

A Hard Day's Night (1964)

Remember what Public Enemy says about Elvis and John Wayne in "Fight the Power"? I pretty much feel the same way about the Beatles.

In the Mood For Love (2001)

Hunh?

It Happened One Night (1934)

Clark Gable and Claudette Colbert are hysterical. I wonder, if they remade this movie today, what Colbert would have to flash in order to get the car to stop. I mean, she had a mighty nice calf, but I just don't think it would cut it nowadays.

It's a Wonderful Life (1946)

"Yeah, I hate *It's a Wonderful Life*. I hate Jimmy Stewart. I hate Donna Reed. I hate apple pie, puppy dogs, the American flag, God, and my own mother!"

Anyone who would dare say this *deserves* to be burned at the stake!

Jaws (1975)

Even with decades of copy cats, *Jaws* is still a great-ass movie.

King Kong (1933)

The story of my people. Stolen from Africa, enslaved, forced to entertain whitey and make him money, and as soon as you fall for the white woman, the police shoot your unarmed, monkey ass in New York City. Ain't *that* about a bitch?!

The Lady Eve (1941)

Haven't seen this one.

Lawrence of Arabia (1962)

I just want to thank T.E. Lawrence for leaving us with a legacy of colonialist bullshit and the war we're still fighting to this day. Way to go, hoss! Also, you gotta love my Mexican brother, Anthony Quinn. Here, he plays an Arab. He's also played Native American, Greek, *and* Ethiopian. Here's to Old School Racial Ambiguity! You know Vin Diesel's still jealous.

The Lord of the Rings (2001, 2002, 2003)

Honestly, I only liked the second one (though I do give Peter Jackson props for avoiding the apocalyptic race war that was in the books). However, someone who shall remain nameless was in love with that git, Orlando Bloom, for all three movies.

M (1931)

This movie started my love affair with Peter Lorre. Even the subtitle-averse would love this one.

M*A*S*H (1970)

One of my mom's Movie Appreciation flicks. This movie marked the first time I saw a nude woman on film. What up, Sally Kellerman? Other than that, I was confused because it was nothing like the TV show at all. This is probably one of the only Altman films I actually like.

Bill Campbell

The Maltese Falcon (1941)

Bogart, Greenstreet, Lorre directed by Huston based on Hammett. Is there anything about this movie that ain't cool?

The Matrix (1999)

I was only but so impressed when it was fresh, and I doubt this bad boy ages well.

Modern Times (1936)

You know, I was just typing how I hadn't seen this one. But now I realize that I have. I guess I need to see it again, though. I'll get back to you. In the meantime, go watch *The Great Dictator*.

Monty Python and the Holy Grail (1975)

I've been terrified of bunnies ever since.

National Lampoon's Animal House (1978)

Yeah, I've never quite understood the big deal behind this one. I'll take your suggestions.

Network (1976)

This is another *Lefty Film*. My favorite, in fact.

Nosferatu (1922)

It's on The List. My wife can tell you, the only thing longer than our Netflix Queue is The List.

On the Waterfront (1954)

Kazan was a rat-fink bastard! Aside from that and that old-timey rape/"love" scene, this is a really good movie.

One Flew Over the Cuckoo's Nest (1975)

Graduation summer I was over at a friend's house, getting ready to go out. While we waited for more of our friends to get to the house, we started killing time by watching *Cuckoo's*. We *had* been pumped to go out. But as the movie wore on and more and more people arrived and then sat down, we all found we couldn't pull ourselves from the movie. As the movie went on, we found ourselves more and more depressed. By the time the damned thing ended, we felt more like shooting ourselves in the head than flying all around town in search of a good time. The resulting depression was worth it, though.

Paths of Glory (1958)

You guessed it, *Lefty Film*.

Princess Mononoke (1999)

Another one I have no clue about. I guess I'm a flag-waving troglodyte if ever there was one. Crank up the Lee Greenwood!!!

Psycho (1960)

Being a Slasher Film Baby, how terrifying could I have ever found *Psycho*? I respect it, though.

Pulp Fiction (1994)

Back during the *Pulp Fiction* furor, a white friend of mine asked me one night, while drinking, if I thought Quentin Tarantino were a racist. I thanked him because I'd thought I'd been going crazy because the racial aspects of the film were driving me crazy and yet nobody, at the time, had mentioned it. Other white people started eavesdropping and soon joined the conversation and, before I knew it, I was "Little Big Horned" by a bunch of angry white people calling me a "racist." It was a pretty crappy night, but it sparked my first foray into cultural criticism with a piece called "Art and Pulp Fiction" (I wish it were still on the internet, but I couldn't find it). At the time, I did like this movie but I hated the fact that Q-Dog took every opportunity to demean black men in his movie (from "dead nigger storage" to Ving Rhames' being cuckolded and sodomized by white guys—only to be saved by the White Messiah, Bruce Willis). Nowadays, though, I just wish Tarantino would go away. I find his stuff pretty boring.

Bill Campbell

Raging Bull (1980)

I often think that whenever people wax poetic about *Goodfellas*, they're just rhapsodizing about the glorious afterglow one receives after watching *Raging Bull*. But that's just me.

Raiders of the Lost Ark (1981)

Oh yeah, this one's still fun.

Raise the Red Lantern (1992)

Hm, each night having to choose which of your three wives you're gonna get a li'l nooky from ... You know, one night in Paris, I spent the night with six Swedish nurses. Sounds great, doesn't it? Sounds like the night you've always dreamed of, eh? Well, I slept on the floor. And they slept in their bunk beds. Some things just always sound better than they turn out to be in real life.

Rashomon (1951)

There are few things better in this world than Toshiro Mifune being directed by Akira Kurosawa.

Rear Window (1954)

Ya know, I think Hitchcock is pretty cool, but I *know* Jimmy Stewart is God. I love all their movies together.

Rebel Without a Cause (1955)

I love "Rebel without a Pause." I'm guessin' they ain't related. After watching *Celluloid Closet*, I've been meaning to watch this. I just haven't gotten around to it, yet.

Rocky (1976)

If you can overlook the constant desire to put the uppity nigra (Muhammad Ali) in his place and can try to forget all the reactionary, racist bullshit sequels that followed, you can really get into *Rocky*. Instead of basking in American triumphalism, this one is about a working class slob who wins just by showing up. I like that message. I would've liked it more if Apollo Creed just woulda whupped his ass and called it a day, but that was before Denzel and Will Smith. Sly wouldn't have a shot in hell nowadays. Where's Gerry Cooney when you need him?

Roman Holiday (1953)

Sorry. I got nothing here.

Saving Private Ryan (1998)

I think that Steven Spielberg's probably the best action director of all-time. But any time he deals with adult themes, I find his movies at best annoying and, oftentimes, infuriating. I mean, in *Amistad*, why the hell did that one Muslim slave become a Christian just because he liked *the pictures* in the Bible?! Anyway, *Saving Private Ryan* is a great example. Those battle scenes are absolutely amazing. But, when they start expounding on the "hell of war," you feel like ABC made a WWII after-school special. I mean, the plot was so fucking stupid, throughout the entire movie, the characters are complaining about how fucking stupid the plot is. They should've just cobbled a bunch of old *Sgt. Rock*s together and called it a day. It would've been cool to see Tom Hanks shoot down a Stuka.

Schindler's List (1993)

Personally, I've grown sick of Nazis, World WWII, and Holocaust films. I realize it was the last good war and that the Germans were pure evil, but enough is enough. I mean, more Nazis have died in Hollywood than in the African and European theaters combined. I liked *Schindler's* all right, and Spielberg got megaprops for the flick. But, when Roberto Benigni can win Oscars for making a slapstick Holocaust romp ("Zyklon B! The New Laughing Gas!"), how hard can it be?

The Searchers (1956)

If I had a dollar for every white film connoisseur who ever praised *The Searchers*, I could fucking bail out AIG (throw in *Birth of a Nation* and I'd rescue Detroit, too). Now, I'll give it to the Duke on this one.

Bill Campbell

John Wayne comes dangerously close to acting in *The Searchers*. He plays a cowboy whose daughter (Natalie Wood) is kidnapped by a band of Indians and who's hellbent and determined to find his girl. As the movie progresses, you start to realize that his determination is actually racism; that he's obsessed with the idea that his precious, little white daughter has been turned out by the red man and that she's whiling away the time, sucking on his teepee; and that when he says "save" he actually means to blast his girl between the eyes. Now, the logical conclusion is that this obsessed racist is going to blow his daughter away for defiling the white race no matter what she says. The Hollywood conclusion goes something like this:

Duke: "Did you ...?"

Nat: "Ewww ... Daddy ... with them ... *gross!*"

Duke: "Aw shucks, pilgrimess, I guess I was bein' right silly."

Nat: "You sure were, Dad."

Hugs, smiles, fade to crap.

Seven Samurai (1954)

What I said about *Rashomon* times ... uh, seven.

The Shawshank Redemption (1994)

My wife loves this movie. So I love this movie (that's how I came to be able to quote *Dirty Dancing* verbatim -- yeah, I'm gonna pay for that one). But seriously, I like it. The Catholic in me always quibbles that this movie isn't about redemption at all, but hey, when was the last time I've been to mass?

The Silence of the Lambs (1991)

I have never understood the big deal about this movie. But I haven't found Anthony Hopkins scary since he stopped his ventriloquist dummy from killing folks in *Magic*.

Singin' in the Rain (1952)

I think there *may* be about five or six musicals that I've ever liked. *Singin' in the Rain* is definitely one of them. I think it's all because of "Make 'em Laugh," I'm not sure, but I do find this one a lot of fun.

Snow White and the Seven Dwarfs (1937)

You know, I've actually never seen *Snow White*. Does that make me racist?

Then I guess I shouldn't mention that there are only two "black" movies in this whole, damned list. Whatever happened to Affirmative Action?

Some Like It Hot (1959)

For years I avoided this movie, determined that it was going to suck. It's actually a lot of fun. Of course, Jack Lemmon was most definitely the Man during this period. If you don't believe me, check out *The Apartment*.

The Sound of Music (1965)

I hate to admit it, but this is one of the other musicals that I like. If you're seriously questioning my masculinity by now, the others are *Camelot* and *Damn Yankees* (see, knighthood and baseball, I'm still a man).

Star Wars (1977)

I can't believe I spent some twenty years loving this franchise. It was when Lucas reissued those new, digitally-remastered "director's cuts" back in '97 that I realized that *Star Wars* actually sucked. It was a rough epiphany to digest. I became depressed, abandoned my family, and went on a two-year bender. Only the love of a good woman made me realize that life was still worth living, it was OK to hate *Star Wars*, and that love was all that mattered. When the prequel trilogy came out, I felt secure in my newfound hatred.

Sunset Blvd. (1950)

I challenge each and every one of you to point out one thing wrong with this movie. Go ahead. I'll wait.

Bill Campbell

Terminator 2: Judgment Day (1991)

Someone must've been smoking crack on this choice. I'm no pacifist, but even I couldn't swallow the bullshit moral they tacked onto this piece of cow piss. I mean, "If a killer cyborg can learn the value of human life, why can't we humans?" I'm sorry, didn't the Schwartze spend the entire film mutilating people with high-powered automatic fire? Sure, he didn't kill them, but he permanently maimed them. Is that really what we want to teach the kiddies?

The Third Man (1949)

My second favorite stiffy, Joseph Cotten, in my second favorite Joseph Cotten movie. (God bless him, but the man never did try; in *Gaslight* he plays a Scotland Yard investigator who sounds like he's straight outta Peoria, Wales—and the man was actually from Virginia). A great tale of moral ambiguity in our post-WWII world. And wasn't Orson Welles cool as hell?

This is Spinal Tap (1984)

Lick me love pump, Stonehenge, "But this goes to 11." God, I love this movie, and I pretty much hate the music they parody. Go figure.

Titanic (1997)

I still find it hard to believe that I liked this movie. Of course, I saw it before the hype machine went off its nut. As I've said before, that makes all the difference.

To Kill a Mockingbird (1962)

Never saw it, never read it. Tell me, what did I miss?

Toy Story (1995)

I wonder why this one made the list. I mean, it was cute, and all, but it's no *Fritz the Cat*—at least not the version I saw.

The Usual Suspects (1995)

Yeah, this was dope, wasn't it?

Vertigo (1958)

"I'm not afraid of heights. I'm afraid of parents!"

Oh, wait, that's Mel Brooks' *High Anxiety*. Well, you have Hitchcock and Stewart and that new camera technique Hitchcock invented for the flick. I'd rather watch *Rope*, but this is still cool. I'm sure they exist, but I can't think of a Jimmy Stewart clunker.

When Harry Met Sally... (1989)

Well, shit, I already told you I loved *Annie Hall*, wasn't this the sequel?

Wild Strawberries (1957)

Hey! I saw *The Seventh Seal* and I have a tattoo of Max von Sydow on my ass. What more do you want from me?

No, I haven't seen this one.

Wings of Desire (1988)

Yeah, I tried watching this movie once with a ... friend. I got a bit distracted. Did Peter Falk get the girl in the end?

The Wizard of Oz (1939)

"Can you feel a brand new day?!"

Yeah, I like both versions.

Women on the Verge of a Nervous Breakdown (1988)

Why don't I remember this movie? My boy, Dabalou, once told me he forgets movies he doesn't like. I've worked long and hard over the years to acquire this skill. I wonder if that's why I don't remember this one. Sometimes, just looking at Almodóvar pisses me off.

Bill Campbell

The World of Apu (1959)

I'ma plead troglodyte on this one. I don't even think I've ever heard of this one—though I'm pretty sure I've been told to check out Satyajit Ray movies before.

Bow Down for the Bend-Over

Sunday, April 5, 2009

With all the fanfare surrounding our President's European tour, with the *entire* mini-continent all on Obama's Balzac, it's no surprise that America's conservatives are off their collective nut with rage. They've decided that they hate The Big Brother, that his every action makes the bile rise in their throats. Therefore, they are basically *automatically* outraged by the man's every action—and every action of his wife.

Earlier this week, the First Lady got into trouble for putting her hand on Queen Elizabeth's shoulder. Outrage ensued—followed quickly by controversy. "Violations of protocol!" Yadda yadda. Some were so red-faced, you'd think Michelle kissed Liz's head with a bottle and stole her purse. Eventually, Bob Costas, John Madden, and a telestrator were brought in to analyze the tape. Apparently, the Queen put her arm around the First Lady *first*, prompting our Lady to put her hand on *their* Lady's shoulder in what experts are now calling a "reciprocation of affection."

Having finally overcome that controversial obstacle, the White House has stumbled into another with the President's bowing before Saudi Arabia's King Abdullah. Screed Queen Michelle Malkin says the whole thing is "embarrassing" and (ironically, in light of the last administration) complains, "It's like the 'American Hillbillies go to Europe.' He is throwing American power and prestige out with both hands as fast as he can." Defender of the Faith, Gary Bauer, of course, sees a Muslim conspiracy in that nefarious bow. As though the Saudis will now dictate US foreign policy in the region. As though they haven't been doing just that the past eight years.

As Costas, Madden, and the telestrator are once again employed to examine whether or not this was indeed a bow and etiquette experts like Gloria Starr calculate the exact ratio of degree-of-bow to loss-of-American-power, I'll be the first to admit that I actually don't give a shit about any of it. I'll also admit that I didn't care when W. actually held Crown Prince Abdullah's hand during their romantic stroll in Crawford back in '05. Now, don't get me wrong, I made jokes. How couldn't I? But I actually didn't care.

I think whether the President bows, holds hands, kisses, cuddles, or spoons another leader matters about as much as the Pittsburgh Pirates' World Series plans. However, for the past 60-plus years, our country has bent over backwards to please the House of Saud to the point of utterly fucking ourselves, and that's what we seriously have to look into.

FDR started the contortions in 1943, making Saudi Arabia (a neutral country) eligible for Lend-Lease assistance. Saudi security was considered vital to US interests, and that's been our position ever since. The House of Saud could do whatever it wanted (oppress their women, torture its dissidents, spread virulent anti-American Islam worldwide, whatever); as long as they pumped the cheap crude, we'd cover their asses.

It wasn't a pretty relationship, but no junky/dealer relationship ever is. But, during the Cold War, this despicable deal made some sort of realpolitik sense. But the canoodling *really* needed to stop after September 11.

It's not just that 11 of the 19 hijackers were Saudi or even that Osama himself is Saudi. It's that, for decades, while we Americans have made that country rich by consuming their oil, while we've bolstered and equipped their military with aid they never needed in the first place, while we looked the other way when it came to their abysmal human rights record, and while we went to war to save their oil and asses, the Saudis have been funding the very terrorists who aimed to kill us while spending billions to indoctrinate Muslim children around the world to replace the terrorists who died that day.

It would seem that anybody who did all that to contribute to and actively encourage your own destruction would be classified an enemy. But Bush twisted the Saudis into dance partners.

Not only did the main funders and mentors of al Qaeda become our "biggest allies" in W.'s ack-basswards "War on Terror," but Pakistan (the country that formed and funded the Taliban) became our second biggest allies. How our worst enemies somehow morphed into our greatest allies is still beyond me. It's as though, after Pearl Harbor, FDR joined us to the Axis and we went on to invade Spain and Argentina. Has such a powerful country ever been so utterly fucked over by a smaller nation only to bend over and ask for more? Back in the day, we nuked Japan. Rome plowed Carthage under with salt. But now our allies whisper sweet-nothings in our politicians' ears while their underlings blow the living shit out of our soldiers.

Now, Lord knows, I don't want us to nuke Saudi Arabia, and the salt thing seems a little too ... well, Biblical. I don't even want us to invade the peninsula. I just want to know why W. never called these "allies" of ours to task. Why did W. insist on calling them "friends"?

While these cons are screaming about Obama's bow, why have they never answered why Boy George was always so eager to bend over for the Saudis? Our thankfully-former president not only never caught bin Laden, but he never made the Saudis pay *in any way* for their involvement with 9/11 or the global network of Islamic terror. There were no breaking of ties, no economic sanctions. We never curbed our "addiction to oil" or even tried to switch dealers.

I'm thinking Malkin, Bauer, and their brood would better utilize their time if they stopped speculating if Obama gave Abdullah a 25-, 40-, or 90-degree bow and actually get to the bottom of the mystery that was W.'s diplomatic policy towards the Saudis. Perhaps, they can even start speculating on whether or not our relationship with that country is even worth continuing.

Now, look, I understand what it's like to hate, hate, *HATE!* one of our presidents. I spent the last eight years filled with rage every time I saw that Connecticut Texan on the boob tube. I hated that dummy's goofy smile, his chuckle. I even hated the way he *walked* — like something powerfully uncomfortable was lodged up his rectum — you know, Cheney's forearm. But, *more importantly*, I hated Bush's supposed "War on Terror," his lying to get us into Iraq, I hated his constant calling for tax cuts despite growing deficits, and I hated his utter contempt for governance itself, which I believe led to levees breaking, bridges collapsing, poisoned children's toys, and collapsed banks.

So, in the grand scheme of things, how important is Obama's Bow, really? What really matters here is the Bush Bend-Over our country's been experiencing for over seven years now and whether or not Obama's simply going to "assume the position" or actually go in a different, "bold" direction and somehow extricate us from these "Wars" of ours and possibly from the region altogether.

Bill Campbell

The Original Gun Clappers:
Shays' Rebellion
and the Second Amendment

Wednesday, April 22, 2009

Eric Kelly. Paul Sciullo, III. Stephen Mayhle. Those were the names that reverberated throughout the Pittsburgh area Easter weekend. Everywhere we went, their names rang out. Round-the-clock news coverage, flags at half-staff, even gas stations memorialized these three names. Eric Kelly, Paul Sciullo, III, and Stephen Mayhle were the three police officers killed by an NRA fanatic with an automatic weapon, Richard Poplawski. Now, I'll admit that I've often had an ... ambivalent relationship with the cops, but I'd hardly wish death on any of them. And these men died so needlessly—due to the insanity of one man and the failure of the dispatcher to tell these officers that their target collected firearms.

Ed Rendell. Wayne LaPierre. This past Sunday these two men were rehashing the same, old, tired debate on gun control on *Face the Nation*. The Pennsylvania governor and executive vice-president of the National Rifle Association regurgitated the cud that constitutes our nation's gun control debate—as though their arguments were actually new—as though those three officers had not just died needlessly—as though none of it really matters.

And I don't know if it really does matter. The NRA has our nation's politicians on lock. There's no telling how many of our pols are actually on their payroll, but those who aren't run in fear, knowing the NRA will target them in the next election cycle. They continue to have the power to reduce the gun "debate" to nothing more than these meaningless forums. They have been so powerful that their very interpretation of the Second Amendment holds sway over American politics (even that bleeding-heart liberal who's going to take away all their guns, Obama, believes the way they do).

"A well regulated Militia, being necessary to the security of a Free State, the right of the people to keep and bear Arms, shall not be infringed."

This "well regulated Militia," they contend, is an *individual* and he has the *individual* right to bear arms. There's hardly a person on the public stage who disagrees with them. More importantly, in their decision to repeal Washington, DC's gun ban, the Supreme Court made it clear that they will uphold the NRA's interpretation.

Now, I can't put this all on the NRA. It's how we Americans imagine our own history: Thomas Paine writes *Common Sense*; some dudes dump tea into a harbor; we sign the Declaration of Independence and form a nation; we fight a little war with the Brits; win; and we all (except those pesky, little slaves) live happily ever after.

So, we celebrate 1776 as the year of our birth. We somehow gloss over the fact that the Revolutionary War lasted *seven* years. We never really talk about the colonists who remained loyal to the British, how we retaliated against them, or how they fled back to Britain or off to Canada during and after the war. We don't talk about the four years after the War when our fledgling nation was hardly a nation at all — operating under a loose Articles of Confederation whose nebulous powers couldn't even determine whether America was one nation, a confederation of 13 nations, or simply 13 nations out for themselves. Most importantly, we *never* talk about the three rebellions America faced in its first years of existence — especially the one that finally forced our leaders to get their act together and finally forge the country we have today: Shays' Rebellion.

In August 1786, unpaid War veterans and disgruntled farmers tired of being thrown into debtors' prison formed armed units in central and western Massachusetts to forcibly halt property confiscations. In confrontations across the state, sometimes these groups faced off against local militia; and sometimes they actually *were* the local militia, forcing Massachusetts' rich to run scared.

On January 25, 1787, Daniel Shays, a Revolutionary War veteran, led a group to take the weapons from the Springfield federal armory. The governor sent two militias to meet Shays' forces. One general, Shepard, whose forces were unpaid, underfed, and inadequately armed, requested permission to use the armory's weapons. However, Secretary of War Henry Knox said that Shepard's request required Congressional approval and Congress was out of session. Therefore, Knox denied Shepard's *militia* the *right to bear arms*, being *necessary* to the security of a *free State*, Massachusetts (see where I'm going with this?).

Meanwhile, according to Jay Winik in his marvelous history, *The Great Upheaval*, Shays' rebellion also inspired other little dust-ups from

Maine to Georgia. The 13 states were caught with their pants down. Many states didn't even *have* militias to defend themselves and had to beg rich patrons to supply defenses for them. And, when rebels would flee across state lines, these militias didn't know if they even had the authority to pursue the varmints.

Fortunately, those dust-ups didn't amount to much, and Shays' rebellion itself was finally quashed by March 1878. The rebellion showed the nation's leaders that there were serious, potentially fatal flaws in the Articles of Confederation. The country had no institutional means with which to protect itself. In response, the Constitutional Convention convened in May of that same year, the Constitution was drafted, and the Second Amendment was added to address what happened in Massachusetts and across the nation.

In other words, despite the public discourse on the matter we have today, the Second Amendment is not some vague or misworded amendment about an individual's right granted by the Constitution at all. It's a very specific amendment meant to address a very specific problem the nation faced at the time: it did not want to repeat the problem General Shepard and Secretary Knox faced when a state's militia was left defenseless.

The Second Amendment says that a state's *militia* has the right to defend itself and, therefore, does not need Congress' approval to do so. It says absolutely *nothing* about an individual's right. If you don't believe me, look at it again. However, if you want to address whether or not an individual has a right to bear arms, my non-Constitutional lawyer ass would guess that you need to look at the Tenth Amendment:

"The powers not delegated to the United States by the Constitution, nor prohibited by it to the States, are reserved to the States respectively, or to the people."

In other words, since the Constitution does not expressly rule on the issue, it is up to each, individual state and municipality to decide what its gun laws are. Though our "strict constructionist" judges like Scalia *proclaim* to only apply the Constitution as it was originally written, we can see here that they are more "activist" on this issue. The amendment refers only to "militia" and nowhere does it say a thing about the "individual." These conservative judges simply fail to acknowledge the context in which the Second Amendment was written. The actual history simply fails to fit their ideology, and they choose to ignore it. As does the NRA.

Therefore, despite the intentions of our forefathers and their own rhetoric about "states' rights," it was all too easy for the Roberts Court to strip all local governments of their right to determine their own gun policies. And the NRA is hellbent and determined to make sure our local *and* national governments never regain that right. Both will fight for this imagined individual right to own a gun—whether it be single-loading like Cheney's musket or fully-automatic like the gun Richard Poplawski used to slaughter Eric Kelly, Paul Sciullo, III, and Stephen Mayhle. As long as the Court remains similarly constituted and as long as the NRA holds onto the power it's already got, none of this nonsense is going to change.

My Fellow African-American, Jack Kemp

Monday, May 4, 2009

All right, let's get this straight: Jack Kemp was the Original Supply-Sider, and for that, I can never forgive him. I mean, if he hadn't fallen for that damned Laugher Curve (oh, I'm sorry, did I misspell that?), he wouldn't have convinced David Stockman of the lunacy, who wouldn't have converted Reagan to the madness, who may (or may not) have screwed our nation as royally as he did. So yeah, Jack and I have had our problems in the past.

However, I *think* he said and did some interesting things while he was Secretary of HUD. I remember his campaigning to have residents of the projects own their own residences, believing private ownership would inherently better their lot. And I'm not quite sure, but I think he was the one who hired the Fruit of Islam as private security in some of the most drug-infested and dangerous housing projects in the country, which did briefly improve safety until Republicans went after Farrakhan's FOI for being anti-Semitic, racist, etc.

Most importantly, though, I *love* Jack Kemp for providing me one of my most memorable nights in the eight years I've lived in Washington, DC.

It was about six years ago at a benefit dinner for an African development charity that's a fairly big deal in town. They've had Bono, Colin Powell, Bill Clinton, W., and yours truly at their dinner in the past. Well, OK, my wife worked for the organization. So I got to go for free. I also got a free pass to the pre-dinner VIP lounge. So, I was generally pretty lit by the time dinner and the speeches rolled around each year.

I think Jack may have been lit the year he gave his speech before the organization ... for he addressed the audience with "Greetings, my fellow African-Americans."

Oh no, he di'n't!

Why yes, he did.

I wish you were there to truly appreciate the beauty of the moment. There were other politicians, dignitaries, maybe a Supreme Court justice in the crowd. There were old, angry black militant types who still say things like "Whitey" and "honkey." And white folks who blush when they say "N-word" and are afraid to refer to another person's race even when asked to give a description. And there was Ol' Jack talking about "my fellow African-Americans."

Folks wuz Whore E. Fied!

Gasps sucked the air out of the room, threatening to become a vacuum. Silverware was dropped. People clung to their religion and their guns out of desperation. Me? I cheered the man and kept drinking as Jack continued to punctuate his speech about the importance of aid to Africa with little references to his own Negritude.

It was such a beautiful moment of political faux pas-ery I wanted it to last forever. But we all know nothing lasts forever. However, they *can* end with a bang. And Jack Kemp went supernova with ...

"If only God would've left me in the oven long enough so I could've been black, too."

After the speech, even the Sudanese had blanched in terror. People questioned his sanity. Others were beside themselves in indignation. One woman asked me what I thought got into Ol' Jack there. I shrugged, "I don't know. Maybe O.J. when they played in Buffalo together."

She left my irreverently drunk ass alone after that, obviously determined to be offended the rest of the evening. I just kept laughing and drinking. I mean, think about it, our public figures (political or not) have manicured their personae so closely we hardly ever even see a hang nail. They're just manufactured mannequins with canned opinions tailored to never offend a single soul. We hardly see a drunk or candid moment—hardly ever see them as human beings. It's only when they're washed up like Michael Richards do we see their hair out of place.

But it's not like you can blame them. Our 24-hour news cycle manufactures outrage faster than GM can produce a crap car. If I were a celebrity, you'd never hear me say another honest thing again in fear of becoming America's latest "controversy."

And then there was Jack Kemp that night—former AFL star, United States Congressman, Secretary of Housing and Urban Development, Republican leader, Vice-Presidential nominee, closet black man—telling us to screw C. Thomas Howell, that he, Jack French Kemp, was the Original Soul Man. And, in that light, supply-sider or not, how can I hate a white politician who had the (high)balls enough to say some stuff like that to an African-centric charity's donors?

It was the absolute *wrong* thing to say in the absolute *wrong* place at the absolute *wrong* time. Here, in a town where everybody's so careful to hit the *right* note with any given audience, this man went completely

Bill Campbell

off the scales. It was almost a thing of beauty when you think about it. I still think of it as one of the best political speeches I've ever seen.

But you know ... I'm a satirist.

Rest in Peace, Jack.

Pants Down and Shirt Off:
Obama and Gay Marriage

Tuesday, May 12, 2009

A conservative friend-who-shall-remain-nameless of mine sent me a link to *Iowahawk* with the photo of a topless Obama and the headline, "Breaking News: Gay Marriage Opponent Topless Photos Leaked." This was a play on the controversy surrounding Miss California Carrie Prejean getting even more flak for her opposition to gay marriage, with folks threatening to come out with topless pics of her.

Hawk, and I'm sure other, disingenuous conservatives, are rightfully pointing out liberals' hypocrisy in decrying Prejean when their own, *liberal* president also opposes gay marriage.

As much as it galls me, as much as I hate to contribute to what will later turn into Gorgeous White Woman Redemption and a Prejean the Plumber book and concert tour (followed by a brisk business of CDs, DVDs, and swimsuit calendars), I'll have to agree with the conservatives on this one. Though for completely different reasons, I believe they *should* point out liberals' hypocrisy here. While they feel somehow vindicated that The Big Brother's on their side with gay marriage, I believe that they are *all* on the wrong side of civil rights and history when it comes to this issue.

Obama's need to appear as a moderate and mediator has him reaching out to a constituency who's never quite believed him and is always champing at the bit to have that hand returned as a stump. With the abortion issue, where he constantly talked about "curbing the need for abortions" on the campaign trail, he's found that there is no mythological "Third Way." Even before he was elected, Pro-Lifers were considering him "the most pro-abortion candidate" ever to step foot on the American political stage. And the furor over his appearance at Notre Dame and his rescinding the Mexico City Policy, which blocked federal funding to overseas facilities that provided abortions, proves that there really is no middle ground when it comes to abortion rights. I don't know why anyone would be surprised at this. The woman's right to choose is a civil right—either one is for it or against it. There simply *can* be no middle ground.

That's the funny thing about civil *rights*. There are no half-measures. Or rather, the half-measures ones come up with are often tragic. Could there ever be three-fifths of an abortion?

As the Supreme Court decision *Loving v. Virginia*, legalizing interracial marriage, proved, marriage is indeed a civil right. Moreover, it's a property rights issue, determining who rightfully inherits what and who has authority over one's person if incapacitated, etc. "Civil union" is a cute compromise that falls far short of the rights bestowed upon marriage. These rights are what the state, the *secular* state, have to concern themselves with. The so-called "morality" of gay marriage is nothing the state needs to worry about. Leave it up to the individual and churches to wrangle over that. Any politician, including Obama, who kowtows to the "civil union" argument is laying our own Constitution prostrate to the whims of the mob.

And what happens when we Americans allow civil rights to be dictated by plebiscite? It's not simply California's voters re-implementing their state's ban on gay marriage. Just look at slavery and subjugation of African-Americans. Political cowardice had our forefathers backing away from abolition, which extended the institution of slavery by some 80 years, giving us the Three-Fifths Compromise, a civil war in Kansas, and the Civil War itself. The Republicans' weak will led to the collapse of Reconstruction and the ultimate passing of Jim Crow laws all across the South. Millions were oppressed, thousands murdered, and we are still (despite Obama's election) struggling against the legacy that slavery left our country.

No, the gay marriage ban has not had such drastic consequences. However, when it comes to this fight for civil rights and human dignity, Obama's looking more like George Wallace ("Straight marriage now! Straight marriage tomorrow! Straight marriage forever?") than Martin Luther King—or, if we are to believe current and historical rumors about breast-bearing, more like Carrie Prejean than Sojourner Truth.

We Need a Hero

Tuesday, May 19, 2009

Good vs. Evil. The Good Guy against the Bad. It's the stuff that almost all fiction (whether good or bad) is made of. Whether it's a romantic competitor or an evil mastermind bent on worldwide destruction, we know there is *one, single* person our hero must defeat in order for all to be right in the world.

It makes for entertaining storytelling. However, as I said before about Philip Roth's *The Plot Against America*, sometimes it just doesn't make much sense. In that novel, Roth blamed the imagined Nazification of America on the election of Charles Lindbergh. When Lindy wasn't re-elected, everything simply went back to normal. But, in the case of this alternative history, the problems faced by Nazi America would've been a societal, *systemic* evil. The elimination of "the bad guy" simply would not have solved the problem. A single hero could not have stood up to the task.

Currently, our country faces more problems than I have time to enumerate. We've tried to offer up bogeymen for each one, to purge ourselves of evil and live happily ever after. But each Evil One seems to fall short. The execution of Saddam didn't end our problems in Iraq. Afghanistan's problems won't stop if we ever catch bin Laden. The prosecution of Lynndie England and The Abu Ghraib Gang did not kill torture as either a debate or a policy. And the banking crises didn't end with Bernie Madoff's pleading guilty.

These problems continue to persist—nobody's ridden off into the sunset, no credits have rolled—because they simply don't fit into the format of simple storytelling that we're accustomed to and our press uses way too often. This ain't no romantic comedy here. What we're facing are deep, ingrained system failures.

But even in the face of such grave challenges, in the past, heroes have arisen, people who stood in the face of powerful opposition to do, what they felt, was the right thing to do. FDR did everything he possibly could to end the Great Depression. Truman (after staring at 100,000 casualties after three weeks of fighting on Okinawa) dropped the atomic bomb on Japan. He also found the cojones to desegregate the military when segregation was pretty much the law of the land. LBJ pushed through Civil Rights legislation knowing that the "Solid South" would flee the Democratic party. Nixon (yeah, Nixon), no Friend of the Negro by any stretch of the imagination, found the courage to extend and *expand* that same Civil Rights legislation.

Now, none of these men are your prototypical hero and, in many respects, they are villains themselves. However, these men flew in the faces of their own parties and powerful interests when the time came for them to do something. They could've easily dissembled, demurred, or disregarded the impolitic and done absolutely nothing. But they weathered the storm and took somewhat heroic action in order to do what was right.

But, when I look at all the ills facing America today, I can't help but wonder where are those people willing to take similarly heroic action? Where are our heroes?

It's not as though I want the government to take over the banks, reorganize and re-regulate them, sell off as much bad debt as possible, and then sell the banks off out of some imagined vision of revenge or "class warfare." I definitely don't want to screw the shareholders. I want the government to do all that with these failed banks because that's how we emerged from the S&L crisis of the '90s with minimal damage. Because that's how Sweden emerged from their banking crisis that same decade. Because every US Treasury Secretary before Paulson said that's how you rescue banks. Because what we're doing now is what Japan did during their "Lost Decade." I want Uncle Sam to take over the banks because it is *the right thing to do.*

I don't want universal health care because I want to be French or Canadian or even French-Canadian, *comprenez-vous*? I want it because tens of millions of Americans don't have health insurance. Because tens of thousands of Americans go bankrupt because of illness and mounting medical bills. Because these problems persist despite the fact that America spends more on health care than any other country. I don't even want to "stick it to" the insurance companies—though they stick it to us every day. They spend millions to deny us the care we pay for in order to save themselves billions. They are the arbiters of life and death in order to make a profit. So, people suffer and die, they live with illness or delay treatment because they fear being diagnosed with a "pre-existing condition" and being dropped from their insurance, never to be picked up again. Patients can't afford the system. Our employers can't. OB/GYNs are constantly driven from the business. I want universal health care because it is *the right thing to do.*

I definitely want more than a Truth and Reconciliation panel for this torture debacle. I want prosecutions. Not because I hate America. Not because I hate Bush and Cheney. I want people punished for torturing detainees because torturing is morally reprehensible. Because it is against international and *US* law. Because torture was much bigger than Lynndie England and The Abu Ghraib Gang. I want it because our former President and Vice President openly bragged about torturing prisoners. Because our own Justice Department wrote legal briefings sanctioning torture. Because it looks like it was not only the Bush Administration and Republicans in on the whole thing but also their Democratic "opposition." Because the CIA, FBI, our own soldiers, and even *private contractors* appear to have tortured people. I want prosecutions because all these people tortured in my name, they did it as *Americans*. And it was wrong and a systemic failing and I never want to see America sanctioning torture *ever again*. I want people prosecuted because it is *the right thing to do*.

But where are our leaders who believe in doing the right thing? Who has the courage to stand against the powerful interest groups and lobbyists, the pundits and donors?

Instead of the government's taking over the banks like they did with the S&Ls, we have Geithner and Bernanke pouring our *grandchildren's* money down the drain. They don't want to hurt or offend or even hold their Wall Street cronies accountable for the disaster they've created. People aren't fired. They're given retention bonuses even if they've left their jobs. They don't want the shareholders to lose their money. They want their buds to reap all the rewards of capitalism and the American taxpayer to assume all the risks—to the tune of $700 billion and counting.

The Obama team, who promised us some sort of universal health care while campaigning, has a heart-to-heart with the insurers and now says all options *except* a single-payer system are on the table.

Obama himself, our Constitutional scholar president, has reversed decades of human rights legislation by openly condoning the Nuremberg Defense. No, we won't be prosecuting individual CIA agents for torture. They were "just doing their jobs." He even, despite mounting evidence to the contrary, reached into a tried and true fiction trope by saying that it was only "a few bad apples" who committed torture.

We live in an era where no one believes in accountability and personal responsibility, where no one should suffer the consequences of their own misdeeds if they're rich and powerful enough.

Bill Campbell

The bankers get away with it. The torturers. Hell, even A-Rod has gotten away with taking steroids.

There is no such thing as personal responsibility. And our own elected officials can't be entrusted to enforce it because they can't even regulate themselves. Responsible for our money, they're running up an historic national debt. While it's only to be temporary, they refuse to take any action that will make it just that.

They squawk about fiscal responsibility, but none of them are going to give up their own pet projects. They refuse to curb spending but also refuse to raise taxes on the people who can *most* afford it. No, capital gains must remain taxed at 15 percent while everyone else gets taxed at higher rates. Ultimately, we all know taxes will be raised, but those who reap the most benefit from living in this country won't bear the brunt of the burden, the rest of us will.

And war crimes? What war crimes? Yes, Robert Mugabe must pay for *his* war crimes. Those despots in Sudan, North Korea, Burma, etc., must pay for *theirs*. But, when the rubber hits the road, Congress will scream, "We don't commit war crimes. We're Americans!"

Now, I am not naive enough to believe that there was some mystical "Golden Age" when the rich and powerful did *not* escape justice. However, there have been instances when the Michael Milkens of the world had to do at least a little time for their crimes. When the CIA was taken to task for their misdeeds. And I can't help wondering where those times have gone?

I don't expect a storming of the Bastille and the streets to run with blood. But, with all that has been going on, I do *desire* a return of the notion of The Common Good. That people have to take responsibility for their actions and their positions. These bankers were trusted with our money and squandered it. They must pay. These agents and soldiers and *private contractors* violated US law. They must be prosecuted. A-Rod sucks ass. He must die! Health insurers are bad actors and run an exploitative business. They must be taken to task or driven out of business. Our President and Congress were elected to create and *uphold* the laws of this land. They must *enforce* them.

These are not the rantings of a lunatic (I think) who lives in some sort of paranoid delusion. These are all parts of the social contract we sign onto by being members of society. These are the responsibilities of the positions these people hold. I am only asking them to do *the right thing to do*. Obviously, this is too much to ask from mere mortals. So, I guess, what I'm asking for is heroic action. I guess I'm asking for a hero.

Whatever Happened to Loving?

Saturday, June 6, 2009

The older I get, I realize, the less I know, and there are simply some things I just don't understand. For example, I just don't understand all the controversy over gay marriage. Don't get me wrong, yet again, I'm not some naif fresh out the womb who needs to suckle on the teat of "civic" discourse. It's just something I don't get.

I don't understand why people feel the need to mask their morbid curiosity, dread, and hatred over what goes on in other people's bedrooms in such dramatically indignant, "moralistic" tones, using the Bible, Koran, Torah, or McDonald's Dollar Menu to justify their aversion to homosexuality. Let's face it, people: you either hate gays, kinda wanna *be* gay (or at least have an "experience"), or they just creep you out. Why mask this with such high-falutin', florid, religious language (you know, like "God Hates Fags")? I'm not saying, "Get over it." Some of you will. Most of you won't. Just admit it and leave God out of it!

You used to say He was down with slavery and stoning adulterous women. He seems to have gotten over those little disappointments. Maybe He'll get over this little gay marriage thing, too. But, until I see you conversing with a burning bush or bringing down a plague of locusts, shut the hell up and let God speak for Himself.

I also don't understand why our government listens to this vitriolic, hyperbolic, pseudo-religious hate speech and allows this claptrap to dictate the law. Now, if these different "God-fearing," "Bible-believing" churches want to ban marriage ceremonies in their own "houses of God," that's one matter. But how does that dictate what goes on in the State House?

The last I checked, the religious ceremony was all pomp and circumstance signifying nothing in the eyes of the State. The *real* marriage happens when two people sign that paper and file it with you.

And I could've sworn that, in the eyes of the State, marriage was not some mystical, magical, holy union to unite man and wife. I thought, to them, it was a straight-up *property rights* issue: who can sign for whom; who can speak for whom; who gets whose stuff when somebody dies. I mean, aren't there *thousands* of rights conveyed to a married couple that single folks don't have? And let's face it: nobody looks into my moral character when I buy a house (though it *is* a rather invasive procedure), and nobody seems to care who I diddle when I hit the Dollar Menu. That's not the issue when it comes to property rights. Now, is it?

I'm simply baffled as to why these same states allow the gay marriage issue up for referenda, too. Since when has granting Civil Rights been up for popular vote? Could you imagine the campaign speeches back in 1860?

"Now, my glorious, urbane, civilized, Christian, *white people! Let us take this filthy, barbaric, lazy, son of Ham, heathen nigger and* raise *him up from slavery! Let us unshackle this beast of burden! Let us give him* full *and* equal *rights with us, the civilized, master race of Caucasia! Let him live among us! Let him compete with us for the same jobs...*

"Yeah, yeah, I know. Funny, right? But I'm on a roll here.

"Let this dusky brute marry our pure, virginal-white daughters! Let him father our mulatto grandchildren! Let him vote! Let him hold political office! Hell, let him run for President of these here United States of America! What say you, my glorious, urbane, civilized, Christian, *white people?!!!"*

"Hoorah!!! Hoorah!!! Hoorah!!!"

"You gonna let them niggers vote?"

"Hush now, Susan B. Anthony!"

Exactly.

Civil Rights have *never* been granted at the ballot box. American Civil Rights have been won in the streets, on the battlefield, through judicial rulings, Constitutional Amendments, and hard-fought legislation. But never have the people voted on the rights of a despised minority and *granted* them. Anybody serious about the issue ought to know this by now.

But what I *really* don't understand about the gay marriage debate is whatever happened to *Loving v. Virginia*? I mean, haven't we had this fight already?

For those not in the know, *Loving v. Virginia* was the landmark, 1967 Supreme Court decision that forever struck down anti-miscegenation laws and bans on interracial marriage. Mildred (black) and Richard Perry Loving (white) were Virginia residents who moved to Washington, DC in order to get married. When they returned to Virginia, the local police raided their home, hoping to catch them doing the Mandingo (interracial sex being a crime), and arrested them in their bed. When the Lovings produced their marriage license, the cops hauled them in (interracial marriage being an even bigger crime). The couple was sentenced to one year in prison, but the sentence was commuted to 25 years probation if they promised to never return to the commonwealth. They moved back to DC and later sued with the help of the ACLU.

The Supreme Court decided that Virginia's anti-miscegenation laws violated the Due Process and Equal Protection clauses of the Fourteenth Amendment, and stated:

"Marriage is one of the "basic civil rights of man," fundamental to our very existence and survival.... To deny this fundamental freedom on so unsupportable a basis as the racial classifications embodied in these statutes, classifications so directly subversive of the principle of equality at the heart of the Fourteenth Amendment, is surely to deprive all the State's citizens of liberty without due process of law. The Fourteenth Amendment requires that the freedom of choice to marry not be restricted by invidious racial discrimination. Under our Constitution, the freedom to marry, or not marry, a person of another race resides with the individual and cannot be infringed by the State."

They also stated that these laws were racist and perpetuated white supremacy:

"There is patently no legitimate overriding purpose independent of invidious racial discrimination which justifies this classification. The fact that Virginia prohibits only interracial marriages involving white persons demonstrates that the racial classifications must stand on their own justification, as measures designed to maintain White Supremacy."

Now, I ain't no lawyer and definitely no legal scholar or nuthin' like dat, but it is absolutely *beyond* me as to how this does not apply to homosexuals and their right to marry. Substitute "black" for "gay" and "white supremacy" for I don't know, "hetero homodoxy," and you pretty much got your answer to this entire debate.

I know a lot of my fellow African-Americans don't like equating our Civil Rights struggles with others and think that our hard-won rights should not be expanded. However, the Due Process and Equal Protection clauses have *already* been expanded to other groups.

Due Process has been used to protect the "freedom of contract," so employers and employees could negotiate wages without state interference. And it's been used to interfere in said contract in setting maximum hours for workers. It's also been used to uphold states' prohibition laws and federal drug laws as well as the right to privacy and parental rights.

Equal Protection expanded to protect Chinese-Americans in 1886 and all other racial groups in 1954. It's also been expanded to protect women and illegitimate children. Hell, it's even been used to regulate voter redistricting.

How so far-reaching an Amendment and a Supreme Court decision incorporating said Amendment does not apply to gays and their right to marry is utterly incomprehensible (I'm almost certain that it applies to all other facets of their lives). And how any law or court ruling that does not utilize the Fourteenth Amendment and rules against gay marriage is *not* deemed unconstitutional just boggles the mind.

Marriage is a Constitutional right. Plain and simple. Any legislator or judge who believes otherwise is simply neglecting their duty as protectors of the Constitution and playing with people's lives under some false pretense of morality. Morals are for individuals to grapple with. Your jobs are to uphold the Constitution. Start doing it.

"Surrounded as I am now by wonderful children and grandchildren, not a day goes by that I don't think of Richard and our love, our right to marry, and how much it meant to me to have that freedom to marry the person precious to me, even if others thought he was the "wrong kind of person" for me to marry. I believe all Americans, no matter their race, no matter their sex, no matter their sexual orientation, should have that same freedom to marry. Government has no business imposing some people's religious beliefs over others. Especially if it denies people's civil rights.

"I am still not a political person, but I am proud that Richard's and my name is on a court case that can help reinforce the love, the commitment, the fairness, and the family that so many people, black or white, young or old, gay or straight seek in life. I support the freedom to marry for all. That's what Loving, and loving, are all about."

--Mildred Loving, 2007

Puns

(actually, mostly satire, but that would've screwed up the alliteration)

Visions of Blood

Tuesday, September 30, 2008

If there were no hell, man would need to invent it. So many people do so much evil here on Earth and escape punishment, there has to ultimately be a place where justice is finally meted out. Some are consoled with the death penalty, but that's mostly for the poor. What about the rich and powerful? No matter what they do, no matter how many lives they destroy or end, they seem to always get off scott free. Most never see the insides of a courtroom; if they do, they generally get off; if they're sentenced, the Michael Milkens of the world are shuttled off to Club Feds with manicured lawns and tennis courts crying about doing "hard time"; and bastards like Augusto Pinochet, Slobodan Milosevic, and Ken Lay would rather die than face terrestrial punishment. So few receive a righteous gunning down like Anastasio Somoza, eternal damnation seems to be our last hope for retribution. And we console ourselves, singing, "If there's a hell below, they're all gonna go."

But sometimes our fantasies can't wait, and we resort to dreams of good ole-fashioned street justice. "Boy, if I caught that bastard in an alley … on the street … alone …" Oh, we'd take that jerk to task. Beat him down like the punk he is. Take a pound of flesh out of that ass. That would teach the powerful a real lesson. Even in our fantasies, it's not enough, but it makes us feel better believing that our fists could knock the rich and powerful down a notch.

The problem with living in DC is that the powerful truly walk among us. Tim Russert was a neighbor of mine. My wife was ten feet away from W. when he and "Condi" were condemning "nation building" after the Afghanistan invasion. I've been in the same room as Bill Clinton, Sandra Day O'Conner, and Ted Kennedy; the same bar with Barbara Bush the Younger; met Bono en el baño; been given free cartons of Camel Lights by a powerful tobacco lobbyist; gotten drunk off of the telecom lobbyists' dime; and was even had an assistant director of the FBI buy me a drink. And I'm not even in politics.

So, when you cry for the opportunity for street justice, in this city you have to be careful what you ask for. Because, sooner or later, you may just get it. I sure did. In 2004.

It was a nice, fall morning. I'd just genuflected to middle age, eating my All Bran "shit rods", grabbed my water bottle, and was off to the gym. I walked outside to see three, official-looking black SUVs. Paranoid Black Man Instinct instantly kicked in, checking to see if my shit was correct. *You got any drugs or guns on you, Bill?* I asked myself. *Wait, you don't do drugs and hate guns.* Somewhat relieved, I hesitantly walked by—hoping these bastards (whoever they were) wouldn't pin a gun and/or drug charge on me.

When I turned the corner, I faced a squat, powerful brother with Pecs o' Steel that spanned all six lanes of Connecticut Avenue and a white coil sprouting from his left ear. Three black SUVs plus this black behemoth equaled one, powerful sumbitch. Before I had a chance to speculate who, a little lump of graying timidity popped out of the dry cleaners. I gasped, coming face-to-face with the ultimate apparatchik of evil.

Paul Wolfowitz. At the time the Deputy Secretary of Defense. The face of the Iraqi invasion. God, I hated that bastard. I hated all those neocons—that cabal of pseudo-intellectual dweebs who couldn't fight their way out of a high school locker who got their menopausal machismo on by heralding others' deaths and tortures. During Vietnam, Wolfowitz studied math at Columbia to get a deferment, Bush had his Daddy get him into the Texas Air National Guard, and Cheney was "too busy" all the while trumpeting the war effort, while folks like my Uncle Bob eschewed college, volunteered for the Marines, and received two Purple Hearts—his Jeep getting blown to bits in the jungles outside of Saigon. And while my little brother was bogged down in Baghdadi firefights, these paper patriots were busy wrapping themselves in the flag, questioning the patriotism of Max Cleland (who lost three limbs in Vietnam), and circle jerking to "Shock and Awe" casualty reports. God, I wanted a piece of them. And here was Wolfowitz, right in front of me, hunched over with dry cleaning, scuttling along as though he were still traumatized by the wedgie Biff Tannen gave him back in Hill Valley High.

Come on, Bill, I urged myself as Wolfie walked toward me. *You can do this, Negro. Sure, you're fat and out-of-shape. Sure, you haven't been in a fight since 1994.* (My last fight was the first fight I ever started, and, in a fit of divine justice, I broke my hand in the fracas. Taking my punishment, I never got it fixed, figuring I'd re-break my hand if I ever fought again. But this would be worth it. Besides, could you imagine the parades they'd throw for me in San Francisco if I said, "I broke my hand on Paul Wolfowitz's face"?) *You can do this, Campbell!*

No, you can't.

"Who?" I asked.

"What?" Wolfowitz asked.

I suddenly realized that Supa Brotha was looking at me. Interested.

Have you ever head-butted yourself, Campbell? he telepathically asked.

What?

It's a process where a powerful, virile brother—such as myself—takes your head, shoves it up your ass, all the way up through your entire digestive tract, and out through your own mouth to where you're actually looking at yourself. Then, said powerful, virile brother proceeds to smash your head into itself until the victim is rendered completely unconscious.

Damn. You can do that?

The brother just looked at me, Sphinx-like. Wolfie was just a slug away. It was now or never. I looked at the brother again, at Wolfowitz, at the sight of my head traveling past my morning bran through my large intestines, back at Wolfowitz again, Supa Brotha.

I sigh. "Good day, Mr. Wolfowitz, mighty fine job you're doing."

I bow reverentially.

"Why, thank you," Wolfowitz smiled. The Brotha smiled. I went on to the gym promising to punish myself with extra stomach crunches.

Bill Campbell
Obama Campaign Targets Deadly Disease

Monday, October 6, 2008

For centuries, medical and social scientists have been plagued by questions concerning the debilitating African-American disease, CP Time (or "Colored People's Time"). Apparently striking in adolescence, CP Time renders your typical person of African descent literally incapable of ever being punctual. Victims are chronically at least 15 minutes late every day for work and may not show up to social engagements for hours.

Founder of American psychiatry Benjamin Rush first discovered this malady in 1781, claiming it to be "a fundamental weakness of the negro physick." Many slave owners at the time just chocked it up to malingering and attempted to cure this deadly genetic disease with healthy doses of horse hide. Thomas Jefferson, along with many other slave owners, thought they themselves caught the disease from their slaves. Jefferson claimed to have contracted it from his slave Sally Hemings, reporting that on several occasions he couldn't get himself out of bed for days on end after being visited by the woman. It was their own chronic tardiness that had detractors believing presidents Abraham Lincoln and Warren G. Harding were indeed part-Negro.

The mystery of CP Time has led to many far-flung scientific "theories." Phrenologists believed that the African's skull was too small to include the concept of time. Louis Pasteur was absolutely certain it was caused by a Negro-specific virus. Albert Einstein even thought there was perhaps an exclusively Negro dimension of time. However, it wasn't until 1995, when scientists realized that those of mixed race were only on average five minutes late to work, that the causes of CP Time were known to be genetic.

Though the Genome Project has yet to identify a CP Time gene, the evidence is quite striking and the consequences can be deadly. Recent research has shown that those of African descent spend on average 5.7 years of their lives waiting for other blacks; Latinos waiting for other Latinos, 3.2 years; Europeans, 1.2 minutes; and while South Asians lose 6.2 years, East Asians actually gain 5.3 years, chronically being early to work and social occasions.

Former Surgeon General Louis B. Sullivan stated, "This is a serious health crisis. Something needs to be done."

Al Sharpton cried, "This is racist! Tawanna told the truth!"

While there still seems to be no cure in sight, this past week encouraging news has emerged out of Georgia. The southern state is currently conducting early voting for this year's election. While African-Americans only constitute 29 percent of registered voters, they have made up nearly 39 percent of votes already cast (74,961 out of 194,138). With Senator Obama garnering roughly 93 percent of the African-American vote, it can only be assumed that the Democratic nominee's campaign is responsible for this medical breakthrough.

It is too early for scientists and the medical community to garner any meaningful data on the recent phenomenon. However, they are hopeful and are gathering information while trying to figure out what exactly about the Obama campaign has caused African-Americans not only be on time but actually early for this election. We reached the senator for comment.

"I don't know frankly," Sen. Obama said, frankly. "I myself have been plagued by CP Time my entire life. I never understood it. I barely knew my Kenyan father, was raised by my white mother and white grandparents, went to Harvard, became a successful attorney, community organizer, and politician, and never smoked menthols, and yet I could never be on time for anything. My campaign will do everything within our power to find a cure."

Geogia Republican Senator and owner of one of the largest real estate brokerage companies in America, Johnny Isakson, represents much white ambivalence about the news of a possible cure. "In all honesty," Isakson said, "we in the GOP depended on blacks to show up on November 10 [for the November 4 election]. While as an employer, I'm excited to see my workers finally show up on time; but if this means that McCain could possibly lose Georgia, I'm afraid the price may be too high."

Isakson's feelings are not shared by most, however. With the global proliferation of rap music and the worldwide prominence of Oprah Winfrey, Denzel Washington, and Will Smith, outbreaks of CP Time have been reported in such far-flung places as London, Beijing, and Tel Aviv. In Tblisi, Georgia, government officials have abandoned designated times for meetings altogether. "Something needs to be done. Our government barely functions," stated Iraqi President Jalal Talabani. "We are still waiting on a time table from the Bush administration." CP Time may indeed be a worldwide pandemic. With Gov. Palin's recent

Bill Campbell

"shout out" in last Thursday's Vice-Presidential debate, scientists have rushed to Alaska in search of a new outbreak in the "Last Frontier."

Joe the Plumber Goes Postal

Thursday, October 16, 2008

Joe never wanted to be a plumber. He wanted to dance. It all started in the summer of 1984. Joe was but a misunderstood lad. He didn't understand why he didn't want to play football and baseball like the other lads. He couldn't quite figure out why he was so obsessed with *Fame* and why Leroy was such a hero to him. At first, he thought he might be gay. But that fateful summer it all started to make sense. That was the summer he saw *Footloose*.

Like Kevin Bacon, Joe was stuck in a town that had outlawed dancing. Like Kevin, Joe was misunderstood. Like Kevin, Joe wanted to "dance in the sheets." Everything started making sense. He *was* holding out for a hero, and it wasn't Brian Sipe or Ozzie Newsome or any of those other crappy Browns. It was Ren McCormack! And like Chris Penn, he worked hard to copy every one of Ren's rebel moves.

No one understood Joe's newfound love. They ridiculed him. Once, in the boy's shower, Joe flashed "Jazz Hands" and was beaten ruthlessly within an inch of his life. All was lost. He almost gave up.

And then he saw the Mikhail Baryshnikov/Gregory Hines vehicle, *White Nights*. He came away from that Soviet-era movie knowing three things: he loved Isabella Rossellini (see, he wasn't gay after all), he hated the Soviets, and loved dance. He wanted to study ballet like Mikhail and tap like Gregory.

But his parents were adamant. His father roared, "I didn't raise no faggot!" Actually, his Dad did understand. He had a secret love of macramé that he could only exercise during "hunting trips." Unfortunately, Youngstown Steel had just closed; he no longer had a good-paying union job, and was stuck as a line cook in the local diner; he just could not afford to indulge his son's dreams.

Joe's life became a covert campaign of dance. He videotaped every episode of *Fame*, bought *White Nights*, watched PBS, the *Breakin*'s, all the musicals—especially Bob Fosse flicks. He watched *All That Jazz* at least once a day. Once, he even sneaked all the way to Cleveland just to see the Dance Theater of Harlem. And he practiced, practiced, practiced.

In 1987, he got his chance. An audition to Juilliard. He worked overtime, closing the local McDonalds every night for three months to pay for his bus trip to New York. He came into the studio with his cut-off shorts, Van Halen T-shirt, and a boombox. They openly scoffed. But when he turned on Nu Shooz' "I Can't Wait" and busted his Hollywood hip-hop moves, he really moved the judges. "Well," one of them started, "we usually only accept students who are more ... well, um, classically-trained, but you had me once you danced on the table and flicked my tie. Welcome to Juilliard, son."

The elation died as soon as he returned to Ohio. "No, son," his father said, "it's too risky. You're gonna be a plumber. There ain't no union no more, but there will always be shit."

Joe's life became shit. But he did what his father wanted (not realizing that it broke his father's heart—he would never weave a pot holder again). He tried to find the poetry in polybutylene but just couldn't. With a broken heart, he got married, had kids, worked his way up the ladder.

"I always got a feeling Joe hated plumbing," a co-worker recently said, "but, boy, you should see him move across the construction site."

"Joe always hated being called a plumber," a former girlfriend confided. "He used to fly into such a rage. I remember he broke a bottle over one guy's head when he called him that. And then, one night, he put two guys in the hospital when they joked, 'You must lay plenty a pipe there, Joe.'"

It all apparently came to a head last night during the presidential debate. The constant references to his unchosen profession just unhinged him.

"I don't know," his wife said. "We were watching that boring debate, and I kept telling him I wish I could vote Sarah Palin in for president. And he just kept getting angrier and angrier. 'Joe the Plumber, Joe the Plumber,' all night long. I could see the rage boiling over. I'd never seen Joe like that before. And then, Senator McCain said, 'You're rich, Joe!' I don't know where he got that. We live in a double-wide. But then Joe told me to get his shotgun."

Mrs. Joe did just that. Joe took it, left their trailer, climbed into his '74 El Camino, and has not been seen since. The authorities are now looking for him.

Joe the Plumber Goes Postal

Thursday, October 16, 2008

Joe never wanted to be a plumber. He wanted to dance. It all started in the summer of 1984. Joe was but a misunderstood lad. He didn't understand why he didn't want to play football and baseball like the other lads. He couldn't quite figure out why he was so obsessed with *Fame* and why Leroy was such a hero to him. At first, he thought he might be gay. But that fateful summer it all started to make sense. That was the summer he saw *Footloose*.

Like Kevin Bacon, Joe was stuck in a town that had outlawed dancing. Like Kevin, Joe was misunderstood. Like Kevin, Joe wanted to "dance in the sheets." Everything started making sense. He *was* holding out for a hero, and it wasn't Brian Sipe or Ozzie Newsome or any of those other crappy Browns. It was Ren McCormack! And like Chris Penn, he worked hard to copy every one of Ren's rebel moves.

No one understood Joe's newfound love. They ridiculed him. Once, in the boy's shower, Joe flashed "Jazz Hands" and was beaten ruthlessly within an inch of his life. All was lost. He almost gave up.

And then he saw the Mikhail Baryshnikov/Gregory Hines vehicle, *White Nights*. He came away from that Soviet-era movie knowing three things: he loved Isabella Rossellini (see, he wasn't gay after all), he hated the Soviets, and loved dance. He wanted to study ballet like Mikhail and tap like Gregory.

But his parents were adamant. His father roared, "I didn't raise no faggot!" Actually, his Dad did understand. He had a secret love of macramé that he could only exercise during "hunting trips." Unfortunately, Youngstown Steel had just closed; he no longer had a good-paying union job, and was stuck as a line cook in the local diner; he just could not afford to indulge his son's dreams.

Joe's life became a covert campaign of dance. He videotaped every episode of *Fame*, bought *White Nights*, watched PBS, the *Breakin'*'s, all the musicals—especially Bob Fosse flicks. He watched *All That Jazz* at least once a day. Once, he even sneaked all the way to Cleveland just to see the Dance Theater of Harlem. And he practiced, practiced, practiced.

In 1987, he got his chance. An audition to Juilliard. He worked overtime, closing the local McDonalds every night for three months to pay for his bus trip to New York. He came into the studio with his cut-off shorts, Van Halen T-shirt, and a boombox. They openly scoffed. But when he turned on Nu Shooz' "I Can't Wait" and busted his Hollywood hip-hop moves, he really moved the judges. "Well," one of them started, "we usually only accept students who are more … well, um, classically-trained, but you had me once you danced on the table and flicked my tie. Welcome to Juilliard, son."

The elation died as soon as he returned to Ohio. "No, son," his father said, "it's too risky. You're gonna be a plumber. There ain't no union no more, but there will always be shit."

Joe's life became shit. But he did what his father wanted (not realizing that it broke his father's heart—he would never weave a pot holder again). He tried to find the poetry in polybutylene but just couldn't. With a broken heart, he got married, had kids, worked his way up the ladder.

"I always got a feeling Joe hated plumbing," a co-worker recently said, "but, boy, you should see him move across the construction site."

"Joe always hated being called a plumber," a former girlfriend confided. "He used to fly into such a rage. I remember he broke a bottle over one guy's head when he called him that. And then, one night, he put two guys in the hospital when they joked, 'You must lay plenty a pipe there, Joe.'"

It all apparently came to a head last night during the presidential debate. The constant references to his unchosen profession just unhinged him.

"I don't know," his wife said. "We were watching that boring debate, and I kept telling him I wish I could vote Sarah Palin in for president. And he just kept getting angrier and angrier. 'Joe the Plumber, Joe the Plumber,' all night long. I could see the rage boiling over. I'd never seen Joe like that before. And then, Senator McCain said, 'You're rich, Joe!' I don't know where he got that. We live in a double-wide. But then Joe told me to get his shotgun."

Mrs. Joe did just that. Joe took it, left their trailer, climbed into his '74 El Camino, and has not been seen since. The authorities are now looking for him.

My Dinner with Bill

Saturday, November 29, 2008

I sit down at the bar and am immediately greeted by a gritty blond and a Rolling Rock draft. God, it's been so long. I used to be a regular here at Clagaire's, my favorite Irish pub, the place I always used to go when I wanted to get back in touch with my roots. But that was a lifetime ago. I live in the suburbs now—Washington, DC but a faint memory.

My guest slumps into the bar. His designer suit is wrinkled and tan and is hanging awkwardly off his bulky frame. His goatee is graying and spreading haggardly across his face. I wave him over, and he sits down next to me, wreaking of pathos.

"Wanna beer?" I offer.

"Yeah. Bud. And a shot of Jack."

"Not tequila?"

He looks offended. "No. Why?"

"Oh, no reason," I quickly say.

I don't want to cause my boy any more heartache. He's had a rough year. Chock full of disappointment. Who needs to add insult to his innumerable injuries?

"So, how you doing, Bill?" I ask.

"Fine, Bill," he says, stonily. Suddenly, his lower lip starts quivering. "Just fine," he blubbers.

"You should try the corn beef and potatoes," I quickly offer. "They use cilantro."

"Cilantro, Bill?"

"Yeah. Cilantro, Bill. The cook's Mexican."

"Ahh," he says, mistily, "*mi gente.*"

"Yeah. Your *gente.*"

See, my boy and I have a lot in common. We both inexplicably call ourselves "Bill." We could both stand to lose a few pounds; we're both Third Culture Kids; both products of immigration. He's half-Mexican, half-white. I'm half-Jamaican, half-African-American. He's bilingual ... I could stand to lose a few pounds. We both have an utterly *magical* way with the ladies. And no matter how hard we try, no matter how immensely qualified we are, we both tend to end up screwed in the end quarters.

"Commerce?" New Mexico Governor Bill Richardson squeaks, as our corn beef comes. "Secretary of Commerce, Bill?!"

"I know, Bill," I say, heavily. "Another round, please?!"

Too late.

"I served 14 years in Congress," Richardson starts, heatedly. "I was deputy majority whip. I was chairman of the Congressional Hispanic Caucus. I've negotiated with Saddam Hussein, met with Slobadan Milosevic, the Sudanese, and those wacky North Koreans."

"They *are* wacky."

"I've been Secretary of Energy and the US ambassador to the United Nations. I've brokered peace—no matter how temporary—between the Palestinians and Israelis. I strengthened the UN's Environmental Programme, promoting 'ecologically sustainable development'—whatever the hell that means. *I'm* actually the governor of a state, worked for Kissinger's State Department, and I've still got a mean, fucking curveball."

"I know, Bill. You're preaching to the converted."

"Did I mention I have a way with the ladies?"

"Well, Bill, that goes without saying." I pat him on his beefcakey shoulder. "If life were a meritocracy, you'd be President-Elect. You were the only candidate who was truly qualified for that office."

"But Hillary stole my Experience argument, and now she's stolen my State Department."

"The brother screwed you, what can I say?"

"Commerce," he weeps. "It's like being rejected by Blair, rebuffed by Jo, Tootie and Natalie don't want anything to do with you, and, next thing you know, you're screwing Mrs. Garrett, wondering where it all went wrong."

"Ah, yes," I sigh, heavily. *"The Facts of Life."*

"What the hell am I supposed to do with Commerce, Bill?"

"I don't know, Bill," I confess. "I guess you could tour the country, test out all those weigh stations on the highways."

He groans.

"Human trafficking?"

He sniffles.

"Ooh. I got it!" I pipe up. "You could 'investigate' the dangers of internet porn. Hold hearings. 'Interview' some of the stars. You'll be swimming in silicon for *months*, my brother!"

That seems to do the job.

"Hm," he ruminates. "I wonder what Vanessa del Rio's doing these days."

"Hell, the way you have with the ladies, Bill," I smile, "*you* come March."

"You're a good man, Bill Campbell."

"And you're a *great* one, Bill Richardson."

We raise our shot glasses and down more Jack, my patriotic duty done for the day.

Ha! I Still Got It

Thursday, December 11, 2008

A lot of guys in my situation (looking at 40 and ever-decreasing levels of testosterone and married with chilluns) sometimes find themselves in a lonely bar hitting on a woman damned near half their age in desperate need of a number, a modicum of attention, anything, all in the vain hopes of reaffirming what they know ain't true: that they "still got it." Fortunately, I've yet to find myself in that situation. No, it's not that my ego is all that strong. It's just that I'm old and schlumpy and never really had it in the first place. Besides, who has the time to go out drinking?

However, my ego *is* fragile. It can always use a little boosting. And last night it got just that. Thanks to Montgomery County's Finest, I know I do "still got it."

Now, as many of you know, many males of the Negroid persuasion have often had and continue to have a rather, let's say, contentious relationship with our nation's law enforcement. A lot of us deserve it—drug dealers, gang members, professional athletes, and the like. But others are innocent babes in the woods, victims of an evil world not of their making. That'd be me.

This poor, little integration baby has been pulled over more times in more states than he can count. They're always looking for the same things—attitude, guns, drugs. My wife and I even got the drug-dog treatment driving through South Carolina while going the speed limit. There have been countless eyefuckings between po-po and me. I can't tell you how many descriptions I've fit, how many walls my hands have been against. The cops even tried searching *my* apartment when *I* called to complain about a neighbor. And I've been stopped WWB (Walking While Black) in four different states (in high school, I was stopped walking in the neighborhood I grew up in—the cop apologized after he realized he knew me).

But that was back when I was a young, *dangerous*, black man. In other words, a looooong time ago. I don't know what happened—maybe there was a memo, or something—but, when I turned 30, suddenly the coppers no longer hated me. Instead of hot stares, I'd get a "Good afternoon, Mr. Campbell." It was like they respected me, or something. At first it was confusing, then a relief, and then just downright depressing. Somehow, the po-lice knew I was no longer in the main crime-commiting demographic, no longer a threat. They knew I was … *old*.

Yeah, nobody likes being a target for the cops—moving or stationary. But there's something kinda flattering about their derision—especially for a nerd like me. Really, I'm just a labium with legs who fancies himself a writer. Not only could I not hurt a fly—that fly could seriously kick my ass. But, for a brief moment in my life, Officer Friendly thought me so threatening, so dangerous, they'd stop what they were doing, search their databases for my crimes, approach me with apprehension and their hands on their guns. You can't buy an ego boost like that. No nubile, winking co-ed could even come close. For the last decade I wouldn't quite say I missed that experience exactly but … well … who likes feeling old?

But last night I was young again.

It was after midnight, drizzling, and I was coming home from work. I was approaching a red light on a deserted, four-lane road. The light turned green before I had to stop, and I swung a left onto another four-laner, passing a stationary cop as I did so. Before I knew it, I was pulled over.

Since the kid, I've pretty much become a Sunday driver. So, I knew what this was about. I knew he probably got a good look at the face and the hair and decided to pull me over.

The officer approached from the passenger side window and informed me that he clocked me going 35 on a 25 mph road [it's actually 30 mph]. I wanted to say, "Yeah, right. You just had your radar going while you were sitting at a stop light with only one other car on the road." But I learned the hard way (a 13-hour stint in a Chicago/Cook Co. jail) that one should never argue with the police. (Hell, once in Atlanta, I got a cop to confess before the judge that he didn't actually see me violate the law he gave me a ticket for. The judge said, "What's your point?" and made me pay the ticket, anyway.) Besides, I knew why he pulled me over. He knew I knew. We just had to go through the routine.

Now, despite what Johnny Cochran said, a person can sound black, and a person can definitely sound white. I sound so white Lawrence Welk calls me "cracker." So, except for Chicago, when a cop hears my cadence, they quickly lose interest. The same was true last night. You could see the guy's ears straining for even the slightest hint of Ebonics, a double negative, one misplaced "be," so my ass could be grass.

Bill Campbell

I am ever so sorry to disappoint, dear chap. To make it worse, I live in a fine, upstanding zip code, and I work for a company that produces books for the blind. Johnny Law was looking for a Tupac and all he got was a damned Cosby Kid. He almost deflated and washed away in the rain. Instead, he took my license, wrote me a little bullshit warning, and, to make it look good, said, "Now please, slow down, Mr. Campbell. It's a little nasty out here tonight."

"I'll do that, son," I said, and drove off.

I was tired and, for a moment, annoyed. But then my chest inflated, and I started singing:

"Nah, nah, nah, nah, nah, I was racially-profiled,
Nah, nah, nah, nah, nah, I still got it."

Decisions Made E-Z

Monday, December 29, 2008

In these historically catastrophic times, we need bold, decisive leadership. The world needs people who are unafraid to take the reins and lead us out of the darkness. We need imaginative heroes who will not blink when ... at least filling Illinois' and New York's vacant Senate seats.

After this historic year and election, after all the soaring rhetoric and braggadocio, we at *Tome* have come to realize that our politicians are still full of it, mealy-mouthed, and, at best, mediocre. And, because of these glaring facts, we do not understand why it is not glaringly obvious that New York's and Illinois' politicians simply do not resort to the greatest tool mediocrity has ever known: nepotism.

New York's case is so incestuous it's simple. Governor David Paterson, son of a former state senator and New York secretary of state, must fill Hillary Clinton's Senate seat (who got it because her hubby was POTUS) with either (as conventional wisdom would have it) Andrew Cuomo, the current state's attorney general, or Caroline Kennedy, the ... uh ... Kennedy.

Andrew's argument is that his father was governor and that his brother, Chris, is one hot dude. His dad could give a pretty mean speech. As far as Chris goes, I don't know. I'm still obsessed with the fact that the *Today Show*'s Lester Holt is the only man in African-American history without lips.

But, if we're talking simple pedigree here, you've got to go with Caroline. Her uncle Ted's now being called "The Lion of the Senate," and he's about to kick the bucket; her uncle Bobby held the same Senate seat; her father was JFK, for godsakes; and every one of Caroline's cousins who isn't in rehab has held some sort of public office. If W. could win the Presidency just on the laurels of his *father's* mediocrity, isn't Caroline *due* at least a Senate seat—if not the Presidency, or at least the Papacy?!

I'm sure Gov. Paterson knows this. I'm almost certain he'll do the right thing and choose Caroline Kennedy.

Now, Illinois' seat is definitely a bit trickier, what with Gov. Cowpadour (get it?) on tape trying to sell the vacancy. For awhile there, it looked like Blagojevich was headin' to the slammer. Everybody was crying out for his blood. His own attorney general has been hacking away. But now things look a little murky. Blago refuses to step down. People are now doubting he can be impeached. They're even starting to wonder if the man can actually be charged with anything at all. The only thing that *is* known right now is that Illinois has a vacant Senate seat.

Of course, it's understandable why the good people of Lincoln's Land wouldn't want their governor to fill the same seat he just put up on eBay. But, what are you going to do? You're running out of time. We strongly urge the people of Illinois to find some useful, expedient criteria to fill that vacancy. I suggest nepotism. After all, it's not as though Illinois politics is unfamiliar with that concept.

Many would then suggest that Blagojevich give the Senate seat to Jesse Jackson, Jr. His is definitely the most recognizable name in the game. However, he'll more than likely lose re-election in 2010 (which was why he was not on Obama's short list). Therefore, it is time for bold action, imaginative problem-solving. It is time to think outside the box. It is time to select actress Jeri Ryan as Illinois' junior US Senator! At first, you may scoff, but there are very good reasons for Blago to choose the woman:

1) Like Caroline Kennedy and Sarah Palin, Jeri Ryan is a mother

2) As the former wife of Republican pol, Jack Ryan, Jeri is no stranger to Illinois politics;

3) As the former wife of Republican pol, Jack Ryan, Jeri is no stranger to international sleaze—as her ex-hubby kept taking her to sex clubs in New Orleans, New York, and Paris;

4) This Northwestern grad is no carpet bagger, and her Theater degree suits her perfectly in our media-saturated political world (she even played Sen. Lafe Smith in *Advise and Consent* her sophomore year);

5) Being half-human and half-Borg, Ryan has the perfect balance between logic and compassion and understands the political need to obliterate one's opponents with cold, calculating ruthlessness;

6) As a former teacher in one of Boston's most melodramatic city high schools, Ryan has faced and understands the challenges our

nation's children and schools encounter every day: drugs, gangs, premarital sex, teen pregnancy, social promotion, and, knowing David R. Kelley, transgender-anorexic-bestial-sex with neurotic goats;

7) As the former wife of Republican pol, Jack Ryan, she is owed way too much by Obama. If it hadn't been for the Ryans' sex scandal, Obama wouldn't have had such an easy road (Alan Keyes) to the Senate and would've come nowhere close to the Presidency. An adept pol like Jeri Ryan can use that fact as leverage to get Illinois the pork it needs in these hard, economic times;

8) And while we cannot vow for Jeri Ryan's integrity, we do know that, as Senator, Ms. Ryan will *not* be performing live sex acts on stage in either America or Europe. And that's the kind of decency we Americans deserve from our politicians.

Paying the Bills

Saturday, January 17, 2009

Oh, crap.

"Bill! ¿Que honda, mi perro?"

Note to Self: Find a new bar.

"Not too much, Bill. Guess you're hiding out, eh?"

He plops down on the bar stool next to mine. Oddly enough, he's looking much better than the last time I saw him. Somehow fitter? Haler? Happy? Is that Armani?

"From what?" he asks, jovially.

Jovially.

I roll my eyes—maybe hiss, too. It's hard to say. He ignores me and raises a finger to the bartender.

"A Tecate and a shot of Patrón for me."

"That's pretty expensive," I mumble.

He looks at me. "No," he corrects, "make that a Negro Modelo."

"Funny."

"And a Red Stripe for my friend. Hell, give him a shot, too."

"Thanks, Bill, but that's not necessary."

"What is, Bill?"

"Oh, I don't know," I shrug, "coming clean to the Feds."

Bill Richardson laughs heartily. Funny, when I tell a joke, you can hear a pin drop; but when I'm deadly serious, the room explodes in laughter. The bartender puts down our drinks.

"Ooh," Bill coos, "how about that lovely corned beef and potatoes?"

"They're out," I damn-near scream. The bartender gives me a queer look. "They're *out.*"

"Yeah. We're ... uh ... out."

"Maybe I should go back to the kitchen, talk to *mi hermana*, see what she can rustle up for her Mexican brother."

"She's gone, quit," I say, hurriedly. I just want him gone. "The new cook's Russian. All she can make is *pork.*"

"Whatever," the bartender sighs, and walks away.

"That's no problem, Bill. I love pork."

"So, I've heard."

Bill gives me a quizzical look. "What's the problem, Bill? I thought we—I thought—you know—I thought we'd made a connection. You wrote some really nice things about me in *Tome*."

"You read that?"

"Well ... one of my aides ..."

"Of course."

"So then, what's the problem, Bill?"

"Well, Bill," I exhale deeply. "You *are* under federal investigation for corruption."

"Oh, that," Bill pee-shaws. "These things happen."

"Pay-to-play *happens*?"

"That's Blago. Not me."

"Hmph."

"Do they have me on tape?"

I look at him. Incredulous.

"No," he whispers, harshly, "do they? What have you heard?"

"Dude, I take care of Poohbutt all day. I don't hear shit."

"Oh yeah," Bill chuckles. "'Talkin' Shit ... Literally.' That was funny—or, so my aide says."

"Some company gives your PAC a couple grand, so you, *Governor*, give them a fat *million-dollar contract*?!"

"You're oversimplifying things," Bill says, stiffly.

"Damnit, Bill. What happened to-" I start whining mockingly- "'I served 14 years in Congress. I was deputy minority whip? I met with Saddam and Slobadan and the Sudanese?' What the hell happened to Blair, Jo, and Tootie?!"

"Ahhh, Tootie—"

"What the fuck happened to Vanessa del Rio, nigga?!"

Someone gasps. Bill jerks back.

"Oooh ... ahhh," I stammer. "Did I just say that? I'm sorry. I've been watching a lot of *Boondocks* lately." I inhale ... exhale. "It's just that—well—now more tha—why the quick buck, Bill? Just why?"

Before he can respond, there's a commotion at the door. We all turn. A well-tailored, well-muscled, well-armed phalanx of crew cuts, sunglasses, lapel pins, and funny, white ear-wires quick-step into the bar. Between them flows a river of Saudi robes. Suddenly, the place reeks of petrodollars. On the next wave of visitors comes a hearty, twanged laugh. The entire bar gasps.

"Bill?!"

He and his Saudi/Secret Service entourage head directly to us. Immediately, thoughts of Rodney King flash through my mind. Old habits die hard. I cringe when this Bill slaps me and the other Bill on our backs. I hope someone's getting this on their camera-phone.

"Ha, ha," he chuckles. "Bill ... Bill."

"Bill."

"Uh ... Bill?" I ask.

"A round on me! For everybody in the hooooouuuuuusssse!" the new Bill trumpets.

The crowd cheers. The bartender gets to work. New Bill gives me a deep, penetrating look. Damn, he's creeping me out. He *does* have charisma. Suddenly, I want to find a cigar and a little, blue dress.

"Now, Bill," he says to me, "don't be so hard on my boy, Bill, here. He's a good man, a fine politician, a fine *Latino* politician—a key demographic, you know."

"Oh, I know."

"One day he'll make a fine Commerce Secretary when this all blows over and, who knows, maybe one day, a fine President. Insha'allah."

The Saudis give a crude chuckle.

"Besides," Bill continues. "I taught the man everything he knows."

I give Bill a heated glare. He shrugs uncomfortably. 'Nuff said.

"Now, I'm off to go 'make a speech,'" Bill concludes. "See ya in the funny papers!"

Bill, the Secret Service, and the Saudis flow out of the bar. I watch, dumbfounded. The bartender slaps the tab down before me.

"That'll be $247.82."

"He didn't pay?!" I gasp.

The bartender shrugs.

Bill shrugs.

"We're always paying for what that man does."

Cold Case: The Hip-Hop Sagas

Sunday, January 25, 2009

In an attempt to expand their audience beyond the "old white people" demographic, CBS has announced a bold new programming decision for the upcoming May Sweeps. According to network executives, CBS's hit crime procedural, *Cold Case*, will become a reality show of sorts, tackling the real-life murders of some of hip-hop's preeminent martyrs. Kathryn Morris and other cast members will take the skills learned from playing homicide detectives for the series and apply them to the actual murders of rappers and DJs who have been slain and whose murders remain unsolved. "It's hard to believe that authorities have yet to solve these murders," said Morris in a recent interview. "As a citizen, as an American, I feel it is my duty to bring these murderers to justice. That is what the show is about. That is what this country is about." CBS executives, who knew hardly anything of these murders nor the music, are still enthusiastic about the ratings these reality-based episodes can bring. Many within the hip-hop community are "ecstatic." Noted "hip-hop activist" and journalist, Harry Allen (also known as "the Media Assassin"), says, "It's about damned time somebody do something about this bullshit

Planned *Cold Case* Episodes

Sunday, May 3--Lamont "Big L" Coleman

On February 15, 1999, this noted Harlem rapper was gunned down just blocks away from the apartments in which he grew up. It had been rumored that Coleman was just about to sign with Roc-A-Fella Records just weeks before he died. Though a childhood friend, Gerard Woodley, was charged with Coleman's murder, he was later released. Woodley is currently serving time in prison on federal gun charges

Sunday, May 10--Jason William "Jam Master Jay" Mizell

Legendary, pioneer rap DJ of Run-DMC, Jason William "Jam

Master Jay" Mizell was shot and killed on October 30, 2002, in a Merrick Boulevard recording studio in Queens, New York. Twenty-three-year old Urieco Rincon was also shot in the ankle during the incident. Ronald "Tenad" Washington was named as an accomplice in the murder by federal prosecutors back in April 2007. They had also suspected Kenneth "Supreme" McGriff, a convicted drug dealer and friend of Murder, Inc., heads Irv and Chris Gotti. Most promising has been Washington, though, who's also suspected for the murder of a former Tupac Shakur associate, Randy Walker, in 1995. Neither has gone to court, yet, and many are skeptical. As Washington himself has put it: "They want to blame me for all the blood in rap."

Sunday, May 17 and Sunday, May 24--Pac and Biggie

Was the US Federal government really behind the September 6, 1996 assassination of Tupac Amaru "2Pac" Shakur and the March 9, 1997 assassination of Christopher George "Notorious B.I.G." Latore Wallace? In this two-part episode, Kathryn Morris and Crew dig deep, interview previously reluctant witnesses, go through previously classified government documents, and grill CIA, FBI, ATF, and FDA agents to finally get to the truth the government doesn't want you to hear.

Sunday, May 31--The Black-Eyed Peas

Cold Case: The Hip-Hop Sagas finally answers *the* burning question that has been plaguing hip-hop heads since 2003: Did Stacy Ann "Fergie" Ferguson really and truly kill William James "Will.i.am" Adams, Jr., Allen "Apl.de.Ap" Pineda, and Jaime "Taboo" Gomez, more popularly known as The Black-Eyed Peas?

Pres. Obama's Record-Shattering Day

Wednesday, February 4, 2009

February 3, 2009--Washington, DC (AP)

Amid the snow and ice, a gaggle of White House reporters gathered in DC's Malcolm X Park to witness Presidential history being made. Having lived in DC for far too long, the press corps lacked the prerequisite "flinty Chicago toughness" and soon grumbled to leave. However, the record they were about to see smashed was not a formidable one, though it has stood since the Truman administration. The new president stepped to the free-throw line at the park's asphalt basketball court and sunk bucket after bucket with a hardened, slick ball. The press corps, Secret Service, and gathering crowd of spectators soon marveled at President Obama's efficiency and poise as he drained 273 consecutive free throws, smashing President Truman's previous record of 12 set on August 9, 1945.

As is often the case, President Obama was humble in the face of this historic accomplishment. "Really," the President said, "I must thank Bill Bradley for this day. If it weren't for my trying to top his Senatorial record of 553 [consecutive free throws], I don't know if I could've ever overcome President Truman's formidable record. The credit really goes to Bill."

However, Obama's triumph and ice cream social were cut short as news broke of Tom Daschle's withdrawing his name for consideration for Secretary of Health and Human Services. With a burgeoning tax scandal looming over his head, Daschle decided that his nomination was too much of a distraction for the new administration. His withdrawal threw Washington into a tizzy—as everyone expected him to weather this storm and become the new head of HHS—causing yet another scandal within the new administration.

Quickly, President Obama went into action, shedding his sweaty gym clothes, grabbing a shower back at 1600, and calling in reporters to explain his actions. It is with these words to Fox News's Chris Wallace that the new POTUS once again broke a presidential record:

"I mean, I think that Tom took responsibility for the mistake on his taxes. I think it was an honest mistake and I made the assessment — I made the

judgment — that he was the best person to achieve health care reform and bring people together.

But, you know, what became clear to me is that we can't send a message to the American people that we got two sets of rules: one for prominent people and one for ordinary people. And you know, so I consider this a mistake on my part, and one that I intend to fix and correct and make sure that we're not screwing up again."

On February 7, 1984, President Ronald Reagan claimed full responsibility for sending the Marines into Lebanon only to withdraw them after a suicide bomber killed over 200 American soldiers. Only days before, Reagan presciently said, "If we do [cut and run], we'll be sending one signal to terrorists everywhere: They can gain by waging war against innocent people." While never quite claiming defeat, Reagan told the American people that if there were any person to blame for the Lebanon debacle it was him and that he took all the blame.

Not since that day in 1984 has a single President taken blame for a single mishap, mistake, or wrongdoing committed by himself or his officers. From "I did not have sexual relations with that woman" to the ubiquitous W. Bush claims of "mistakes were made," there has not been one mea culpa issued from the Oval Office in over four administrations. This streak of 9,127 days of denial has far outstripped the previous record of Ulysses S. Grant's denial of the Whiskey Ring Scandal. That lack of culpability only lasted some 3,653 days.

Reached for comment at Dupont Circle's Subairi Salon, TV historian Michael Beschloss noted with his trademark wry grin: "While this may indeed be a sad day for American politics, it is also a great day for the American Presidency. 'The Streak,' as it were, has lasted for far too long. While President Obama may not be able to 'change the tone in Washington,' we might see him actually bring at least an ounce of credibility and responsibility back into the political process. How's my hair?"

His hair fine, Beschloss then went on, *"Team of Rivals,* my ass. I made that—!!!"

Neither President Bushes were available for comment. However, we did catch up to President Clinton on his way back from Davos, Switzerland. Clearly, he was disappointed in seeing "The Streak" end. The President said, ruefully, "Hillary would've kept it alive," before he rejoined his Saudi entourage.

Beyonce Song Creates
"Commitment Ring" Trend

Monday, February 9, 2009

"Oh, this makes me the happiest girl in the world!" cheers Chanté Hall, 23, of Washington, DC. "For the first time in five years, I really and truly know I am his."

The young office assistant is not alone in her euphoria. Young women all across America are dancing for joy, flashing their "commitment rings" to all who are willing to look, and they and their men are crediting Beyoncé Knowles' song, "Single Ladies (Put a Ring on It)," for their newfound happiness. The smash hit single has been listed for a combined 103 weeks on 13 different global music charts including *Billboard Hot 100*, *Canadian Hot 100*, *Australia Singles Top 50*, *Bulgaria Singles Top 40*, *UK Singles Top 75*, and *Portugal Singles Top 50* since its release in November 2008. However, this "commitment ring" trend has only appeared in American cities, and everyone is more than happy to credit the newlywed Knowles for their newfound relationship status. "Well, the song got me to thinking," Danté Mickens, who recently gave Ms. Hall her commitment ring, admits, "and she was right. I do like it. I should put a ring on it."

"It makes the girls so happy," said Donna Mills, a local tattoo artist and piercing technician. "I love doing it. To believe such a simple procedure can give a girl such pleasure. I'm just glad to be a part of it."

Mills explains that she simply numbs the area for roughly five minutes and then pierces the outer labium with said commitment ring.

"There's only a quick second of pain and, as long as you keep the area clean, very little risk of infection. Any discomfort the girl may feel is most definitely clouded over by the ecstasy she feels with now being committed to her man. The couple then comes back a few days later for follow-up counseling and to pick out their 'leash.'"

This "leash," which is attached to the commitment ring, comes in several fashionable alternatives ranging from cloth, nylon, leather, or light- and heavy- silver- or gold-plated chain. It runs exactly 24 inches with a hoop on the other end, which the man can either hold or attach to his wrist. Mills informs *Tome* that most men opt for the heavy chain.

"When I showed it to my folks, they were so happy for me," beams Ms. Hall. "Well, my dad was a little disgusted, but my mama and aunts were absolutely beside themselves. We were going to go out to a bar to celebrate, but Danté said, 'No.' He had to be somewhere else. So, we just got tore up at home."

"It was the least I could do for my girl, you know. See how happy she is," smiles Mr. Mickens. "It's like the song says, I'm the man. I'm supposed to make Chanté and take her and deliver her. With the ring and leash I can deliver the girl anywhere she needs to be.

"Sure," he continues, "she doesn't like having to wear a mini-skirt and no panties all the time. Especially last month was the coldest January in DC history. And those poor girls freezing to death up in Minneapolis. But that's the only way this whole thing can work. And it's like they say, a man's gotta do what a man's gotta do. And so does his girl. We're committed, after all."

Tome's repeated attempts to have Ms. Knowles comment on this new trend have been thwarted by Jay Z's camp, who informs us that Beyoncé's camp is not available for comment. However, the rapper has been quoted as saying that "'Put a Ring on It' has done more for the black family unit than even the Obamas' moving into the White House."

Mother's Finest Was Wrong

Friday, February 20, 2009

In 1976, Atlanta funk/rock band Mother's Finest made one of the most racist, most ignored challenges known to music (only to be eclipsed by the careers of New Kids on the Block and Kenny G.). With "Nigizz Can't Sing Rock 'n Roll," lead singer Glenn Murdock threw the industry into a tizzy.

"I still don't know what they're talking about," rapper/singer/actor Mos Def recently commented on the 30-year-old controversy, "rock-n-roll *is* niggi music."

The challenge was soon taken up by George Clinton and Funkadelic with the release of *One Nation under a Groove* and their song, "Who Says a Funk Band Can't Play Rock?!" However, the "blacklash" was monumental.

"It was an outrage," says noted black revolutionary and jazz activist, Gil Scott-Heron. "We already had Charley Pride singing *country music.*"

"I told them nobody wants to hear black people singing rock music. It would never sell," music potentate, and then head of Arista Records, Clive Davis claims. "I made sure of that."

Through Davis' efforts, *Saturday Night Fever* was released and disco was born, forever closing the debate.

In the '80s, Davis' hegemony was challenged with the signings of black rock groups Bad Brains, Fishbone, and Living Colour. However, he made a concerted effort to quash their careers. At one point, Davis even threatened Madonna with exile when her Maverick label signed the aforementioned Bad Brains. Maverick hardly supported the group's album, *God of Love,* and soon dropped the group. Davis even succeeded in crushing the fledgling career of funk/metal Atlanta band (and one-time acquaintances of the author) Follow for Now. Because of their racial ambiguity, Rage against the Machine escaped Davis's wrath, but with the release of *The Chronic* the renascent debate was once again silenced.

However, with the signing of Executive Order 3865 (otherwise known as "E.O. Funk") in May 2007, President Bush has freed black musicians to once again explore their rock capabilities.

"Oh yeah, I'm proud of that one," Bush commented from his new refuge in Dallas. "I hope those bastards enjoy the Cuban sun. Guantanamo is where they belong."

When told what E.O. 3865 really was, the former president changed his tune.

"You know, I just signed those things. I never looked at them. Damn you, Condi."

The response has been small so far but very promising. There are the "Brooklyn boho weirdos", TV on the Radio, whose *Dear Science* was voted the Best Album of 2008 by *Spin*.

Philadelphia-born, former ska/punk rocker, Santigold (née Santi White, musically née Santogold) also made a huge splash in 2008 with her musically-née eponymous debut.

Somehow circumventing the "Buy American" clause in E.O. 3865, the U.K. has also contributed the hard-driving funk/rock of The Heavy, who some have compared to "Tom Waits backed by the Stooges" (though this author thinks they are more like Curtis Mayfield backed by early Earth, Wind, and Fire or Sly and the Family Stone).

"Oh yeah, the future of blacks in rock is limitless," comments Tunde Adebimpe, lead singer of TV on the Radio. "With The Big Brother in the White House, anything's possible."

Fellow band member, Kyp Morgan (who many have confused for Cornel West), raised a beer. "I heard that!"

Rush Limbaugh on Black Men

Tuesday, March 3, 2009

With his recent attacks on President Obama and the head of the Republican Party, Michael Steele, people are once again openly questioning whether or not conservative radio talk show host, Rush Limbaugh, is indeed a racist. Personally, I don't know what's wrong with these people. I mean, Rush is a *true patriot*, an *American hero*, who only speaks *the truth* to save his country from sure *destruction*. It personally fills me with nothing but joy to see Rush take his rightful place as the head of the GOP. No one deserves it more.

And, if you *really* and *truly* believe that Rush is *racist?!* (how *dare!* you?!!!) just look at all the great things he's had to say about the black man over the years:

On Barack Obama

"I hope he fails."

On Michael Steele

"Why are you running the Republican Party?"

On Donovan McNabb

"Sorry to say this, I don't think he's been that good from the get-go. I think what we've had here is a little social concern in the NFL. The media has been very desirous that a black quarterback do well. There is a little hope invested in McNabb, and he got a lot of credit for the performance of this team that he didn't deserve. The defense carried this team."

On Colin Powell

"Secretary Powell says his endorsement is not about race. OK, fine. I am now researching his past endorsements to see if I can find all the inexperienced, very liberal, white candidates he has endorsed. I'll let you know what I come up with."

Bill Campbell

On Jesse Jackson

"Have you ever noticed how all composite pictures of wanted criminals resemble Jesse Jackson?"

On MLK

"You know who deserves a posthumous Medal of Honor? James Earl Ray [MLK's assassin]. We miss you, James. Godspeed."

On Slavery

"I mean, let's face it, we didn't have slavery in this country for over 100 years because it was a bad thing. Quite the opposite: slavery built the South. I'm not saying we should bring it back; I'm just saying it had its merits. For one thing, the streets were safer after dark."

On an Assumed Black Caller

"Take that bone out of your nose and call me again."

On His Dealer, Datavius Markell Washington

"That was my nigga, right there! He was *always* on time!"

See, he loved Brother Markell. I think all of you racist, race-baiters need to just shut the hell up! After all, who would *you* rather have lead the Republican Party in these times of trouble?

I have a feeling Rush is going to lead them, feverishly goose-stepping into oblivion.

I say you give the man a chance.

Gettin' the Finger

Thursday, March 5, 2009

The lights are intense. They burn your skin. They blind you. Sweat pours into your eyes. Your throat's parched, and you swear you are about to die. How did you get here? How did it go so wrong? You were never supposed to be here? How did it all come to this?

You want to hold your daughter. But she's a toddler. She's got other concerns. Like how many blocks can she stack on top of each other. Or does a doggy go "arf! arf!" or "me-ooh." Besides, you should be strong for her. She can't see you whimpering like she does when you're about to put her in her crib.

The nurse is nice. Cute. Roberta. She greets you with a pleasant smile. The one that tells you she *can* be bothered—though she really can't. But it comforts you. After all, you know the doctor's just going to rush in, invade you, and rush back out. At least Roberta will know your name.

She takes your pulse. It's thumping a little. She takes your blood pressure. It's a little high at the moment. Can you blame it? It knows what's about to happen.

"Please, Mr. Campbell, be patient. The doctor will be in any minute."

She goes to leave and then turns around, suddenly remembering something. She produces that horrible hospital gown, the one that never closes in the back, and hands it to you.

"Could you please strip totally down and put this on?" she asks, with that smile.

"Sure," you gulp.

Your daughter's sitting on the floor, "reading" her ABC book.

"Arf-arf."

You look. It's the cat.

"No, baby. Meeow."

"Me-ooh."

"That's my girl."

You strip. You don't want to lie to yourself, don't want to act like you're too cool for school, you *are* a prude. You hated the shower after swim class, and you were never a fan when the doctor ordered you to turn your head and cough. But the day you always dreaded is now here.

You're looking at 39 while 40's jumping up right behind him, waving vigorously. There was a time you thought you'd never see 25, but, now, here you are. The doctors aren't caring so much about whether or not you have a hernia. They have waved your balls good-bye. They have moved onto bigger and better things: your prostate. Yeah, yeah, the wife wants to know what you're complaining about. She's like, *You should see what we women go through.*

Yeah, I know. I was there for the prenatal exams. But hey, we men don't have it so easy, either.

"My boy, Leroy. They once used the jaws of life! *to check out* his *prostate. Couldn't sit down for* months."

"His farts sounded like yawns, yo."

Those light sure are bright. You blink. Sweat gets in your eyes.

Our Father, who art in heaven,
hallowed be thy name...

"Good afternoon, Mr. Campbell."

The doctor sweeps in. His pen has a corporate sponsor. So do his pocket protector and lab coat. You have the feeling that you're leaving here with prescriptions.

He brusquely probes your eyes, nose, and throat. He thumps your chest, tells you to breathe deeply. Consider it foreplay.

He quickly gets down to business. He smears a jelly over his gloved fingers. You know that jelly. Yes ... you know that jelly.

"Now, stand here, Mr. Campbell and rest your elbows on the table."

You tearfully look over at your little girl. Wow, six blocks. A personal best. You're proud, but ...

"Hey, Doc, could you take her to the waiting room?" you ask, gravely. "I can't have her see me like this."

He hisses, "Roberta!"

Roberta hustles in. She's not smiling now. She plasters one on for the kid. "Oh, you are so adorable."

Your daughter reaches out for you, but Roberta whisks her away. You can hear the girl cry through the door.

You bend over.

Thy Kingdom come,
thy will be done,

on earth as it is in heaven...

Pop!

Your sweat splashes across the wall.*read!Andforgiveusourtrespasses! AsweforgivethosewhotrespassagainstUS!!!*

What the hell is this guy looking for?

"Would you please stand still, Mr. Campbell?"

I will not stand still for this!

Hey, wait ... a ... second ...

Have the lights dimmed? Is that a cheesy sax you hear? Is that ... no ... Barry White?

'Cause deeper and deeper
In love with you I'm falling

What is that?

Your doctor's voice drops a few octaves. It's like he's whispering in your ear.

"That's your prostate."

Really?

Sweeter and sweeter
Your tender words of love keeps calling

"Hm. It feels healthy. Of course, I can only reach the one side."

A little to the left, wouldya—Oh my God! What the hell?!—Isn't this what Jerry Falwell used to warn us about?!!!"

Pop!

"Hey!"

Suddenly, it's very cold. When will they make hospital gowns that close in the back?

The doctor icily snaps off his jelly-smeared gloves. "There are tissues over there in the corner," he states, dumping the gloves in the trash and quickly exiting the room.

It's just so cold.

You shuffle over to the corner, feeling exposed. Vulnerable. Just like Coco in *Fame* when they made her strip down to her brown boobies. The lights are harsh again. But a different song is playing. "Don't Leave Me This Way" by Thelma Houston. You grab some tissues and start wiping.

Roberta pops back in the room with your daughter. She sets the girl down on the floor with her ABC book. She looks at you, says, "Welcome to middle age, Mr. Campbell," and giggles out of the room, shutting the door behind her.

Your baby girl points at her ABC book, and declares, "Me-ooh."

Super Exitos Para "Change"

Sunday, March 22, 2009

As recently reported in *The Washinton Post*, the US Border Patrol has a hit on its hands. Over the past two years, the department has been releasing a five-song CD all across Mexico, featuring upbeat tejano tunes, warning of the dangers of illegally emigrating to the United States. These anonymous "bouncy ballads of death, dashed dreams, and futile attempts at manhood" are a smash—though the audience has no clue who's behind the recordings.

After some hours
Abelardo opened his eyes
And in the middle of the cold night
Discovered his dead cousin at his side

--"The Biggest Enemy"

Before you cross the border, remember
that you can be just as much a man
by chickening out and staying
Because it's better to keep your life than ending up dead

--"20 Years"

In fact, these songs have become so popular, the Border Patrol is planning a follow-up CD later this year as well as cumbia, marimba, and merengue discs for countries south of Mexico's border.
Taking notice of the Border Patrol's apparent musical success, other departments in the Obama administration have decided to use the new propaganda tool:

Defense Secretary Robert Gates has recruited Lebanese sexpot, Nawal al Zoghbi, to record "Please Don't Kill the Infidels" for release all across the Arab market.

Incoming Commerce Secretary ~~Bill Richardson~~ ~~Judd Gregg~~ Gary Locke has already recruited Taiwanese R&B sensation, Jay Chou, to release "Buy American!" in Taiwan and China.

And with no governmental prompting whatsoever, country music star, Toby Keith, has recorded "GOP STFU," to be released this Tuesday.

Michael Steele: "Nobody's Bitch"

Sunday, April 12, 2009

For the longest, Michael Steele was all hip-hop and one-armed midgets. He was everywhere. You couldn't get out of bed without tripping over a Michael Steele quote. But then the Rush controversy happened and Steele followed it up by rightfully calling abortion a "choice."

I suddenly couldn't think of the last time I'd heard from the GOP leader. My Black Paranoia kicked in. Surely, he couldn't be among all those angry white folk for this long, claiming to be their leader, and something not have happened to the boy. I'll be honest. I was getting a little worried.

Using my *Tome* press credentials, it still took awhile to find the Republican leader. It took even longer to convince him to grant this interview. I had to come with some booty—a Boppy pillow, a box of finger cots, some Ho-Hos, and a whole lot of grape Kool Aid.

I got off the train at Farrugut North and went up the escalators to K St., where Steele's new offices were. I was greeted by the strangest sight. A long line of white people—and only white people—that stretched for blocks and blocks. My first inclination was to write it off, thinking Wayne Brady must've been in town, but, with the demise of print journalism, this blogger suddenly found himself a journalist and needed to investigate.

The line had grown to over three blocks long. There were some women, but the crowd was overwhelmingly male. It was a jubilant crowd, with lots of loud drinking and crude joking. They refused to tell me why they were all there, but they were more than happy to tell me where they were from: Heritage Foundation, American Enterprise Institute, Hoover Institute, Manhattan Institute, American Civil Rights Institute, Focus on the Family, NRA, National Right to Life, Operation Rescue National...

It quickly became obvious that this was a Republican line and that we both seemed to be heading to the same source: Michael Steele. As I moved farther up the line, the faces became more familiar, the mood even more jovial: Gary Bauer, Dick Armey, Newt Gingrich, Eric Cantor, Michele Bachmann.

When I finally reached Steele's office, I found myself surrounded by

Bill Campbell

Republican royalty: Mitch McConnell, Lindsey Graham, Ann Coulter, John McCain, Laura Ingraham, Megan McCain, Sarah Palin, John Boehner, and Sean Hannity. The GOP was supposedly in disarray and everybody at each other's throats. But drinks flowed like blood and hugs and kisses like automatic gunfire.

My Black Paranoia kicked in again. All these happy, conservative white folks together could *not* be good. I wanted to get the fuck outta Dodge, but I had a job to do. I was a journalist—I heard on NPR this morning. Besides, it was Michael Steele making all these white people so happy. The brother must've been doing *something* right.

I announced myself to the receptionist and was about to sit down when Steele's office door was thrown open. Rush Limbaugh emerged, sweaty and smiling, with only a towel covering his genitalia. He pumped his meat fists in the air. "It's good to be the king!"

Everyone cheered and slapped his back in congratulations. Someone gave him a Cuban. Suddenly, the room reeked of Rush sex and cigars. I wanted to vomit.

"Chairman Steele will see you now," the receptionist informed me.

For those who don't know, Michael Steele is a very imposing man. Well over six feet and 200 pounds, Steele has an athlete's frame and keeps it extremely fit. In other words, if you met Michael Steele in a dark alley, you'd definitely be giving up the wallet. However, now seeing the GOP chairman in rouge, cherry-red lipstick, a pink tube top, stilettos, and denim mini-skirt, I was suddenly wondering who was giving up what to whom exactly.

"The Boppy please," he groaned.

I handed him the large, padded donut pillow. He placed it on his seat behind the desk and sat down with a wince.

"Did you bring the cots?" he asked.

I handed him a box of what I thought were called finger condoms. "You turning a lot of pages around here?" I chuckled, uncomfortably.

"No, we use them for condoms," he informed.

"But they have neither a receptical tip nor lubricant."

"They fit, OK?" Steele whined. "We're talkin' Republicans here, ain't we?"

"Yeah, but—"

"Why do you think we become Republicans in the first place?!"

"What would I know? I used to be an anarchist."

"The Ho-Hos and grape Kool-Aid please."

I handed over the rest of "the booty," and he immediately began chomping and guzzling down my offerings. Amongst the chews, though, I could hear sobs, and, before I knew it, Michael Steele, former Lt. Gov. of Maryland and current chairman of the National Republican Party, was *weeping*.

I knew the interview was over at that point. I could never report this, what they had done to this man. I never really agreed with Steele on any issue, never really liked him all that much, but I never wished this on the man. I mean, Steele was from DC. Petworth. I'm not sure, but I heard it used to be rough. Now, these Republicans had this big, bad brother hopping around in Daisy Dukes?!

There were so many questions to ask, but I couldn't bring myself to ask even one. Steele downed another glass of the grape Kool-Aid, burped, and looked me intently in the eye. He saw the pain on my face. I saw the pain on his. We shared a moment. I was just about to say something. He raised a massive hand to stop me.

"No, you're right," he anticipated, gravely. "I should've never backed down from Rush Limbaugh."

Things That Work!

Sunday, April 26, 2009

If you're in a hurry to get from Point A to Point B, prudently ignore all red lights and stop signs that impede your progress—you know, all of them.

If you're short of cash, go through your parents' and/or co-workers' belongings until you find the required amount.

If you can no longer tolerate working with someone, carefully plant drugs in their desk, locker, automobile, etc., and instantly notify either your employer or the authorities. The resulting embarrassment and possible criminal prosecution will force this person to terminate their own employment—if your employer has not already done so for them.

If you meet someone at a party, bar, or club you're interested in but are afraid they will not accept your sexual advances, carefully place a dose of Rohypnol ("roofie") into their drink. No doubt, they will soon be going home with you.

If you are tired of arguing with your partner over such triflings as the tardiness of your dinner, kindly go upside their head a few times or until your partner is no longer "needin' it." Not only will dinner be served in a prompt and timely manner, but your partner will more likely become more accommodating in the sexual arena as well.

Similarly, if you find yourself with an impertinent child, we have found that a riding crop to the hindquarters is not only good for horses. Your child will climb to new heights of obedience with only a few, well-placed thwacks.

We here at *Tome* have decided that it is utterly futile to argue with the Right over the *effectiveness* of the Bush administration's "enhanced interrogation techniques." And since their *effectiveness* seems to be the only thing we should even be considering with the EITs, we have decided to utilize the *effectiveness* argument in other aspects of our own lives (*see above*). Also, knowing that the CIA got the idea for waterboarding from the Khmer "Killing Fields" Rouge, we've looked into other highly *effective* techniques that our United States government may want to consider when next *interrogating* a terror suspect.

*****

The Rack

The rack enjoyed centuries of popularity in Europe from the Tower of London to the Spanish auto da fe. Stretching the victim across its wooden frame, interrogators can then fasten the suspect's legs to one roller while chaining the wrists at the other end of the device. While interrogating the suspect, the *interrogator* can ratchet up the chain's tension, causing what some have called "excruciating pain." However, one must be careful. During interrogation, some suspects have been known to have their muscles and joints dislocated and separated. Cartilage, ligaments, and bones have also been known to snap. As with the other methods we find most *effective*, we strongly suggest a physician be present during one's *interrogations*.

Bamboo

During World War II, the Japanese Imperial Army was known for shoving bamboo splints underneath a *suspect's* fingernails.

Electric Shock

During the 1960s and 1970s, Brazil's military junta was known for attaching electrical wires to a *suspect's* genitalia and delivering shocks during *interrogations*.

GBV

While rape has always been considered an *effective* weapon in war, we are certain that the CIA can modify this *technique* to serve their purposes during *interrogation*. The raping of entire villages and towns was reported frequently during the Bosnian conflict. However, in the Democratic Republic of the Congo, rebels have been noted to not only rape entire villages but have the villages' family members rape each other. As noted by Liz Cheney, if a physician is present while these *techniques* are being utilized, it will not be considered rape.

We feel that the Right is correct in stating that *techniques* such as waterboarding are, indeed, *effective*. However, we also feel that, if our force's *only* criterion for any *technique*'s being utilized is its *effectiveness*, our CIA should consider employing our own suggestions above as well as any other *techniques* they may find scanning the annals of *interrogation* methods. We are most certain that other beacons of security such as the Taliban, the Pakistani ISI, the Saudis, or the Syrians have a lot to teach us about "enhanced interrogation techniques." We should not quibble over other, frivolous matters. It is only our *safety* that is of concern in this "torture memo" debate. Therefore, use these methods, use any methods you find *effective*. They will not only keep us Americans *safe*, but it will make us all proud to *be* American.

You Barbaric Fuckers.

Dick and the Big Rock

Saturday, May 23, 2009

Beautifully-mustachioed Peter Kirsanow of *National Review* took time away from barbershop quartet practice long enough to write a *glowing* defense of Dick Cheney's torture speech this week at the American Enterprise Institute. In it he posited the *ever*-pertinent question on *everyone's* minds these days:

"When that big asteroid finally heads toward Earth, who's the person you'd most want to be in charge?"

And concluded: "I suspect Cheney would score at or near the top."

Now, never ones to question the veracity of *anything* coming from *National Review*, we here at *Tome* have asked ourselves WWDD if The Big Rock came hurtling toward our beloved Third Rock? and came up with this list:

**Top 10 Things Dick Cheney Would Do
to Stop an Asteroid from Obliterating Earth**

1. Shoot it in the face.

2. Go on a media campaign of outrage! Outrage, I say! against the asteroid for referring to his daughter as a "lesbian." His wife, Lynne, will ride shotgun on this one.

3. Declare it a "weapon of mass destruction," make allusions to "smoking guns" and "mushroom clouds" and never find the damned thing.

4. Join the circle-jerk séance with Rudy Giuliani and Bill Kristol, repeatedly chanting "9/11! 9/11! 9/11!" in the hopes of ... wait, why do they keep chanting "9/11!" again?

5. Cut taxes!

6. Defy all rules of logic—and the law of gravity—and waterboard

the asteroid until it confesses that Saddam was involved in its hurtling toward Earth.

7. Nothing. Like military service in Vietnam, he'll have "better things to do."

8. Nothing. He doesn't believe that Big Government can solve all our problems.

9. Nothing. He'll be too busy testifying in the Hague.

10. Have another heart attack and recuperate by spooning Scooter Libby in an "undisclosed location."

A Queer Qase in Reverse Reverse Racism

Saturday, May 30, 2009

It was a blustery, cold, January afternoon in Baltimore's Fell's Point, when Shamekia Watts lost her baby.

"It was my husband's birthday, and he wanted that movie, *Putney Swope*. So, I went down with my daughter, Tamara, to pick up the DVD."

Ms. Watts, a Harvard Law graduate and partner at the law firm, Watts, Day, Fuchs, and Associates, had just picked up her three-year-old daughter, Tamara, from day care when the incident occurred.

"We were just about to enter the CD store, when three white men approached," Ms. Watts stated. "They were big, and there was something wild in their eyes. I tried to rush into the store, but Tamara bent down to tie her shoes. That's when it happened."

What happened is still confused in Ms. Watts' own mind, but apparently these "three white men" with "something wild in their eyes" proceeded to jostle the mother and her child, knock the mother down in the middle of the street, took her purse, and her daughter.

"It was absolutely horrific," the 35-year-old mother wailed. "They took my baby!"

But the horror was only compounded when the authorities arrived.

"They didn't believe me," Ms. Watts claimed. "They didn't believe three white men would abduct my daughter. They didn't believe I had a daughter. They didn't believe I only had one child. They didn't believe I went to Harvard or that I had my own law firm. No matter what I said or did, they wouldn't believe me."

The police held Ms. Watts overnight in jail and ultimately charged her with filing a false report. She served six months probation and was expelled from the Maryland Bar Association. She and her husband are yet to find their daughter.

"We've received absolutely no assistance," Ms. Watts continued. "No one would believe us. We provided lie detector tests, hospital records. One security camera had even caught the three men on tape with my daughter. Yet, everyone decided to treat it as a hoax. We didn't even get an AMBER Alert."

The AMBER Alert (a "backronym" standing for America's Missing:

Broadcasting Emergency Response") is a child abduction alert issued nationwide via commercial radio stations, satellite radio, television stations, and cable TV through the Emergency Alert System whenever there is a suspected child abduction. After much investigation, we at *Tome* discovered there actually was never one issued for three-year-old Tamara Watts.

"No parent should have to go through this," Ms. Watts moaned.

When asked about the failure to issue an AMBER Alert and asked about Tamara and Shamekia Watts, Baltimore Chief of Police Harry Quim was incredulous.

"It was a hoax," Quim guffawed. "Shamekia Watts is a con artist. She got what she deserved. Like she went to Harvard!"

He continued, "I mean, come on, three *white* guys, stealing a *black* baby? Who's ever heard of such a thing?!"

The local media was equally unimpressed with Ms. Watts' story.

"What? Does Harvard have affirmative action?" WFUN producer, Liam Sacco-Shipp asked.

"She was graduated summa cum laude," I informed him.

"Still."

Nanny Mace, the host of cable network WNN's *Mace Up Her Sleeve*, didn't believe Shamekia Watts' story either. Mace's nightly show focuses on murdered women and missing children. According to National Center for Missing and Exploited Children, some 264,000 black children under the age of 18 go missing every year. The Violence Policy Center reported that, in 2005 (the last year such data were collected), "574 black females were murdered by males in single victim/single offender homicides." None of these stories have been featured on *Mace Up Her Sleeve*.

"That was all a hoax, right?" Ms. Mace questioned. "She was the one who claimed carjackers took her kids and drowned them in a lake?"

"No. That was Susan Smith."

"Oh, right. She's the one who said she got kidnapped and ended up going to Disney World with her daughter."

"That was Bonnie Sweeten, and that just happened this week."

"Got me there," Ms. Mace smiled. "She was the one who got mugged, and they carved a backwards 'O' on her forehead for being an Obama supporter?"

"What the hell is a backwards 'O'?"

Ms. Mace shrugged and smiled impishly.

"No, that was Ashley Todd, a backwards 'B' because she was a

McCain supporter, and a hoax."

"Right," Ms. Mace conceded. "She was the one who shot her pregnant wife in the stomach and blamed it on car jackers."

"What the hell kind of sense does that make?"

Ms. Mace shrugged once more.

"That was Charles Stuart," I finally huffed.

"Who knows?" Ms. Mace concluded. "Maybe her baby daddy took the kid."

"You mean, her *husband*?"

"Ooh, that reminds me. What has O.J. been up to lately?"

She reached for the phone to talk to her production assistant.

"It's a damned tragedy!" exhorted self-proclaimed civil rights leader, J.C. Sharktowne. "A white woman go claimin' a black man hurt her, and *all* the national media come runnin' to her side! Say he hurt one of her children?! Hoax or not! There's an all-out manhunt! Brothers are rounded up and thrown in jail! AMBER Alerts go up in *Sweden*!!!

"But, you ask me! That AMBER Alert be lookin' *mighty* alabaster! What about our black babies?! Where Nanny Mace then?! Where CNN?! Where BET at?!

"No, forget the AMBER Alert! We black folks need a EBONY Alert! Something to protect our black babies!!!"

Shamekia Watts could not agree more.

Poohbutt

(with a couple other people thrown in for good measure)

Talkin' Shit ... Literally

Sunday, August 10, 2008

Way before our daughter was born, I was on a mission to have my first child potty trained by the time s/he was one. I mean, so many places around the world train their kids by six months. We Americans, on the other hand, wait until our children are out of college before we teach them shit from Shinola. I felt it was my patriotic duty.

Nothing reinforced this conviction more than those first, fecal diapers. Parents/caregivers, you know what I'm talking about. That grey/green/yellow/brown slop (*all the colors of the rainbow!*) that runs like a mighty river all over the damned place. And like napalm, it sticks to everything. There are days when you, the baby, the walls, your neighbors, innocent bystanders are just covered in shit. You're scouring your hands with Brillo, hand-washing everything your baby's ever touched, sterilizing entire communities, and cursing Luvs for the crap diapers they truly are. Like Sherman heading to Atlanta, I was fierce and determined and had a fire in my eyes that would've scared Al Sharpton's hair curly. My girl would *be* potty-trained!

Now, some nine months later, I've relaxed a bit. Now that our girl's eating solid foods, I just don't feel the same urgency. I never realized how convenient a turd really is. Small, compact, easily flushable. Absolute genius! I will never look at shit the same way again.

Of course, it wasn't that way at first. The transition was rough, and our poor, little baby spent those first few days constipated ... and miserable. She would strain and strain, her face cherry-red, and would cry in frustration and pain. It was so hard to watch. We were powerless, and those pureed prunes didn't seem to be working.

Then, on the third day, it was finally starting to happen. I was holding her, walking through the apartment. Her face started turning red, and she started trembling and grunting. I knew the look.

"Oh, crap," I said. "Ha, ha. I'm funny."

The grunts quickly gave way to ear-piercing screams. I set her on the changing pad. The poor girl started thrashing around frantically. Her face was so red and hot I contemplated setting up solar panels and powering the neighborhood. I ripped off the diaper and looked.

There it was. A little brown round turd. And it was stuck. And she was screaming. And I was a first-time father. I'd never dealt with this shit before. No, not funny this time.

"WAAAAHHHHHHHH!!!!"

"Oh, it's OK, baby," I soothed. "It'll be all right."

"WAAAAHHHHHHHH!!!!"

"Uh … push? … push? Naw, that was for your mother."

The damned thing wasn't moving, and my words weren't going to push it along. It looked so damned painful. Finally, I grabbed up my baby's little legs and pressed them against her belly. I thought the pressure would help. It didn't. I had to do something.

And I did it. Something I'd never thought I'd do. Something I'd never once in my life contemplated. But what could I do? My baby was in pain. So, I did it. That's right, I did it.

I pulled a Bobby Brown.

I grabbed a baby wipe and gently placed it over the turd. She screamed and squirmed. I ignored her and carefully, slowly pulled. It finally came out, and my girl instantly forgot the terror and torture—as only babies can do. I gave her a new diaper, snapped up her clothes, and disposed of the little, brown terrorist. I placed my giggling, babbling daughter in her crib, and headed to the bathroom to wash my hands. Soaping up and listening to my little girl's "goo goo gah gah," I looked up at the mirror and smiled a little proudly, thinking, "Damn, I'm a father."

PS. Yes, I will be saving this blog entry for when *somebody* thinks she's grown enough to start dating. Some lucky, little boy is going to have some reading material on his way to the movies. :)

Arresting Development

Thursday, August 21, 2008

As most of you know, when a baby enters the world, everybody becomes intensely curious about the kid's progress. Folks want to know where your baby is on the evolutionary ladder. Is she crawling? Has she teethed yet? Is she walking? Is she eating solids?

You can't blame folks, they're just interested in new life, but as new parents, you start feeling a little defensive. When *will* she start crawling? Why doesn't she take her first steps? What is so *hard* about the Pythagorean Theorum? Why isn't Poohbutt getting it?

I try to ignore the pressure, but we all greet each new development in our babies' lives with a sigh of relief. That is until recently. I've discovered that some things your baby does are just downright disturbing.

It happened yesterday afternoon. Daddy (when did I start referring to myself in the third person?) thought he would encourage his little girl to nap by laying her down on the floor next to him and napping himself. I don't know if it worked for her, but I got a few, much-needed winks. And then it happened. Our Grand Poohbutt displayed her new, mad skillz.

I blame genetics and her cousin Taishan (he's a month and a day older than our girl and I'm really questioning his role model status). See, that boy can scream. And not your normal, run-of-the-mill, *Psycho*, blood-curdling scream. No, this is glass-shattering, ear-bleeding, banshee screams that flay the skin, madden the mind, and make you beg for a merciful death. And every time I pick that boy up, he squirms right up to my ear, and lets loose. I hold on tight while my eyes roll back in my head and my eardrums start bleeding. Once, I came to to find a whole pack of wild animals outside the in-laws' door looking as though they were awaiting orders. I've tried everything—bribery, intimidation, pleas for familial solidarity. Nothing. That boy cannot be bought. He just loves screaming in Uncle Bill's ear. The *only* thing that gave me any solace was knowing that Pooh could never scream like that.

I rested peacefully in that knowledge until yesterday when I was rocked by *that* scream coming from my daughter. I gasped. My girl's face was red, blood trickled down my lobes, wedding china shattered, wolves bayed, there was a ten-car pile-up on I-495.

As I'm typing this, my wife and daughter are fighting in the bath tub, my daughter's newfound gift on full display. I guess I should go help, but, frankly, I'm scared. Right outside our sliding-glass door are four deer, six dogs, and 32 chipmunks awaiting my daughter's command.

Chris de Coeur

Sunday, August 24, 2008

Last night, just before going to bed, I went on the internet, and suddenly my world didn't make sense. One of my boys, Chris "Crash" Pryor, died ... 10 months ago. And I just found out last night?!

It made no kind of sense. I kept reading all these loving posts on Mog Music Network about his life, his writings, his spirit with disbelieving eyes. I thought it was some kind of joke. I mean, who the hell dies two days before their 36th birthday?! It just doesn't happen. Eighteen, in a way, makes sense—something tragic and stupid—car crash, gunshot ... Seventy-two, all right. You lived a full life. I hope you made it a good one. But a brother just doesn't up and die walking to an ATM machine! Not at 36!

And I didn't know. While my wife and I were waiting for our first child to enter the world, an old friend was leaving it. And I didn't know. Chris and I were no longer a part of each other's worlds. But shouldn't I have known? There was a time when something like that couldn't have happened. And now ...

Chris was one of the first people to befriend me when I'd moved to Atlanta back in '93. I'd been deported from the Czech Republic and Great Britain and moved to the ATL, broken, broke, and friendless, because my dad was there. I was lonely and really lost, and Chris and Hop quickly became my friends, my boys, my ... you know.

For three years, those two were such a huge part of my life. Looking back, I'm amazed how much time you spend with your friends when you're young, single, and unattached. The stupid things you do. The fun you have. And Chris was a blast—a wise-cracking, acerbic, too-smart-for-his-own-good blast. And we were boys. When I had, he had. When he had, I had. He was there when things were good, there when they weren't, and was a good enough friend to tell me when I was screwing up.

But those things never last. They can't. You grow up, and we Gen Xers move. For millennia, people never went more than 12 miles outside of their place of birth. But our generation is nomadic. I'm not alone in having friends all over the country—even friends in other countries, on other continents. It's what we do. And you never think much of it. You miss your friends for awhile, but it's not that big a deal. You'll see them again. Hell, you'll probably end up in the same city again at some point. My one friend and I have ended up living in both Atlanta and Washington, DC after college.

There was no reason to think something like that wouldn't happen with Chris and me. After all, it wasn't like we had fallen out or had grown apart or anything like that. He'd just moved away. We'd lost touch. But a friend is a friend for life. We'd hook up again, shootin' the Shinola in a bar, ranting politics, race, women, and music, music, music.

We'd gotten back in touch briefly last year. I found his blog and shot him an email. He called me, and we laughed for a minute. Chris was rapid-fire funny the whole time—like he wanted to cram the last ten years into one phone call. It wore me out, but I loved it. He was still the intense, wry intellect I remembered, and we were still friends—like that last decade apart didn't mean a thing. And age hadn't mellowed him one bit. He still gave a shit.

He called again, but I was driving and DC had just banned cell-phone driving. I told him I'd call him back. I didn't. I was about to go on tour. At the time I'd thought I was going to be in LA and told him as much. But I later changed my mind. With a pregnant wife, I didn't want to be too far from home. When I got back, life took over: moving to a new place, nesting, having the baby, caring for a newborn. And then, I just forgot.

I didn't remember until last night—ten months later—ten months after my boy's death.

It's not like I feel guilty, or anything. Just sad. A couple years ago, when I had to eulogize my uncle, I said that life is a collection of moments and that we need to hold those moments dear because they are what makes life worth living. I meant those words, but I don't really live them enough. I get busy. Sometimes, I don't appreciate all that I have and all the people around me. I don't keep in very good touch with the people who are important to me, and it doesn't make me feel any better knowing I'm not alone in this. Chris was important to me; he was there during a very difficult period in my life; and I hadn't talked to him in ten years.

I'd thought we'd always meet again, that we'd always be friends, that one day we'd be those two, old coots talkin' bookoo shit at the end of the bar. But that moment is never going to happen.

But we did have some times. I stayed up late last night, crying off-and-on 'til 4 am, thinking about them. And while I'm sad now, I'm so glad we had them.

Like how my former (?), bourgie self used to cringe when he used to greet me with "What up, my nigga?"

That time when my wife and I went to enemy territory, the Buckhead neighborhood of Atlanta, to celebrate Chris's birthday. We walked into a wack-ass reggae bar, confused ('cause Pryor *knew* his music, why the hell were we there?). And there was Chris, sunglasses in the dark bar, sipping on a drink, watching the band play.

"What's up, Chris?"

"I hate soca."

Or that one night how he was vehemently ranting about how the white boys, Red Hot Chili Peppers, had stolen the funk and how there weren't any brothers or sisters out there strong enough to take it back. And then forcing me to listen to the Peppers until I conceded that Flea was indeed a *bad* mother. He is.

And I'll always remember the night when Chris dragged me to the Dark Horse Tavern to go see some of his old band mates from Full Stop. At some point he got up on stage. He'd always talked about how he used to rap, but I'd never seen him. But there he was, bald head shining, rocking the crowd. Folks around me jumping and screaming and dancing … to Chris. When he finally surrendered the mic, he was beaming like a little kid. If you didn't know the man, he could have a pretty mean, intimidating grille. And there he was—beaming! And I remember thinking, proudly, "That's my nigga right there. Here is where he belongs."

There's so much in our lives that we forget. So many specifics that are lost to us over time. There are so many things about Chris that I've already forgotten, and I'll forget more still. But I'll always have that moment at the Dark Horse. I'll always know that he was special to me. And looking at all the loving eulogies last night, it means a lot that he was special to so many others—even to people he'd never actually met—even as far away as Sweden and France.

Last night, during one of my little crying jags, I was thinking I was being stupid. I mean, Chris and I hadn't hung out in over a decade. But now I'm thinking it's less stupidity on my part and more of a testament to just how special Christopher Alonzo Pryor was. Maybe we hadn't been close in all that time, but even with time and distance, I still feel we were friends. We will always be friends. Friendship's like that—transcending time and space and even death. Even on that October morning when you died alone on that L.A. sidewalk, you were loved by so many. You touched so many people and will always be a part of their lives. You will always be a part of mine. Fuck, Chris, I don't know

Bill Campbell

why you had to die. What the hell is that all about? It ain't supposed to be this way. But I do know, even though our time together was so short, you will always mean the world to me. You will always be my friend, my boy, my … you know.

The Grandparent Effect

Monday, September 22, 2008

Now, don't get me wrong. I love my family, and, though you better not tell them and swell their heads, I actually like my in-laws. While most liken their visits to the in-laws to prison stays in Siberia, I look upon it as merely a jaunt to Wisconsin, a pleasant, amiable place where you'd think they'd serve more kielbasa.

And Poohbutt absolutely *loves* the grandparents. Who wouldn't? God, they spoil that girl. No longer is it "just you and me, kid" or just her boring, old parents. There are suddenly parents, grandparents, uncles, aunts, great-uncles, great-aunts, cousins, neighbors, random passersby, all collected to lavish attention on her—which I'm pretty sure is how it should be in her mind.

I mean, we're all born narcissists, right? And how wouldn't we be? As soon as we're born (if we're lucky), there are at *least* two grown people running around like lunatics trying to satisfy our every need. I cry, they feed me. I whimper, they pick me up. I clear my throat, they give me something to drink. These suckers are *so* into me, they even change my clothes when I soil myself. Heck, *I* don't even do *that*.

Throw the extended fam into the mix, and my li'l girl is in kiddie heaven. All these people are climbing over themselves showing her just how special she is. They cheer her every babble, offer her all kinds of toys, feed and clothe her, hug and kiss all over her. The Grandparent Effect—where every baby is a star!

(Which is how it should be.)

And this past Fourth of July, Poohbutt was in a parade to help her granddad's run for city council. And all those people came to see *her*. I mean, what is this "Independence Day" all about, anyway? The girl did not disappoint her adoring public—laughing and smiling and being all coy and cute—giving the people what they want. It's the least she could do for her adoring fans.

But then the weekend ends, and it's just her and her lame Daddy. She suddenly looks around, nothing, then looks at me, still glowing from all the adulation. She declares, haughtily, "I'm ready for my close-up, Mr. DeMille."

"Close-up?" I ask. "Wait, you've seen *Sunset Boulevard*?"

"Why, of course, father."

Bill Campbell

When did she get a British accent?

"But Poohbutt," I apologize, "I don't—well, life isn't a movie, baby."

"Hm." She contemplates. "Well, dearest father, are you familiar with Ice Cube's oeuvre?"

"You are? God, you mother's going to kill me. Wait, are we talking about his kids' movies?"

"Oh, silly man," she scoffs.

"Yeah, I guess that was foolish of me," I admit.

"Perhaps, you are familiar with the line, 'Once again, it's on.'"

"Yeah, yeah. 'No Vaseline.' I love that song. Why?"

She stares at me—waiting for me to get it. I get it.

I gasp. "Oh, shit."

"WAAAAHHHHH!!!"

"But baby, it was just a *visit*. We'll see them again!"

"WAAAAHHHHH!!!"

And then, for the next several hours, yours truly gets a Basic Training workout—doing thousands of jumping jacks, slaloming through countless obstacle courses, climbing ropes, dodging live bullets and barbed wire—trying to calm down my daughter, who suddenly misses all that grandparent attention.

As I said, I love my family and the in-laws. I love that Poohbutt makes them so happy. When you see the joy and love that everyone exudes—one big, happy fam playing together—you realize this is the way life should be. Not this rat-race, "nuclear family" fiction isolated in our single-family dwellings hooked to the cathode-ray babysitter. There's something *whole* and natural about the whole experience. Somehow, we've gotten it all backwards. Nothing can replace the *entire* family. Besides, with all those built-in babysitters, maybe Moms and Pops could go see a movie once in awhile.

But there's a flipside to each visit—no matter which side of the family's visiting. It's the Monday morning hangover. The Grandparent Effect is pretty powerful stuff. Sometimes it takes entire *days* for Poohbutt to get all that affection out of her system. Apparently, it's a pretty painful withdrawal process 'cause that little girl can cry and cry for hours on end.

This weekend was cousin Taishan's first birthday, and Poohbutt hammed it up as usual, showing off her nascent crawling skills, becoming the Queen of Babble-On, cracking jokes, making people laugh, claiming she's more qualified than Sarah Palin to be V.P. Sure, she had to share the spotlight with her cousin, but I'm sure she feels she stole the show.

This morning, it's back to Daddy's meager love. *I mean, the old man's all right, but…*

Wish me luck, people.

A New Kind of Man

Friday, October 3, 2008

Unlike most people, I don't believe that gender roles have ever been written in stone. I don't believe there has ever truly been a time when "girls were girls and men were men." I definitely believe there has always been misogyny. I just don't think that all our forefathers were John Wayne and every woman, June Cleaver. Within every relationship there is negotiation, and I'm sure within every marriage there has probably never been a strict delineation of who did what every and all the time.

Despite what conservatives say, identity politics is nothing new. There has always been cultural battles over what a "real" man and "real" woman were. I once read about one cultural critic excoriating WWII vets for being too effeminate, letting their women work in the '50s. And of course, there are the Platonic love codes that told us "real" men could never love an "inferior" woman—best to go with little boys.

Personally, I've never bought any of it. Who are you to tell me what a real man is? Besides, I'm an artist and a proud nerd. While no Alan Alda, I've never been a "man's man" (still trying to figure out what that means). Sure, I played sports as a kid, but flat feet and asthma led me to the books. I chased the P like any other fine, young gentleman. While in the Czech Republic, I drank and fought so much that they deported me and prohibited me from reentering the country for seven years. And when I worked on a loading dock, I did have to tone down my aggression levels, but I've never been "hard," a "gangsta," or a "thug." Nor have I ever wanted to be. But I've never really been a softie, either.

All that changed a year ago with the birth of my daughter. As soon as a lock of her hair popped into the world, I was flooded with so much emotion, I damn near cried on the spot. And the sappiness hasn't really stopped. Now, I know a lot of this is natural: our levels of testosterone drop as we age; and my wife read that a baby's caregiver's estrogen levels increase (I guess so we don't leave them in the woods or ingest their heads, or something). Since I spend at least 11 hours a day taking care of Poohbutt, I guess mine remain pretty high.

But damn, it can be annoying sometimes. I used to be fairly cool and detached. My dad used to chastise me for being too "cavalier." But now, it's all switched up on me. Things that I used to scoff at as corny now tug at my heartstrings. Watching an old episode of *Freaks and Geeks*, I choked up when Bill had a heart-to-heart with the gym teacher who was dating his mom. When friends now close an email with "Love," I don't go like Riley with an, "Ooh, you gay." Instead, I think (earnestly, no less), "Yeah. I love you, too, man." If there's a loving scene with a father and daughter, my chest gets all warm and fuzzy. I can't stand hearing about dead children. I used to hate the local news because all their "special reports" are designed to scare parents. Now, I can't watch the local news because all those "special reports" scare *me*. It's so bad, I'm sure if *Bambi* came on, I'd run from the room screaming and crying.

Last night, during the vice-presidential debate, was no different. Joe Biden got me when he started talking about losing his wife and daughter in a car accident. My eyes genuinely started steaming. Then, when he said that "Don't tell me I don't know what it's like to raise a family because I'm not a woman" and he had to stop because he was about to cry, I damn near lost it myself

My wife and I often talk about gender (gender analysis is part of her job). Right after that moment, she was champing at the bit, wanting to discuss it. "How interesting," she said. "That's something Palin couldn't do."

Intellectually, I was ready to respond. After all, this past year has been choked with race and gender politics, hasn't it? If I'd been capable, I would've said, "Well, Hillary choked up in New Hampshire, and that worked for her. But Ferraro, Thatcher, a Golda Meir or Indira Ghandi, I think they would've been crucified as soft or mentally unstable." Then I probably would've gone on: "This evolution of men and crying is interesting, though. I mean, Edwin Muskie's political ambitions were dashed when he choked up. Bill Clinton had that biting-the-lower-lip-'I-feel-your-pain' schtick. But this…"

But that Biden moment had me. I don't know if it was manufactured or not, but the Senator, at that moment, seemed so real. So vulnerable. And I (the punk I no doubtedly am) was just caught up in the speculative horror of losing my wife and daughter. And he had two injured sons he had to care for at the same time. Damn. I couldn't imagine it. Yet, I was trapped doing just that—all misty-eyed, and shit. Annoyed, I didn't know whether to go to a bar, down a couple of shots, and slug the next guy I saw or just grab my daughter and let her fall asleep on my chest. Damned estrogen. Of course, I chose the latter.

Project P.O.P. (Political Operative Poohbutt)

Friday, October 31, 2008

She came like a thief in the night—well, actually, like a toddler being wheeled around in a polka dot stroller wearing a pink hoodie in the middle of the day—it was slightly overcast, though. Through the blood, the sweat, and the tears (diaper changes *can* be harrowing), she appeared—grim and determined. She had to save the day.

Liberty was in peril. Good, patriotic Americans were being exploited. Children, endangered. Cattle, raped. Someone had to stop the madness. So, the good people of East Bumble, VA, called on their last, best hope: Poohbutt.

A small, college hamlet nestled comfortably within the Shenandoah Valley, East Bumble's going through some hard times. Greedy, fat-cat land speculators are gorging themselves on the public trough. They hold these good townsfolk hostage with their shady land deals and Repugnantcan tax breaks! tax breaks! TAX BREAKS!!!

Schools go without books. The police are reduced to pea shooters. And the fire department just held a bake sale to buy a new garden hose. All the while, the robber barons and their Repugnantcan cronies get fatter and fatter on the money that should be funding the local orphanage.

Only Poohbutt's grandfather, Grandpoo, and his valiant partner, Slingin' Sammy, can save the day. But they need help. They suffer ruthless, vile, and vicious attacks daily. Hoodlums haunt their doorsteps, and their email boxes are flooded with spam. In utter desperation, they initiated Project P.O.P.

Poohbutt immediately swept in, no questions asked, dragging along her trusty sidekick, Pop (who frankly doesn't feel the same genetic obligations as P.O.P. and, though poor now, can always win the lottery; and therefore feels that the government should get off our backs and cut *all* the taxes for the rich—cause he may one day be one of those … rich and like hell you'll get his hard-earned money—even if it means running up huge deficits, selling government airplanes on eBay, being literally owned by China, and mortgaging away his, Poohbutt's, and Poohbutt's grandchildren's futures away—can I get an "Amen," people?!). This courageous duo has scoured East Bumble, knocking on every door, being immensely adorable (well, P.O.P. has), bringing freedom and democracy, and slowly wresting liberty from the gnarled, despotic clutches of those dastardly Repugnantcans.

But there is still a lot of work to do until Tuesday night, people. More doors to knock on, more pamphlets to hand out, more freedom to let ring. East Bumble ... all of America ... will soon be free. P.O.P. and Pop are doing their part. How about you?

All Hail P.O.P. aka Queen Victorious!!!

Sunday, November 16, 2008

While her mother's off in Belgium hobnobbing with Princess Astrid (really, I can't make this up—my wife's life's so much more interesting than mine), Political Operative Poohbutt is receiving a retinue of her own, offering her gifts, gratitude, and praise.

My little pol went to East Bumble with a mission. Through the blood and grit, grime and corruption, our girl has emerged bloodied, scarred, and, most importantly, victorious. Her terrible, swift sword and doe-like eyes won the voters of that little ville over. They just couldn't resist the little bugger.

Now, our Queen Victorious has those greedy developers and their Repugnantcan cronies on the run. They have melted into the shadows of the Shenandoah, vowing to return again. But for now, they are defeated. Grandpooh has won his city council seat, and reforms can now be implemented. For the next four years, at least, these developers' pockets will not be lined with taxpayers' dollars (if we could all be so lucky!).

And now, thankful Democrats line up before Poohbutt's crib—I mean, throne—bearing gifts. Binkies, onesies, every toy that flashes lights and/or sings a tune (and *every* child's toy does that) crowd the room. It's all lost on her, though. She only likes the boxes.

Everybody asks her advice.

"Any advice?" asks David Axelrod.

"Baabaabaabaah," she advises.

They look at me for translation.

"Uh," I screw up my face, "she says avoid nuts and always keep your diaper clean."

"Out of the mouths of babes," gasps Donna Brazile.

"Balderdash!" screams Karl Rove, storming out of the great hall.

"Where did he come from?" I ask.

"The diaper pail," Steve Schmidt, McCain's campaign adviser, announces—from the diaper pail.

"Baabaabaabaah."

"All right, people," I announce, clapping my hands. "Audience over. Thanks for everything. And see you all in '12—when we can finally end this Palin mess for good."

"Damn you all *to hell!!!*" Schmidt screams, and rushes out, leaving a trail of stained diapers in his wake.

Kickin' My Butt Down the Home Stretch

Thursday, November 20, 2008

I need a vacation. Not Aruba, not Jamaica, nor Fiji. Nothing fancy like that. I'm so desperate I'd be cool with some militia man's basement in North Dakota for a week. Just give me an internet connection, a remote, cable, and maybe Netflix Instant Watch, and I'd be happy. Any little vacation will do.

As many of you know, I've been watching Poohbutt solo 24/7 for the past three weeks now. My wife's been off globetrotting for work. Well, not exactly. She's been in Belgium, and now she's in Ethiopia. I think it's been pretty tough on her, being away from our daughter for so long. I get it. I've been bummed the few, short instances of my being away from Poohbutt. But the depths of it, being a man, I'll never get. Aside from rage and despair, I've never really had anything growing inside me. I've never had a little organism depending on me for its very existence. I've never spent yet another year giving a baby life through my own glands. There's a connection between mother and child that we men sadly miss out on. Then again, that labor was something like 22 hours. There are just some experiences I'm cool with missing.

But, I'll tell you what, I don't see how single parents do it. I'm exhausted and wondering why I didn't want her in day care too soon. Keeping a toddler entertained all day is pretty rough stuff. Really, I'll drink PBR and talk about the UN black helicopters priming to take away our Second Amendment rights, I'll brave the North Dakota cold, I'll even watch NASCAR—just give me a break.

The Adventures of Poohbutt and Pop (which only have two more days to go) started out fun enough, going down to East Bumble and electioneering, then capping it all off with the Barack-O-Rama in Baltimore. We only had one mishap: The French Fry Incident. We were just on our way, rolling through rural Virginia when *someone* decided that she didn't want to be in a car. Desperately, a starving father stopped off at a Burger King to buy us both some solace. Cheerios are baby crack, but French fries are baby heroin. I decided to drug the little bugger. Unfortunately, in a hurry to silence a crying baby, I accidentally gave the little tyke some piping hot fries. She screamed, something like: "Jesus Christ, you idiot! These things fucking burn!!!" She spasmed and screamed and refused to let the taters go. I had to karate chop them out of her hand.

Still, everything was copacetic until we both got sick. I blame Obama. All that pent-up frustration and anxiety, all that anticipation, and then the victory, the elation. We all relaxed, let our defenses down, and whatever's going around hit us. There's not a single Dem I know who hasn't been sick these past few weeks. I bet you it's a Republican conspiracy, a different version of the Palin Plague we all feared.

Pooh emerged (much quicker than me, of course) a brand new toddler. She's all over the place. When she's not puttering around on her little walker jeep, she's getting into the kitchen cabinets (are kids automatically drawn to Pine-Sol?) or trying to pry the guards off the electrical sockets or trying to dismantle the DVD player or changing the channel when Daddy's watching his Steelers or trying to play in the toilet water or trying to smash Daddy's CD collection or flinging his books off the book shelf or pulling out his facial hair or trying to procure WMD from a former Soviet republic. In other words, my baby girl's curiosity has far outgrown the limits of our humble abode. I now need to record "Poohbutt! No!" and put it on continuous loop.

I've gotten a few breaks. The Baers took her for a Saturday night. Their little Boogie Boy is six weeks older than Pooh and is walking. Pooh came back taking her first steps. It's very cute. She was taking three left steps and was scooting around in a semi-circle before she dropped to her butt and went tearing into my copy of *The Young Lenin*. The grandparents came by for a few days. And Pooh was entertained by the Puppeteers for a day. They kept her so entertained she cried when they left. And now Mrs. Baer spent last night taking care of Pooh and is coming back tonight.

Unfortunately for yours truly, these breaks translate into my going to work. And having been sick for much of it, I've only been more miserable, dreaming of Bismarck snowstorms.

Don't get me wrong, it's been fun, too. I love Poohbutt. She's most definitely the best thing that's ever happened to me. I think I'm doing a pretty good job. OK, I can't seem to get rid of her diaper rash, and I can't get her to get anything green aside from broccoli (the green bean experiment's touch-and-go, but I thought she was going to slit my throat when I introduced cucumber); but I've taught her how to clap during the "Here we go Steelers" chant, been drowning her in whole milk, convinced her to drink water out of her sippy cup, persuaded her to sometimes shake her head "Yes" instead of breaking her neck saying "No!" all the time, and got her to *finally* grasp the Pythagorean theory (you'd think it was hard, or something). We've had tons of laughs and great conversations (you know, "Blablablablabah," "Really, babe, I didn't know that"). We've had Johnny Hartman and Immortal Technique sing-alongs. And there's no greater feeling in the world than having your kid nestling on your chest and falling asleep.

My biggest failing is endurance. Babies can just wear you out. Not having the wife (happy anniversary, babe!) coming in to spell me has just left me ragged. No, seriously. How *do* single parents do it?

My second biggest failing is stopping Poohbutt from headbutting everything. Seriously, my little princess has turned into a soccer hooligan. It's like she goes all Cockney on me, screws up her face, goes, "You spill me bottle?" and rears back her noggin, ready to strike.

She's headbutted my chest, chin, and belly. Most disturbingly, she's even tried to take out the walls. No matter what I do or say, I can't convince the crazy kid to stop hurting herself. Yesterday, in a fit of frustration, sleepy yet refusing to sleep (what's that all about, anyway?), Poohbutt reared back and gave the most vicious head crack to the hardwood floor. OK, that was *kinda* funny, but, boy, did she erupt? She flew into my arms and promptly fell asleep. "But, baby," I whispered, "if it hurts so much, why do you keep doing it?" before I quickly joined her in Slumberville. But before I did, I couldn't help wondering if this is what having a teenager's like.

Punjabi Poohbutt

Tuesday, December 2, 2008

At Bill's Bi-Weekly Buffet (oddly enough always coinciding with payday), yours truly struggled mightily feeding my daughter's new appetites. You've guessed it: she's finally eating all solids (though you can sneak yogurt in every once in awhile). And you've also guessed it: she's become finicky as all get-out. Apparently, *somebody* has never heard of Dr. Atkins. This girl can eat her some carbs now. My biggest challenge is to slip *something* in besides. So far, sliced turkey, mashed peas, and an occasional broccoli spear will pass her lips. Otherwise, it's bread and milk all day (I guess that's how she keeps her girlish figure).

So, in order to not fall back on the usual French fries and noodles at my favorite ghetto Chinese buffet, I went to Delhi Dee-Lite instead. The change of location didn't help any. I failed with carrots, tomatoes, and lettuce. She didn't even want to touch the Tandoori chicken. I was trying to explain to her how rare it was to get tender Tandoori chicken at a buffet, but she was having none of it.

For little Poohbutt, it was all about the batter-fried veggies, the naan, and the Aishwarya Rai retrospective on the flat screen TV across the room. The once-most-beautiful woman in the world was lip-synching and dancing through 20 years of Bollywood hits—in clubs, in the mountains, on desert roads. There was even this steamy, weird-ass dry-humping video *sans* kissing, of course. Poohbutt was all into it, enraptured by the colorful saris, precision hand movements, and dazzling lights. With naan in hand, she boogied on down in her high chair, entertaining the multi-culti crowd that could appreciate tender tandoori and a fox-trotting toddler.

Callous in Suburbia

Tuesday, February 10, 2009

In Washington, DC's latest freeze a couple weeks ago, a man died. Jose Sanchez, 31, was apparently beaten over a bottle of beer and was left to die on a Columbia Heights sidewalk while some 150 people walked by him, not a one calling 911 for assistance. And since all public discourse has been narrowed into one, elongated screech of moral outrage, there has been an ass-backwards crue and hy over big-city indifference, a self-righteous *cri de coeur* over how empty-hearted DCers could leave a helpless man to die (from an internal brain hemorrhage). This is yet another senseless tragedy in the life of the Modern Age, I admit. But, come on. It's not as though none of us has ever passed a sleeping homeless person and thought nothing of it. It's a shame that we've accepted this reality, but we have. We *all* have. Hell, I'm sure even Mother Theresa has stepped over a homeless person or two in her day.

There is a very valid reason to feel disheartened over this incident. But there's absolutely no reason for this breast-beating public scourge of faux outrage. And no reason that DCers should feel especially guilty. After all, man's-insensitivity-to-man can be found far outside city limits. Indeed, one can even see it in all-mighty suburbia. And you need look no further than to yours truly to find a hardened heart among you.

The infamous, cold-hearted incident happened this last, ass-freezing Saturday night. I'd just gotten off a nine-plus-hour stint at work and decided to make the fam a little dinner when I got home. I was chopping tomatoes on the kitchen counter when I heard a loud thud outside the window and a woman yelp. I thought nothing of it and kept chopping.

Now, in my defense, I usually leave work a little spacey. I work for a company that produces audio books for the blind. I read for a living. After our narrators finish recording, I review their work. I have to ensure that they've spoken every word in a book verbatim with the correct pronunciation and inflection. I also watch out for technical glitches, extraneous noises, bad edits, you name it, to guarantee that each recording is as perfect as humanly possible. After nine hours of such intense concentration, you can understand why I might be a little loopy.

So, even after I heard the thump and the yelp, I didn't pay especial attention to what was going on right outside my kitchen window. I was chopping tomatoes and having a pleasant convo with the spousal unit (Poohbutt having been already put to bed).

"Help!"

"Bill, what was that?"

"Oh, some woman fell on the ice outside," I ho-hummed.

It had been warm those past, few days. Just beyond what I call "our driveway" behind our building—but what our Friendly Local Nazihood Association calls an "access road"—is a long, grassy stretch that is mostly in shadow all day long. So, even though the snow had mostly melted everywhere else, our backyard had become a football field of ice from constant melting and re-freezing. There was nothing back there but some patios and very rarely any foot traffic. So, I assumed that a bunch of my neighbor's smoking friends were back there and one of them had slipped on the ice.

"Help!"

I figured they were just having a laugh at the clumsy woman's expense.

"Help!"

"I don't know why they're being such jerks about it," I shrugged.

I mean, I love physical comedy as much as the next guy...

"Are you sure she's not talking to you?" my wife asked.

"Hunh? Why would she—"

"Why won't you help me?!!!"

"Oh shit!" I snapped. "But I don't have my shoes on!"

"Whhhhhhyyyyyyyyyyyyyyyyyy?!!!!!!!!!!!!"

My wife and I rushed for our shoes, threw them on, and flew out the sliding-glass door. There, prone on the ice sheet, was a rather portly white woman whom I originally confused with our neighbor, Spanky (another large woman who likes certain things done to her while screaming to the entire complex what's being done). Spanky once accused me of lying about living in the building so I could gain purchase to her condo and, I guess, spank her. I hate Spanky and thought about leaving her bruised, racist ass there to freeze. But it wasn't Spanky. So I sprang into action.

My wife and I slipped and slid helping Not-Spanky to her feet. I picked up her groceries, skated them over to her condo, and retrieved her behemoth of a boyfriend. Apparently, Not-Spanky usually uses our access-driveway and then drives across the lawn to her place to drop off groceries and then drives back across 300 feet of grass to park her car. But my wife had left our car there that night. So she parked behind us and decided to walk across the ice. Apparently, not her best idea.

Not-Spanky was effusive in her thanks when I returned with the boyfriend. We all introduced ourselves and chuckled over the averted tragedy.

"Oh, it was horrible," our rescued neighbor tittered, still embarrassed. "I thought you couldn't hear me and that's why you weren't coming to help me."

My wife and I looked at each other, more than a little embarrassed ourselves. She seemed to be saying to me, *Yeah. Let's stick with that story.*

Protecting Your Poohbutt

Tuesday, February 10, 2009
(Originally published at the blog, Devis with Babies)

This past holiday season, I saw my future as the father of a little girl, and it contained a shotgun.

It started innocently enough. My 14-month-old daughter, Poohbutt, was playing alongside a two-year-old boy. A cute, little picture of holiday cheer. Suddenly, the boy abandoned his blocks, "yawned" dramatically, and slid his arm across my little girl's shoulders. Before I could react, he turned her head and kissed her square on the mouth. Yours truly said, "Hey" (Note the lack of exclamation points), and the boy snapped back to his blocks while Poohbutt swift-crawled to Daddy's protective leg. All to a chorus of "Aaahhhh"s.

All the adults thought it was cute. Some chuckled. Others giggled. The boy's father high-fived him. Me? I thought I wasn't going to have to suffer this scene for *at least* another decade. I suddenly found myself paraphrasing the beleaguered brother in the Loretta Swit comedy classic, *Beer*, thinking, "This black man has worked too long and hard to come home to a pregnant teenager."

I know. A lot of you think I'm overreacting. But you fathers out there understand my plight. As soon as we saw a future womb emerge from our wife's womb on the delivery table, we were immediately concerned with how to protect it. And our concerns *are* immediate: How did that toddler already know the "yawn" move?

Now, Little Girls' Daddies the world over have spent billions of dollars and countless hours researching scientific means to protect their daughters since the chastity belt was ruled unconstitutional in 1810. The most promising is "the Lesbian Switch." This handy, little device is activated upon the first menses and will shut off on your girl's 28th birthday. The subject reportedly credits her previous sexual experience as "youthful experimentation" and is soon ready to pump out the grandkids.

However, researchers say the technology's decades away from being perfected, and Staples refuses to release the "Not Easy" Button to the general public. So, we fathers are left to more traditional approaches. Physical intimidation is a tried and true device, but I'll be in my 50s when Poohbutt hits puberty. I've hit the gym and have taken up boxing and street-fighting training. But let's face it: My future, geriatric ass trying to kick a teenager's ass will be tragicomic at best. I have to come up with something better.

There's always the shotgun, but those can be messy. I've ordered some mounted animal heads for the den. I can show the young man around, regaling him with tales of "how I bagged the big one" and finish off the introduction with my lovely speech, "The Beauty of Hollow-Point Bullets." I've also gotten Lasik surgery and have enrolled in sniper training. But seriously, I don't want my little girl to grow up with a bunch of sexual hang-ups, and a trail of dead boyfriends can give the girl a bit of a complex.

Also, all these avenues lead to Dad the Bad Guy Boulevard. I don't want to be the bad guy. Sure, I want to be in my daughter's head. I don't want to be her friend. I'm her dad. I want her to think, when handed her first joint in second grade (these kids are fast!), "Dad's gonna kill me!" However, I don't want Poohbutt to picture me with horns and cloven hooves. There have got to be subtler, more passive-aggressive ways for Daddy to protect his baby.

Fortunately, Pops, there are. Studies have shown that education, the arts, and athletics all lessen the chances of unexpected grandchildren. In other words, keep 'em busy! Idle loins are the Devil's handiwork. However, while activities are definitely important, the *kinds* of activities your daughter engages in are what really matter. I've devised a list of fields you should pursue with the girl. Please take heed. You can't afford not to.

1) Quantum Physics.

This is the most sexless field of study your daughter can get into. I strongly recommend it. Yes, nerds wanna get laid, too, but they're generally too timid to try anything. Your daughter will be safe. Besides, when was the last time *Playboy* ran "Those Sexy Sluts of String Theory"?

2) The Drums.

Many fathers make the mistake in pointing their daughters toward classical music and the violin. Sure, the boys in the orchestra are nerds, but you've seen the movies, that conductor is one lascivious bastard. And remember, that bow don't come with no arrow. How will she fend the lecher off? No, my brother, she needs to hit the drums—not the skins. A proper drum kit is a mighty fine barrier that will keep the barbarians at the gate. If they do breech it, however, she has a mighty fine weapon in each hand, and a skillfully placed cymbal crash can leave a boy writhing in pain. Besides, drumming for hours in a rock band can be a heck of a workout. James Brown didn't call Clyde Stubblefield "the Funky Drummer" for nothin'. Your girl's "funk" *will* fend off possible suitors.

3) Field Hockey.

It's the closest thing to a "Lesbian Switch" we fathers have right now. There's also softball, but the girls don't get to take the bats home with them. That hockey stick is a nice, little weapon. Have your girl repeatedly watch *Braveheart* to learn how to properly wield it.

4) Akido.

As a pacifist, my wife's against martial arts training for Poohbutt. Me? I want her to know some '80s *Gymkata* stealthy ninja shit. I want her to be a deadly mix of Bruce Leroy in *The Last Dragon* ("He catches bullets with his teeth?!") and Patrick Swayze in *Roadhouse* (who actually ripped some dude's throat out). A nice compromise is akido, which uses the opponent's attacks against him. While leaving the larynx intact, your girl will be able to fend off any pimply-faced playa without hardly breaking a sweat.

5) 1-800-NUNNERY.

As a recovering Catholic, I was a bit hesitant to go this route, but, after the "yawn" move, I got this bad boy on speed dial. At the first hint of trouble, Our Ladies of Vengeance and Blood are getting a call. No matter what, until girls start serving as altar boys, your girl will be safe in the convent. Give 'em a call, visit. They make the *best* pierogies.
If none of these tactics work for you, Dad, pray. Pray hard. And if that doesn't work, shotguns are running for less than $300 (I recommend the Mossberg) online. While they don't make hollow points for shotguns, a load of buckshot in the ass will make any boy think twice.

A Concert of Moments

Saturday, February 28, 2009

I remember the moment I heard that my Uncle Rodney was about to die. I'd just come home from watching Detroit drop the second game of the World Series with my friend, Amit, and his brother-in-law, Amit. My wife looked grave when I entered. "Your mother called," she announced. "Your Uncle Rodney has lung cancer."

I'd oddly enough just been reading about lung cancer. I knew what that meant.

"So, he's going to die," I said, blankly. Then it hit me. "He's going to die," I croaked.

I cried the rest of that night. My wife held me.

Before then, I wasn't a terribly emotional guy. But I worked at home. Alone, all these memories would come knocking, and, out of nowhere, crying jags would come calling. All those memories. All those moments I shared with my uncle.

Uncle Rod doing crazy stunts on his motorcycle.

Him sitting five-year-old William on his lap and letting the boy "drive" home.

My mother and father divorced when I was five. My mom had to move in with my grandmother. Uncle Rod and Aunt Elaine still lived in the house. Uncle Rod occupied a lot of memories where my father should have been.

Me and my uncle playing football in the backyard.

Me riding on that motorcycle.

Me burning my leg on the bike's exhaust pipe when he let me down. Me screaming. I can still remember the look of horror on my mother's face. My entire family running to my side.

Uncle Rod filled a lot of voids in my life. A surrogate father, of sorts. An uncle. Only 17 years my senior, an older brother I'd never have. He was a kid when I was a kid. He was reckless, irreverent, fun and funny. And he loved me. The moment I realized all this was at the funeral parlor. There was this picture. Me, four, standing. Him, 21, crouched down, an arm around my tiny shoulders. And he's looking at the camera with such affection and love and pride. And it hit me. All that he meant to me. All that I meant to him.

He was reckless, irreverent, fun and funny. Me? I was an only child of divorce. I was an integration baby who never really felt like he fit into any world he stepped into. I read. I drew. I was debilitatingly shy. There were times when I was paralyzed by fear around other people. One time, at my cousin Lisa's party, I stayed in the kitchen, drawing, while she and her friends yukked it up outside. No amount of prompting could get me outside. That never would've happened to Uncle Rodney.

He was reckless, irreverent, fun and funny. He was someone to emulate.

My love of Reese's peanut butter cups is his.

My love of Prince.

My love of profanity?

And the next time I found myself surrounded by a bunch of strangers, I would never be shy and withdraw. I would be reckless, irreverent, fun and funny.

Bill Campbell

I drove onto the campus of Muhlenberg College, determined to be just that. And I was. It was my senior year of high school. The college was honoring "gifted, minority students." Basically, they were trying to add a bit of color to their alabaster student body. I was the only one from the Pittsburgh area to arrive. Kids were mostly from Philly, New York, and New Jersey. *Bill* would've never gone. *Uncle Rodney* would've had a blast.

That's who I became. I was reckless, irreverent, fun and funny. I helped my hosts sneak a beer keg onto the dry campus. I openly mocked the school for suckering us into going for that weekend and said there was no way I was going there. I actually hooked up with the girl I'd targeted and came home with numbers from a number of the girls in attendance (I'm still trying to figure that one out).
My natural tendency is still to be withdrawn in crowds. But, with the help of channeling my uncle's spirit, I can still be irreverent and funny (I gave up fun and reckless years ago). If you ever meet me, you'll know where it comes from.

My uncle was a diabetic. He contracted the disease while pretty young. I think of diabetes as a war of attrition that you can never quite win. Sooner or later, it drags you down, takes you over, and withers you to bone and dust.

My uncle ultimately gave up. He fought by succumbing. His diet was horrible. He continued to drink. He refused to stop smoking.

Just after my thirtieth birthday, I went to Cleveland for a music conference. I stopped by Pittsburgh to see the family before heading back down to Atlanta. I walked into a family skirmish. My Uncle Rodney had given up. The doctors were willing to give him new kidneys, virtually curing him, but he just wouldn't take care of himself. He wouldn't monitor his diet, wouldn't stop drinking, would not give up smoking. He was tearing the family apart.

He was going blind.

He wouldn't leave the house.

I took him for a walk. Only I could get him out of the house. He was no longer reckless, irreverent, fun, funny. He was old and broken. He was 47. And I took him by the hand and took him out of the house.

We talked and we smoked and he cried. I just listened.

No more bike rides. No more playing football. Just a slow, withering creep toward death.

The news was always bad. Always given with a sigh of resignation

Your uncle's totally blind now.

Your uncle's on daily dialysis.

Your uncle's about to lose his foot.

His leg.

My uncle was there for my first ever book reading. My whole family was there. My friend from high school, Bob, dragged his mother and aunt and another friend from high school, Giac, along. There we all were, standing in this small, metaphysical bookstore in Sewickley while I talked about a science fiction protest novel and how it was inspired by my Uncle Bob, their brother, who'd died tragically a decade before. An inauspicious beginning to a literary career that still ain't about much. But it meant so much to have those people I love there. My Uncle Rod sat in the corner behind me, blind and small, but there. Getting my back

Bill Campbell

"Your Uncle Rodney has lung cancer."

He wasn't the man I'd remembered. He used to be a coal miner. He and Uncle Richard used to work on cars. The Uncle Rodney I remembered did motorcycle stunts, took me to Prince concerts, threw a football, snuck me a Molson Golden for my graduation.

We sat in my old '74 Oldsmobile Omega. I'd graduated from high school and was going off to the college of my dreams and he was proud of me. That beer still tastes sweet.

This Uncle Rodney was an emaciated shell. A mere lump in the bedsheets with a stump where his right leg had been. There were all those tubes, all that beeping. He was in a drug-induced stupor, his hands cuffed to the railing to stop him from tearing out all the tubes that pocked that shell.

I was 36, but I was really that scared, five-year-old boy who moved into his grandmother's house. I sat up on the counter, cowering and terrified. I sat there staring at him, dumb. His partner, Carol, asked me to talk to him. I shook my head, mutely. I just couldn't do it.

We had that discussion no family wants to have. It was complicated. My uncle never married Carol, so she legally couldn't make that decision. My family didn't care. It was her decision. But we still had to talk about it. I didn't think I had a place in that discussion, but they asked. It killed me, but I said that life support is no life and that we had to let him go.

On my next visit, it hit me. My uncle's dying was not about me. It was about him. He couldn't talk. I really didn't know how *there* he really was. He writhed, but was he really there? When someone asked him a question, there would sometimes be a nod. But what was that? Was it him? A spontaneous, non-related muscular action? What was it?

What did it matter, really? This was about him. I had to do something for him. He had to know how much he meant to me

Uncle Rodney loved Prince. Because of that, I loved Prince. Uncle Rod took me to my first concert—you guessed it, Prince. *1999*. I pulled out my iPod, put on that album, sat on my knees next to his bed, put one ear bud in his ear, and put the other in mine. And we listened to that album while my Aunt Elaine sat at our sides.

I wish I could say that a miracle happened. That he sat up and thanked me and we sat there talking and laughing and telling each other how much we meant to each other. But those moments rarely happen. It didn't happen that day. Prince would have to do. I left the hospital with my aunt, bawling.

Outside the hospital, my aunt tried to hug me. I shrugged her off, saying, "I'm OK." Then I realized. My uncle's dying was not about me. It was about his partner, Carol. It was about his siblings. They used to be eight, and now they were about to be five. And the one dying up there in that hospital room was the next-to-youngest. And he was about to die way before his 54th birthday. I hugged my aunt, and we cried. And I listened to her talk all the way back home. I got in my car on my way back to DC, promising to be back soon.

I never got to have that last talk with Uncle Rod. I couldn't make it back in time.

Life is nothing but a collection of moments. We drone on from day to day, living our live-a-day lives. But when it comes down to it, those moments—those moments of joy and pain, agony and bliss—those are the things that we cling to. Those are the things that we hold dear. And we share those moments with those we hold dearest. And we should hold onto those moments. Those are the dearest gifts our loved ones give us. Those moments are the very things that make life worth the journey. And we need to thank our loved ones every day for the gift of those moments. What better gift is there?

Bill Campbell

That was part of my eulogy for my Uncle Rodney.

"Will was just talking about moments," my Uncle Richard opened after my speech. "I just wanted him to know that Rod told us about you playing that Prince for him. ... I just thought you should know."

I lost it. My wife put her hand on my back, my cousin Danielle hugged me, and I cried like a baby.

Funerals are sad and tragic, of course. People cried and wailed and held onto each other. The preacher preached, solemnly, as we stood by the casket on that chilly, December afternoon. I looked around as everyone bowed their heads in prayer. I saw my family, the people who raised and love me. On one side was my wife; on the other, my mother; the two most important women in my life, the two women I love more than myself (and believe me, that's saying a lot). And then it happened. I smiled. I was ... happy?

At that moment, on that chilly, December afternoon, I realized my wife was right. It was time for us to have a child. The following October, Poohbutt was born.

My eulogy was about moments, the most precious gifts our loved ones can give us. And, during my eulogy, I told everyone about the most precious moment my Uncle Rod had given me.

It was on this day, 26 years ago. February 28, 1983. I was 12-years-old, and Prince was coming to town. Prince was my obsession. But I wasn't going. I'd never been to a concert before, and I just knew my mother would *never* let me go see that midget sex pervert (after all, he was the one who forced her to explain to her 10-year-old William what "Head" was—Uncle Rod laughing the whole time).

I did my morning paper route with Chopin's "Death March" playing the entire way. I was de-pressed. The most important event of my *life* was happening that night, and I was going to miss it.

I came home that morning, dragging my paper bag and bottom lip. For some reason, my mother and stepfather hadn't gone to work, yet. Mom ho-hummed, "Your Uncle Rodney has an extra ticket."

"Really?!"

"Do you want to go see Prince tonight, William?" she smiled, coyly.

I think I screamed the whole day—to the bus stop to school back home all the way to the Civic Arena.

You know it was great. Vanity 6 was there. They sucked, but what other chance does a 12-year-old pubescent boy with raging hormones get to see grown women in their underwear? The Time, my second favorite musical act at the time, was great. My uncle was great. My cousin was there, and her best friend, Tina, who I had a huge crush on. I stood on the floor, but she stood on the chair behind me and kept her hands on my shoulders for balance. Sure, it was the most intimate we would ever become. But I was 12. I had a crush. It was great!

And the greatest of all! The greatest musician of all-time! Prince! Of course, he was great.

In fact, though I've been a music critic and have gone to more concerts than I would've thought humanly possible, that concert, 26 years ago today, on February 28, 1983, was the greatest concert I've ever been to.

Thanks, Uncle Rod.

I love you.

Sweets for My Sweet

Saturday, March 14, 2009

I don't have to tell you, little kids are adorable. They're lovable, hugable, kissable. Sometimes, you just want to pinch the hell out of their cheeks. They fill us so full of gushy, mushy corniness that we want to take them, hold them, and care for them for decades at a time no matter how much grief, gray hair, and money they cost us.

I also don't have to tell you, Poohbutt is no different. That girl has me wrapped so tightly around her finger, I fear I may be a bit unhinged. I can have her bouncing on my knee while looking at pictures of her with a big, ole Proud Papa smile on my face. It's sad, but true. Cheesy and maybe a little egotistic. But I'm still utterly gaga over my little "Goo-Goo" Machine.

But I also think that Pooh's at an incredibly intriguing age. Sixteen months. It seems just like yesterday, I had this crying, crapping lump on my hands that I had to carry, change, and feed every two minutes. Now, all of the sudden, I have a little *person* running around and being all ... *persony*.

She walks! She talks! She runs! And can still slice this tomato!

It's just a whole new, fascinating experience for me to watch the world through a child's eyes once again. To observe the discovery. And to see, once again, what a challenge the world was to comprehend and navigate.

It's just that, at 16 months, our children are yet to acquire guile. Whatever's going on in their little minds plays out in their little faces. And, without experience to modulate their emotions, they suffer such extremes it's utterly fascinating. When they're happy, they're ecstatic. When they're frustrated with whether the blue cup goes inside the red or vice versa, they can and will go apeshit. When they're hurt, they scream as though you'd shoved bamboo under their fingernails. And when Poohbutt wakes up in the morning, runs with all the energy in her little legs, and squeals, "Hi, Da!" with the biggest smile on her face, you'd think it was the best thing that will happen in her life—and makes it the greatest thing that happens in mine.

And you know, at 16 months, these little tykes are starting to develop their own little personalities. She loves to dance to all kinds of craziness: Henry Mancini, The Slits, Seal. She loves singing Aesop

Rock's "Boom, Boom, Boom." And, while I don't understand most of them, Poohbutt loves to crack jokes. She'll do anything for a laugh. She'll do her little "moonwalk," her Chubby Checker imitations. And the faces this girl makes.

And you can't help but wonder if we actually develop personalities this early. When she's being all full of tantrum, being all willful as though her name were "Stonewall" Campbell, and throwing everything on the floor, I sure as hell hope not. When she's cleaning up all her toys at the end of the night and starts taking to Mama's training her to do the baseboards, I'm definitely hopeful. And, when she's being all adorable and a cut-up, I can't help but wondering, is this a permanent thing? I mean, was yours truly this witty and acerbic when he, too, was shitting his own pants? One has to wonder.

Especially when it comes to the latest development in the Poohbutt Saga ...

My daughter has become a flirt.

Those of you who've read "Protecting Your Poohbutt" know I am forever vigilant over my daughter's honor. So, you know I keep my eye on this shit. And I have indeed observed some very inter-arresting new developments in my daughter's development.

I noted before that children at Pooh's age are without guile. They couldn't deceive if they tried—and I wouldn't put it past the little buggers to be trying even at this early stage. But those little darlings can be coy.

Now, while Poohbutt is the most precious, dearest thing that's ever happened to me and I love her to death, I'm not going to claim she has any special gifts of adorableness, or anything like that (like parents who are always trumpeting how their kid is "really smart for her age"—as often as you hear that, you'd think we lived in a nation of geniuses—yet we elected Bush twice). Kids are adorable. People love them. And, to be frank, people are often captivated by seeing a black man care for his own child. It's something they've never seen before. They can't help but stare.

Daaaaaaaaamn.

So yeah, Pooh and I can sometimes get a bit of attention. I'm generally not one who likes the attention (I mean, the other day, two women were utterly *spellbound* watching Pooh eating broccoli), but what can you do? Folks like babies.

They smile and wave and sometimes act a fool. Seriously, it's amazing what toddlers can get perfectly normal, grown adults to do. Sometimes, when we're in a restaurant, I'll look up from my own plate and see a grown woman making the silliest faces or a grown man doing a silly little jig hoping to elicit a chuckle from the girl.

What I've also noticed is how she actually *encourages* these fools. We'll be sitting there, eating a fine Jamaican, Italian, Chinese, Greek, Indian meal, and then I'll see that my little, dear, innocent Pooh staring holes into someone. She's picked her target. She'll stare and stare while they're mindlessly eating. Then, I guess feeling the heat, they'll suddenly look up. They'll see Pooh and start contorting themselves in the weirdest ways all to make my daughter laugh.

Then my little, dear, innocent Pooh will give a little half-turn away from the person, cock a shoulder, tilt her head down, and give a little titter. Sometimes, she even *bats her eyelashes*. I shit you not.

These fools fall for it every time. They start laughing in earnest, and coo to me, "Oooh, she's so *shy*."

"Uh-huh."

She plays this little "shy" act of hers at pretty much every restaurant we go to. And her victims run the gamut: sex, sexuality, age, race, religion, ethnicity, none of the stuff that divides us matters when it comes to Poohbutt. Black women have done somersaults to entertain her; white women bust into the Electric Slide; Iranian men have danced the mazurka. What can I say? Poohbutt's a uniter, not a divider. I'm thinking of sending her to Israel and have her bat her lashes for peace.

This week, she's also become a dessert magnet. Pooh has a little fan club at our local Chinese buffet. Whenever we walk in, the waitresses' faces light up. They smile and wave. They come by the table and try to entertain her. They *constantly* fall for her "shy" routine. So, it was no surprise when one of them snuck Pooh a seaweed-flavored Konjac brown rice roll. I think it's supposed to be a sweet. It's not.

What *is* sweet, though, is the caramel-anise cookies we got at a local Peruvian rotisserie the other day. Pooh was on fire that day. She had the customers and the employees dancing around. Even the cooks waved their tongs at her. The waitress, who spent a solid 20 minutes playing peek-a-boo rewarded Pooh's good behavior and eyelash batting with these cookies that rocked Daddy's world.

Now, I'll admit I'm a bit ambivalent about this newfound flirting and her being rewarded with sweets. We do live in a world where I will ultimately have to teach her that it is dangerous to take candy from strangers. And I don't want to teach her to use her supposed cuteness to get what she wants in life. I want her to grow up using her brains!

But for now she's only 16 months. Besides, I'm broke and I *love* free food. I'm trying to train the girl to get us a free meal or two down the road!

"Give it a little more *ooomph!* kid! Sell it! Sell it!"

Hell, you've seen this economy.

"Oh, Shit"

Tuesday, April 14, 2009

Two words have not been uttered that have had a more profound effect on my life since the Missus and I uttered, "I do." That's right, little Poohbutt, on Saturday, April 11, 2009, at 1:27 pm, uttered "Oh, shit," in her grandmother's bedroom just seven days shy of her 18-month birthday. My wife had dropped something, and said, "Oh, no." Poohbutt responded, "Oh, shit."

Now, if you haven't guessed, I'm a pretty profane motherfather. Ever since I was seven, when the older Deebee boys moved into our building, cursing up a storm, I've been exhaling profanity like it was CO_2. The prudes would always say, "Profanity is the sign of a limited vocabulary." Your young rebel would reply, "Oh yeah, what's antidisestablishmentarianism?" When answered with the customary blank stare, I'd then smugly add, "That's what I thought. Now, go fuck yourself."

However, I don't want Pooh growing up with a potty mouth. So, I've been working on cleaning up my own palette for about two years now. I've made fairly decent progress, but "Oh, shit" shows me that I need to seriously step up my game.

Now, I know a lot of parents out there don't care to curb their tongues around their children. Hell, some folks take delight in cursing out their little ones. But that ain't me. My parents didn't curse around me. I don't want to curse around my own children.

See, it's all wrapped up in my Bill Campbell's Bullshit Theories on Parenting, or "B-ToPs," as it's known in the industry. Like jokes, I've got tons of 'em. I should write a book. But this post specifically addresses my B-ToP on Boundaries.

I'm not stupid now. I know children are going to push boundaries. It's an integral part of a child's development. They push them to test their parents' love and as a mode of self-definition. So, yes, Poohbutt, as adorable as she can be, will be pushing my boundaries and my buttons. Hell, she's already started. So, in the future, I know that my baby girl will curse, try smoking and drinking, may experiment with drugs, and—Oh God, say it ain't so—have sex.

My B-ToP on Boundaries dictates that my job, as a parent, is to accept this inevitability, but I ain't supposed to make it easy for the girl. Because the more I readily accept her misconduct, the more outrageous her future actions will be in order to get a reaction out of me (LoR=LoL, or Lack of Reaction=Lack of Love, see).

So, Pops here has a two-pronged approach to the Boundaries issue. As I said, I can't make it easy for the kid. Boundaries must be respected. Attacks must be repulsed. So, punishment is key.

I got the switch once, and I know that ain't gonna happen to Pooh. I mean, it's an effective weapon, but the switch *is* a weapon. I understand why my grandmother used it on my behind. She came up in a time and place where a black child's insubordination could realistically result in death. I don't think Pooh needs to really worry about that. So, the switch is definitely part of the Campbell Clan's past.

While I'm not necessarily against corporal punishment, I'm not necessarily *for* it, either. I can't really see myself whippin' a kid's ass, but you never know. The last time I got the belt was when I was 12. I ran off and fell asleep in a neighboring town's arcade (I had Pacman Fever bad). I woke up to find po-po shaking their heads ruefully at me. They drove me home, where I was greeted with the *entire* neighborhood's searching the night for poor, little, old me. Seriously, every street and wooded area was strobing with flashlights, as frantic parents hoped to and dreaded to find me. Oh yeah, my ass got lit up that night. Some of you may think a child never deserves to get whipped, but I definitely think I did that night. Hell, I'm sure there were a lot of parents who would've lined up to do the honors.

However, I think I'm more into severe grounding. For example, when I was 14, at the beginning of summer vacation, I was supposed to spend the night over at a friend's house. While we were out playing tennis, some of my "cool"er friends strolled by with some girlies, asking me to join them. I deferred, but, later that night, I feigned illness, and told my friend I was just going to walk home. You all know where I went. Hell, girlies were involved. After the folks found out, I wasn't allowed out of the house the entire month of June! One helluva summer vacation, eh? But, you know what? I don't think I've sold a friend out since.

So, Part I of B-ToP on Boundaries *does* include a little shock and awe. It accepts insubordination but it don't put up with that mess. It believes that children *must* learn the consequences of their actions. This may be a race thing, I admit. While my grandmother's day is long gone, black children are still treated more harshly than whites by the authorities. Therefore, our children must learn to respect *our* authority. When they get a bit older, we can then pump them full of "Fuck the Man." But let's get them out of puberty first.

Part II of B-ToP on Boundaries does admittedly have a class bias to it. In acknowledging boundary pushing, we must limit our children's exposure to as many of the wide varieties available to them. In the Mayberry suburbs of

Bill Campbell

Pittsburgh where I grew up, there just wasn't that much trouble to get into. I could've, maybe, gotten drunk and TP'ed a neighbor's yard. Meanwhile, I have friends who grew up in places where their teenage trouble-making could've gotten them into drugs, gangs, jails, and coffins. Part II simply says, "Don't live in those fucking neighborhoods!"

Face it, a lot of the aforementioned criminal activity mostly happens in certain neighborhoods. While drugs are universal, gangs, lethal violence, and teenage pregnancy rarely happen out of certain locales. I'm not saying that you cannot raise decent human beings out of those neighborhoods. If I believed that, a lot of the work that I've done in my adult life would be hypocritical. It's just that raising children in those environments is incredibly challenging. Why do it if you can afford not to? Right now, I am fortunate enough to be able to afford not raising my daughter in such a town/neighborhood. So, I choose not to. Why have your kids ducking bullets if they don't have to?

A friend of mine once told me that, when she was a child, her mother took one look at her friends, didn't like what she saw, and moved her out of there as soon as was humanly possible. My friend told me that none of those childhood friends of hers survived high school without at least one pregnancy. That's what Part II is all about. Limit those boundaries 'cause sure as "Oh, shit," your kids *will* find them.

Now, I don't want you sitting there thinking that B-ToPs are meant to be totally draconian—though they may sometimes be. After all, being an abusive parent is just as bad as being a nonexistent one. An abused child can often be out of control, and the legendary "preacher's daughter" *can* turn out to be a little freak. B-ToP recommends a constant negotiation when it comes to said boundaries. Initially, set them fools *real* high and gradually lower them as your child grows and matures. This lowering will promote personal responsibility while reinforcing the correlation between consequences and actions. See what I'm saying—Bullshit.

So yeah, Poohbutt's about to turn 18 months, and her "Oh, shit," was her own declaration that she is, indeed, ready for Daddy's B-ToPs. As said father, I must now diminish, as much as possible, the uber quixotic Bill Campbell Bullshit Theory on Parenting: Parental Hypocrisy ("I got it from you, Dad!"). I must now work even harder to elevate my own language from the gutter to the choir. I must create a hip-hop-less Poohbutt Playlist on my iPod and shuttle my forbidden love of rap into the closet. And I must pray and pray and pray.

Oh, shit.

Wish me luck.

Poohbutt Crushes Crush

Tuesday, April 28, 2009

It was only a year into my relationship with my wife, 1996, when I developed my first crush. It wasn't as though I just woke up one day, said, "Hey, I think I'll have a crush today," went to a bar, and latched on to the first female I saw. No, I didn't plan it. I never wanted it to happen. But I couldn't resist.

I was sitting with my boy, Dabalou, sneak-peeking the Jack Nicholson/Stephen Dorff/Michael Caine mediocrity, *Blood and Wine*, when it happened. There it was—in dewy, morning light and a kinky maid's uniform—"Dat Azz!" Instantly, I gasped, my voice going higher than a heliumized castrato, "Who's dat?!"

Yep. Jennifer Lopez caught my heart. At the time, it was fun to go all *Tiger Beat* in my mid-twenties. I hadn't had a genuine, bona fide crush since Lisa Lisa. Oh, sure, there have been starlets I'd found attractive over the years—Angela Bassett, Nia Long, anyone in the Prince entourage minus Rosie Gaines—but to have an out-and-out, full-blown pre-pubescent *crush* again. Now, that was fun. I suffered through *Money Train* and *Anaconda* and actually enjoyed *Selena*. I may have even looked for her in old episodes of *In Living Color*. It was Tootie all over again. I think my skin even broke out.

But, ultimately, I was no longer 13. I was going on 30. And, as J. hit new lows with Poof Daddy, I had to give up my crush on the woman. However, I did retain the *concept* of the crush. It was just that these silly, virtual-adolescent crushes matured just as my real ones had: physical perfection diminished in importance and was taken over by intellectual excellence (or in the case of Mrs. Unknown Writer, both). That's right: I started developing *The Nerd Crush*.

Look, as a nerd, I know I'm wired wrong. No, it's not like you can hear my lustily slavering, "Look at the CV on that one." I can objectify women with the best of them (after all, there *is* Serena). It's just that I love me a smart woman. I find nothing more attractive than a woman expounding, pontificating, teaching me something. So, a beautiful woman with a Tweety Bird brain loses her sex appeal while a cute woman with a huge frontal lobe becomes a goddess. A 130+ IQ to me is like some D-cups to a 12-year-old.

So I celebrate the Nerd Crush because it reaffirms my circus geek status. Besides, what harm is there in it? It's not like I'll ever meet any of these people. I mean, playing she-loves-me-she-loves-me-not over a co-worker can only lead to disaster. The closest I've ever come to meeting a "crush" was running into Paul Wolfowitz, whom I'd still like to crush between two Mack trucks. But that all changed yesterday, when Nerd Crush 2004, Liz Marlantes, suddenly entered my life.

For those who don't know (and last night my wife was like, "Who?"), Liz Marlantes was for a time with ABC News. I first saw her on *The McLaughlin Group*, talking about the presidential campaign. My Nerdiness fell for this bronzed cutie with the boxer's nose instantly as I watched her struggle, trying to marry the worlds of journalism and the shout-box, infotainment, claptrap that is McLaughlin. The old man had to actually shush Buchanan a few times just so the woman could speak. Afterwards, I found out that the *Christian Science Monitor* reporter had majored in American history and literature at Harvard and got a Master's in English Lit. from Oxford (the perfect combination of a young Dolly Parton's breasts and J Lo's ass to a geek like me!).

Oh yeah, I fell hard. But, you know, crushes are ephemeral beasts. I hadn't seen her in a few years, and out of sight, out of mind, and all that.

That is until Ms. Marlantes appeared at my local toddler park with her own little boy in tow. Of course, being a toddler park, Pooh was with me. And she was having none of it. While Daddy was standing at the head of the slide, going through the slow process of recognition (*Hey, look, a hot mom ... no, wait ... isn't that? ... Holy shit, that's Liz Marlantes! No way! ... Boy, I used to have a crush on her...*), my fiercely determined daughter was steadily toddling toward the top of the slide, with "Who's that heifer?" burning in her little eyes.

I wonder where she's been. I haven't seen her in years.

I didn't even notice the bile rising in my little Poohbutt's gut.

I should say something ... like ... Hey, didn't you used to be Liz Marlantes? ... Yeah, that's almost *clever...*

My girl reached the top of the slide, dead set against her father introducing himself to this strange woman. None of the other women—none of the nannies, none of the well-kept housewives, none of the power career women—ever even deign to turn up their noses at her miscreant father. What if this cow did?

No. Nothing was going to stand in Poohbutt's way.

I can see she hits the gym, Oblivious Dad thought to himself.

"Goo gaehh issimbakhhh!" Pooh said, sitting at the top of the slide.

(*Author's Note: I later discovered that this is BabySpeak for "Enough!"*)

Then ... relying on the only effective weapon an 18-month-old toddler has in her arsenal, Poohbutt opened her pretty, little mouth and **vomited** all over herself and the slide.

Daddy here, obviously no Boy Scout, came totally unprepared and had to clean the mess up with his own T-shirt—stealthily never taking it off so folks wouldn't notice.

I then scooped my girl up and scurried out of the park, never once introducing myself to Nerd Crush 2004.

Poohbutt happily sucked her thumb in her car seat until she fell asleep, a beatific smile resting on that little face all the way home.

Parenting Advice Required

Wednesday, April 29, 2009

All right, I'm new to the whole toddler park scene. Poohbutt didn't start toddling until well into the winter, and I was totally unaware of one of our local mall's play area. However, last month, when the Unions were in from St. Paul (oops, sorry, *Minneapolis*) and Pooh actually played with (as opposed to around) little Norma Rae, I knew she was ready. Besides, my girl's going into day care soon and I wanted to acclimate her to other kids (as well as gear myself up for cutting one of the many of Daddy's apron strings). So, we've been hitting the toddler play areas ever since.

Just yesterday I was marveling at how the older kids just really don't seem to notice the li'lunz playing around them. They can be going at break-neck speeds and magically veer around them. The toddlers must be on their radar, but the big kids just act like they don't exist. However, today was different.

I took Pooh to said mall's play area. It was a crap day out, but I still wanted the girl to get her play on. She was tooling around just fine with the play cars and plastic, hollowed-out log with the other tykes until *Jeffrey*, the Towheaded Terror, came along.

This little Osama bin Lad, roughly aged five, came in with his mother, grandmother, and two siblings and immediately reeked havoc and mayhem on what was originally a pleasant afternoon diversion.
First, he clamped down on Pooh's little shoulders. She tried to wriggle free, but he wouldn't let go. I wanted to jump in, but I figured she's going to have to get used to this kind of thing in day care. So, I let it go. Then he shoved her down to the ground. I retracted my Poppa Bear claws and let it go ... seething a little.

My daughter stoically got back up and smartly moved away toward me. She veered away and decided to play by herself. That was when *Jeffrey* chased after her, clasped her shoulders *again* and shoved her down. *Then* the little [deleted] *sat down* on my daughter. I thought I was going to kill *Jeffrey*. Instead, I calmly snapped, "Hey, kid!"

His grandmother waddled over, screaming, "Jeffrey!"
She snatched the boy up and immediately apologized to me.
"I'm sorry," she apologized. "He doesn't mean anything by it."
I gave her a slow nod, thinking (in my very un-PC fashion),

"Somebody needs to punch *Jeffrey* in his fucking mouth."

I looked over at the only other father in the play area, who gave me a questioning look, wondering if *Jeffrey* and/or I were going to be a problem.

The next 10 minutes made it painfully clear who it was going to be ...*Jeffrey.*

"Jeffrey!" "Jeffrey!" "Jeffrey!" the grandmother continuously screamed as *Jeffrey* pushed down other kids, tugged at them, tried to pull his older sister's shirt off, tried to pull another kid's pants down. All the other parents looked at the Hun rampaging through our plastic village, wondering when the hell his mother or grandmother was going to A) take him out of the play area and/or B) light his little ass up.

I was hoping Jamal, who was also five, was going to save the day and punch *Jeffrey's* lights out (I know, I know, I'm bad ... I need help). However, Jamal's mother had the right idea and left with her boy. Other parents were starting to get the hint.

Finally, *Jeffrey* frantically ran past Pooh and planted a shoulder into her, knocking her down.

"Jeffrey!!!"

I'd had it. I inhaled deeply, staring hot fire at the grandmother ...

"Really, I'm so sorry."

... and scooped up Poohbutt and left.

We went upstairs to exit the mall. I looked down at the play area, and all the other parents were gone. Only *Jeffrey* and his family remained, playing gleefully alone, I guess, until more kids came along to terrorize.

Now, I've been wondering ... Should I have said something? I mean, I know parents can get all crazy if you even *suggest* that their children are acting badly, that they may actually be bad parents, and may actually rear up and punch *you* in *your* fucking mouth. But damn, *Jeffrey* ran 12 kids and their parents out of the play area. I didn't want to get all ethnic on the fam, but, booooyyyyy, I really could have.

So, is there some kind of etiquette or protocol for situations like this? Or do you just do what I did and cower your kids away from the terror?

Just curious.

Samuella L. Chompers

Thursday, May 14, 2009

Yesterday before the Penguins' game, yours truly decided to treat his little Poohbutt. So, he left work a little early, rushed through rush hour traffic, picked his darling, little child up from day care, rushed *back* through rush hour traffic all to take her to her favorite, little toddler park. It was a fine, no, perfect spring day, the kind that you don't get too many of here in our nation's capital. Mid-seventies, sun shining brightly, a nice cool breeze. Our hero and our hero's daughter were having a fine time of it.

However, time was running out. There was a hockey game to watch. Mother had to be met. Car and child dropped off. A train to catch.

Pooh had yet to go on her favorite slide (yes, *that* slide), the one she always makes it a point to go on. Her father had the bright idea that she would want to go on it before we left. He was just trying to avoid a scene.

So, he lifted her out of the little plastic car with the busted wheels that doesn't move. She wiggled a moment, whined a little.

"What's the matter, Pooh?" her father cooed. "We're just going on the sli---*SONOFAMOTHERFATHERBURRRCOCKANOODLE!!!*"

Yes, for all his troubles—leaving work a little early, rushing through rush hour traffic, picking his darling, little child up from day care, rushing *back* through rush hour traffic all to take her to her favorite, little toddler park—our hapless hero was introduced to his 18-month-old daughter's baby teeth. Right on the chest and clamped down with all her might. Mr. Unknown Writer discovered why those bad boys are called "incisors."

Yep, Pooh broke skin.

A New Normal

Tuesday, June 9, 2009

Yesterday evening, I left work and picked Poohbutt up from day care as I do every weekday. We chatted through traffic while she snacked on pretzels. We settled in at home rather quickly, and my 19-month-old daughter began "reading" *Newsweek* to me. When she moved onto *Say Goodnight* and *Baby's Day*, I realized that a new Normal has finally settled in on our household.

As many of you know, the old Normal was my watching Pooh all day and going to work at night. It was supposed to only last nine months—until she turned one—but went on until she was 18 months. I was reluctant to let that Normal go, but it couldn't last forever. Finally, I took her to her first day of day care just a few days after my birthday. It was one of those bitterly ironic, bright and sunny spring mornings. Pooh bounded enthusiastically out of the house, racing her Ma and Da to the car. You wanted to laugh (ain't nothin' cuter than a running toddler), but I was choking back the tears. I fought the crying jag the entire way—from the Metro station to drop off Ma, through the rush hour traffic, all the way into the day care center. I didn't want my baby girl to think anything was wrong. That is my duty.

It worked. She was confused and apprehensive being dropped off that first day. But she didn't cry. Not in my presence, anyway. And I didn't in hers. Afterwards, though, I was a mess. A zombie, mostly, trying to figure out why the hell I was at work in the daylight. Once, bumming a cigarette from a co-worker, trying to talk about day care, I finally succumbed. I had to scurry off to my car and let the tears flow. Caring for a child, day in and day out, for those really long hours, is pretty intense. It's so joyful and exhilarating, so exhausting and enervating, it can simply overwhelm your identity if you let it. Somewhere in the muddle of the soup I call myself, I know that I am a husband and a son and a friend, an employee, a co-worker, and a colleague, and a writer. There are other things, as well. But they all seemed to be buried somewhere as I became a *father*.

There was never a moment my daughter wasn't on my mind during the day. I never lost sight of her. My head was filled with Pooh. What was I going to feed her? When was I going to put her down for her nap? What can I teach her today? What will I learn from her? Where will we go today? Will she *please* eat something other than these damned French fries?!

I had never been so wrapped up in another human being's well-being. Never so concerned with the mercurial, little tyke's moment-to-moment happiness. Never so personally invested in anybody else. And I'd never been closer to anyone than I was with my little Poohbutt for those 15 months. And she'll never know. She'll never know how hard that was to give up.

Or how excruciating it was those first, few days giving her up to the folks at day care. It didn't take her long to figure out what was up. And that she didn't like it. On that second day, she screamed and wailed and had to be pried off of me. I could hear her screams as I climbed the stairs and left the building.

A lot of you know the cloud that hangs over your head when you leave your baby and she screams like you just put her on the last train to Auschwitz. Rationally, I knew it was for the best. She just reached a stage in her development where she needed more engagement than I felt I could offer. Besides, I had to earn money. As I heard one mother say, "Do you rather want to be around for your baby's seventh tooth coming in or be able to provide for her future?"

I also knew that I wasn't anyone special. Ma had to go through this when Pooh was only three months old, and our girl was receiving her very sustenance from her mother's body. That has got to be the deepest bond one must surrender. I know, my poor wife really did suffer when she had to go back to work. But even her suffering isn't unique. There is hardly a parent in this country who hasn't gone through what I went through this past month. I knew that. Rationally. But when your kid starts crying—even within the hands of paid professionals—who, in many ways, can care for her better than you can—you best believe you want to get all Action Jackson, kick down some doors, and save your baby from all that pain.

But Pooh didn't want to be saved—not by me. I was the man who betrayed her on a daily basis. She was relieved to be rescued from day care at the end of the day, but she was absolutely *ecstatic* to see Ma. Not me. She could no longer count on her Da to protect her.

Ma was the one she ran to when she was hungry, when she was happy, when she fell down. She had no need for me, anymore. One night, when she woke up screaming in her crib, instead of crying, "Da! Da! Da!" as she usually did, she screeched, "Ma! Ma! Ma!" When I went into her room to pick her up as I usually did, she ran away from me, tripped, and fell in her crib, and refused to be picked up.

"Well, she wants her Ma now," my wife ventured, "because Mommies are the nurturing ones."

Now, I don't ever want to dog mothers—my best friend is a mother—or rather, the mother of my child. And yall know about black men and they mommas. However, one thing that bugs me about this recent Cult of Motherhood is the either/or false dichotomy our culture foists on us when it comes to parenthood. It seems we can have either good fathers *or* good mothers. But we can never have both.

That "Father Knows Best" myth that countless generations before us grew up with was complete and utter bullshit—as though the mother was just some cooking, cleaning, perfumed uterus that deferred to the "real" parent when he got home. But why replace that myth of a father with the bubbling, bumbling oaf we have today who impedes the real parent at every turn or who, at his best, can only be considered "helpful"?

I was there at the conception of our daughter. I was there for the doctor visits. I was there breathing along, walking the corridors, massaging, holding hands, and coaching and coaxing. I was there ready to slug the doctors when they gave my wife the epidural and she was in complete agony. I was there to stop the overly eager resident from giving her a C-section. After 22 hours of labor, my wife became my hero that day. And I was there with tears in my eyes as little Pooh came into the world and I cut the umbilical cord.

I was there because that is what fathers do. And those of us who give a shit would do a lot more if it were physically possible.

When I took my wife and daughter home, I actually knew what to do (having much younger siblings and cousins came in handy for once—ha!). So yes, I changed diapers and burped and swaddled. I even tried skin time until my daughter started ripping the hairs from my chest. I was up late at night and early in the morning. I heated up the donated meals, entertained visitors, ran errands, dealt with grandparents while my ladies slept. And I went to work.

That is what we fathers do.

And, for the last 15 months, I woke up with Pooh, changed her diapers, fumbled around with that damned Butt Paste, clothed her, fed her, and bathed her, and played with her, and put her to sleep.

When she was hungry, she tugged on my sleeve. When she was tired, she lay her head on my chest. And when she was scared or hurt, she ran into my arms, and I lifted her up and rocked her gently and hushed and hummed and sang and I showered her pain with Daddy kisses.

Bill Campbell

It's what I thought a father should do. While I'll admit I *really* fell down on the housekeeping, I was not the bubbling, bumbling idiot I always hear about. I was an equal *partner* in raising our child. And I know I'm not anything special here. I know there are tons of fathers out there just like me. I just wonder why I never see him in the popular discourse. I wonder where he is.

A little over a week ago, I was at the day care dealing with a brand new pang. I was just coming to grips with Poohbutt's histrionics with my leaving every day when she totally surprised me. Instead of clinging to me, begging me not to leave, she was actually wriggling out of my grasp, wanting to get down to play with her friends. I suddenly didn't know which was worse. Of course, I hated her screaming bloody murder every time I left, but this ...? Her first little step toward independence. "Da, you cool and all, but look at my girl Shanice over there with all those *crayons*."

It wasn't too overly dramatic, no gnashing of teeth, but I did feel it. I now knew that the old Normal was being replaced. But this is what being a parent is, right? The slow, incremental process of letting go. It hurts a little, but you can't help but feel a little proud. There my baby girl was, laughing and playing with other kids.

But I can't lie. There was something quite glorious in that old Normal. Having your daughter running at you, laughing, "Da! Da!" and waking you up in the morning with a kiss. Playing dolls with Campbell Camel and Baby Rose. Going to the Chinese buffet and downing sushi together. Playing in the sand. And that overriding feeling of pride I got doing my damnedest to be a good father.

I guess a lot of my melancholy was because I also got caught up in the Either/Or. Either I could be this loving, caring nurturer *or* I could be that rock-solid, good provider I've been hearing so much about. But life isn't really either/or, is it? It's these infinite possibilities of And, if we allow it to be. So, I can be loving and caring and a good provider and a father and a husband and son and friend and, who knows, maybe even a writer.

Later in the evening, after we all sat down and had dinner together, the three of us played catch on the dining room floor. Pooh sat on Da's lap and we caught the ball and threw it back to Ma together. God, it was fun.

I'll probably always miss the old Normal, and there are some kinks still to be worked out (how does a lazy, no-good bum of a writer finally become a good provider, and, oh yeah, what about that housework?); but I've got to say, I'm really loving this new Normal, too. And I'm really looking forward to all the new Normals yet to come.

Acknowledgements

As every author will tell you, any book is not the product of one's singular effort but one of collaboration. Pop Culture, being a collection of blog posts, of course, is no different. There are so many people to thank in making this happen, I will undoubtedly forget some people. I apologize beforehand for any omissions. But let's face it: I'm getting old; I tend to forget.

Above all, I have to once again thank my wife. As I stated before, she has given me one of the greatest gifts ever. My time taking care of Poohbutt is something I'll never forget. It's a gift I'd love to one day reciprocate.

Of course, there's Poohbutt herself. My God, what an adventure! I'm one of the luckiest fools in the world for being allowed to participate. I know there's more to come. And I look forward to each day.

Family and friends, of course. Your indulgence is well-appreciated.

I have to thank all of the people who helped make The Booty Tour the success it was. I have to thank all the CRMs in all the Barnes & Nobles across the country who let me take up time and space in their stores to hawk my book. I often rant about globalization and the corporate dominance of this country. However, Barnes & Noble is one corporation that occupies a warm ventricle in my heart. They gave this unknown writer a chance to become known. I am forever thankful.

Then, of course, there are the friends and family who let me sleep on their couches, fed me, and made me feel welcome as I toured: Cord, Valerie, Cedric, and Christopher Williams; Terri Onstad and Donald Ball; Eileen Murdock; Karen Baumgaertner and Paul Rohlfing and Baby Jane; Anne, Bronson, Adam, and Luke Troyer; Danielle Frazier; Korol, Rona, and Kara Taylor.

Tome's readers, as always, have a special place in my heart. Grant, Ron Strelecki, ModiK, and Effaridi have been there since the beginning. Their early encouragement and insights were what kept me going. All the others who have added their comments since add so much (oftentimes things I didn't think of while writing) and make reading and writing Tome an invaluable experience. Keep those comments coming!

And last but not least are the bloggers. Special thanks to Wayne Bennett a.k.a. The Field Negro. Field has been there pretty much from the beginning as well, has been very supportive of my efforts, and has steered more than one reader Tome's way. Thanks, yawdie!

Thanks also goes to all those bloggers who have been kind enough to blog roll Tome. And, of course, thank you to all the bloggers who were kind enough to read Pop Culture and contribute a blurb: Deesha Philyaw, Shani Ferguson, Wayne again, Frances Langum, politickybitch, Andi Fisher, Steve Denton, Iasa Duffy, and Paula Behnken. I owe you all. Keep writing. Your words are important.

BILL CAMPBELL

is the author of *Sunshine Patriots, My Booty Novel,* and *Koontown Killing Kaper*. He lives in the Washington, DC, area and terrorizes the countryside with visions of blackface and watermelon.

www.rosariumpublishing.com

Also Available from Rosarium Publishing ...

Sunshine Patriots (Special 15th Anniversary Edition)
Bill Campbell
978-0-9891411-1-6

Rebellion erupts on the "paradise" planet of Elysia, plunging the colony into chaos. In response, the all-powerful United Earth dispatches its elite corps of cyborg soldiers, led by Aaron "The Berber" Barber. For a hero celebrated galaxy-wide for his acts of bravery against alien hordes, a ragtag group of colonized miners with antiquated weapons should be no challenge. But Barber and his soldiers are unprepared to meet the most dangerous enemy yet□humans just like them. And on Elysia, the soldiers discover dangers that neither United Earth nor the Elysians themselves could have foreseen. The secrets Barber and his soldiers uncover lead them to question the true meaning of freedom in a world where nothing is what it seems.

My Booty Novel
Bill Campbell
978-0-9891411-2-3

Thirty-two-year-old writer Damian Cross has just returned from a disastrous first book tour only to be dumped by his fiancee. Now, newly-single for the first time in seven years, he has to pick up the pieces, start his life all over again, and write a second novel.

Damian blogs his way through today's dating scene and all its hazards to find that the only thing that stands between him and success may actually be himself. Can Damian stop his world from crumbling around him and get it together in time to gain a chance at true happiness and write the "booty novel" everyone's telling him to write?

Koontown Killing Kaper
Bill Campbell
978-0-9891411-0-9

All the rappers in Koontown are being killed, and rumor has it that it's vampire crack babies doing the killing. Desperate, the police reach out to Genevieve "Jon Vee" Noire, ex-super model/ex-homicide detective/private eye. Together with her former partner, Genevieve must navigate the dangerous world of gangsta rappers, shady record executives, corrupt cops and politicians, '80s pimps, welfare queens, secret sistah societies, Ubernoggin, and the National Guard. Can the ex-super model survive the chaos and insanity to save her beloved Koontown while it explodes all around her?

www.rosariumpublishing.com

Coming Fall of 2013

Mothership:
Tales from Afrofuturism and Beyond
978-0-9891411-4-7

"When we look up at the night sky, space is black as far as the eye can see. Yet, when we read novels about it or watch something on TV or in the movie theater, it is white beyond all comprehension. With this collection, we hope to give space some much needed ... color, shall we say (and other genres, of course)."

Edited by Edward Austin Hall and Bill Campbell, this groundbreaking anthology features science fiction, fantasy, and horror for, by, and/or about people of color by some of the hottest names in speculative fiction.

www.mothershipconnect.com